U.S. CHESS FEI

OFFICIAL

RULES OF CHESS

FOURTH EDITION

U.S. CHESS FEDERATION'S
OFFICIAL
RULES OF CHESS

FOURTH EDITION

COMPILED AND SANCTIONED BY

THE U.S. CHESS FEDERATION

Edited by:

BILL GOICHBERG, National Tournament Director,
International Arbiter, FIDE Master

CAROL JARECKI, National Tournament Director,
International Arbiter

IRA LEE RIDDLE, National Tournament Director,
International Arbiter

*This book, effective 1/1/94, supercedes the Official Rules
of Chess First Edition 1974, Second Edition 1978,
edited by Martin E. Morrison, and Third Edition 1987,
edited by Tim Redman.*

DAVID MCKAY CHESS LIBRARY

DAVID MCKAY
COMPANY, INC.

Copyright © 1975, 1978, 1987, 1993 by
UNITED STATES CHESS FEDERATION

All rights reserved under International and Pan-American
Copyright Conventions. Published in the United States by
David McKay Company, Inc., a subsidiary of Random House,
Inc., New York. Distributed by Random House, Inc., New York,
and Random House of Canada Limited, Toronto.
Earlier editions of this work were published in 1975,
1978, and 1987 by David McKay Company, Inc., New York.

Library of Congress Cataloging-in-Publication Data

United States Chess Federation.
[Official rules of chess]
The U.S. Chess Federation's official rules of chess / compiled
and sanctioned by the U.S. Chess Federation.—4th ed.
p.   cm.
ISBN 0-8129-2217-4
1. Chess—Rules.   2. United States Chess Federation.   I. Title.
GV1457.U55   1993
794.1—dc20   92-40961

Book Design by Cheryl L. Cipriani

MANUFACTURED IN THE UNITED STATES OF AMERICA
897
Fourth Edition

ACKNOWLEDGMENTS

The editors are grateful for the help of many. Among these, two in particular, Dan Burg and Bob Sutter, put much time and effort into the task. Especially significant contributions were also made by Alan Benjamin, Tim Just, Myron Lieberman, Jim Meyer, Glenn Petersen, Harry Sabine, and Gary Sperling. And among others providing meaningful suggestions are Charles Adelman, John Barnard, Denis Barry, Allen Beadle, Phyllis Benjamin, Walter Buehl, Frank Camaratta, Howard Cook, Bill Cornwall, Garth Courtois, Bob Dudley, Bob Erkes, Mike Goodall, Roger Gotschall, Don Gunther, Jerry Hanken, Thomas J. Harris, Guy Hoffman, Ken Horne, Randy Hough, Steve Immitt, Mark Ishee, Homer Jones, Edith Kellner, Larry King, Al Lawrence, Al Losoff, John McCrary, Parker Montgomery, Wayne Meyerson, Bob Nasiff, Mike Nietman, Mike Nolan, Warren Pinches, Marcus Roberts, Sophia Rohde, Marshall Rohland, Ernest Schlich, Joan Schlich, Paul Shannon, Robert Singletary, Frank Skoff, Bill Snead, Harold Stenzel, Hal Terrie,

Andrew Thall, Fred Townsend, Howard Wachtel, and Harold Winston.

We also wish to express our deepest appreciation for the work of past rule book editors, without whom our task would have been nearly impossible.

The late Kenneth Harkness, the first to compile a USCF rulebook, was a visionary pioneer. Harkness saw possibilities overlooked by others, in an era when American chess was so underdeveloped that the entire membership of the USCF was less than the turnout for certain large tournaments today.

Martin Morrison worked to establish and refine Swiss pairing rules and other tournament procedures. His efforts to modify the rules to require fewer directors for a smoothly run Swiss tournament have helped to make chess even more popular.

Tim Redman further refined rules and pairing procedures and produced a more comprehensive and readable book. Much of his language is retained in this subsequent edition. His modification of the pairing rules to make them compatible with computer algorithms led to the development of computer pairing programs that conformed fully with USCF pairing procedures.

We believe each previous editor has improved upon what existed before his edition. The editors of the rule book now in your hands hope you find that we, too, have continued this tradition, and that this book will be an informative and understandable companion for your adventures in the exciting world of chess, be they as a player, director, or organizer.

Contents

*Introduction: The Evolution
of Chess Rules*   ix

The Swiss System   xvi

1.   Official Rules of Chess   3
2.   USCF Tournament Regulations and
     Guidelines   77
3.   Chess Notation   154
4.   Equipment Standards   164
5.   The Well-Run Tournament   172
6.   Tournament Directors' Checklists   187
7.   Players' Rights and Responsibilities   195
8.   USCF Code of Ethics   198
9.   Tournament Director Certification   205
10. The USCF Rating System   219
11. Correspondence Chess   230
12. Blitz Chess   233
13. Round Robin Pairing Tables   236
14. The Scheveningen System   252
15. About the United States Chess Federation   254
16. How to Read and Write Chess   261

17. Ten Tips to Winning Chess   266

18. World and National Champions   288

19. A Historical Crosstable of the U.S. Chess
       Federation   296

20. International (FIDE) Laws of Chess   299

21. FIDE–Rated Tournaments   324

22. Special FIDE Rules (including Titles,
       Computers, and Faster Play)   336

       Index   357

THE EVOLUTION OF CHESS RULES

The earliest printed rules of modern chess appear in a book by the Spaniard Luis Ramirez Lucena. The book is believed to have been published in 1497, shortly after the moves of the queen, pawn, and bishop were changed to what they are today.

Lucena's rules are sketchy, but he describes the difference between the old and new styles of chess, as well as the various moves, while providing some definitions and advice. One bit of advice states:

> If you play at night, place your candle on your left-hand side, if by day, place your opponent facing the light. It will be worse for your opponent if you play him when he has just eaten and drunk freely. During a game drink water, not wine. Play for a small stake, so that the thought of it may not trouble you.

The trick of placing your opponent with the light in his eyes was apparently an old Spanish custom, for it is repeated by Ruy Lopez in this text published in 1561.

Chess literature in the sixteenth and seventeenth centuries records the rules followed in various countries. In those days there were considerable differences, including castling, pawn promotion, stalemate, and the en passant pawn capture. Some of these differences were still being debated in the nineteenth century.

In the eighteenth and nineteenth centuries, codes were adopted by chess clubs and eventually by national chess associations, but there was no general agreement on the rules. The first international tournament, in London, 1851, was played under "the rules of the chief European Chess Clubs." In the first national tournament held in this country, in New York, 1857, play was governed by the rules published in Staunton's *Chess Player's Handbook* (London, 1847). In 1860 a revised code published by Staunton in his *Chess Praxis* became generally recognized for English and American tournaments.

Although basic chess laws were fairly well standardized by the mid-nineteenth century, the rules governing competitive play were in a state of confusion. The rules committee of the 1880 American Chess Congress refers to its "delicate and difficult task of dissecting the mass of disordered and conflicting codes of chess laws at present in operation." The congress adopted a revised code, but it was copied largely from Staunton. This code was generally recognized until 1897, when New York's Manhattan Chess Club obtained the American rights to laws which had been officially adopted by the leading chess associations and clubs of Great Britain and published them as *The American Chess Code.*

Old chess rules may die hard. Some eighteenth-century chess rules stated that a promoted pawn could only take the place of a captured piece. Even though no book in English has restricted promotion in this way since before the Lincoln presidency, chess clubs and organizations still receive many calls asking whether such a rule exists. Likewise, even some tournament players believe a player who touches a piece that cannot move must move the king, a rule abandoned at least one hundred years ago.

When the World Chess Federation (Fédération Internationale des Echecs, or FIDE) was founded in 1924, an early priority was the formation of a uniform international chess code to supplant the variations practiced in different countries. Such a code was adopted by FIDE in 1929. These rules governed play in most tournaments in the United States and other nations until 1952, with the addition of some supplementary regulations and interpretations by national or local organizations. In 1952, FIDE published a new edition of the Laws of Chess.

Before the mid-1950s, USCF had no official set of rules. The need to supplement the FIDE rules was growing, primarily because of the popularity of Swiss system tournaments. FIDE rules were written for Master round robins, with few participants, in which directors could provide close supervision. Swisses of over a hundred players would be costly to organize on the same basis.

A USCF Tournament Rules Committee was formed in 1953 to write the rules, but its members were unable to devote the necessary time to their task, and its chairman resigned. Kenneth Harkness, the USCF business manager (a position similar to today's executive director) was then appointed acting chairman of the USCF Tournament Rules Committee. He submitted several drafts to the members of the committee, but none responded. Finally, Harkness submitted his draft to Hans Kmoch of FIDE, who provided some additional ideas.

Authorized by USCF president Frank Graves, Harkness's work appeared as the *Official Blue Book and Encyclopedia of Chess* in 1956. David McKay published this edition and subsequent USCF rule books. The book included a USCF rule requiring a player to maintain a "complete and legible record of all the moves of the game" to win on time, a more efficient way to run a Swiss than the FIDE practice of having directors count moves. The book established that either descriptive or algebraic notation (both long and short form) was valid, provided a table of chess symbols in various languages, and included USCF rating-system regulations.

In 1962 FIDE reinstated an old but rarely noticed prohibition on draws by agreement before the thirtieth move, this time with real intention of enforcement: the penalty was to be loss of the game by both players. The rule was tried for two years, but players ignored it or circumvented it with agreed repetitions of position, and directors were unable or unwilling to enforce penalties. It was abandoned in 1964.

Harkness issued the *Official Chess Handbook* in 1967. He included the laws of chess, supplementary rules, chess notation, and some ideas on "how to run a chess tournament." The adjustment of players' ratings by the director after every round, included in the 1956 book, was abandoned as "an unnecessary refinement." Some FIDE rules which were also USCF rules were changed. Rules regarding scorekeeping were expanded and clarified, and a player was allowed to ask (through the director) to borrow the opponent's score sheet if necessary. The rule providing that a player sealing an illegal move loses the game was modified to allow the director to waive this penalty if the player's intention is obvious. The timing and consequences of draw offers and draw claims were discussed in far more detail than previously (though still far less than in today's rules).

Harkness also edited the *Official Chess Rulebook,* published in 1972, the year of his death. This volume was basically an abridged version of his *Handbook.* He added material on notation, chess clocks, and rules for blind players. USCF tournament rules were condensed and put into the book, but current FIDE changes were not included. These 1970–72 modifications to the FIDE laws plus USCF changes through early 1973 were distributed in a pamphlet edited by Martin Morrison, chair of the USCF Rules Committee, and published privately by Paul Masson Vineyards.

Martin Morrison, then USCF technical director, edited the next publication, *Official Rules of Chess* (1974), dedicated to the memory of Harkness. Morrison acknowledged the help of Pearle Mann and John Osness of the USCF Tournament Direction Committee. FIDE had published a new set of rules in 1972, and these were included in this edition.

The USCF time-forfeit rules were clarified. In order to win on time a player must have a score sheet with no more than three move pairs omitted when the opponent's flag falls, a refinement that encouraged those expecting to win on time to keep score move after move. Also, time forfeits were no longer to be called by players or directors, but by players only. This change addressed the unfairness of directors claiming on behalf of some players but not others. Complete Swiss pairing rules were presented, rules for speed chess added, and sections on prizes and tie breaking expanded significantly. No preference was given for tie-break methods, but the following were listed and briefly explained: Median, Solkoff, Sonneborn-Berger, Kashdan, and Cumulative.

Morrison also edited the *Official Rules of Chess*, Second Edition, published in February 1978. The "corrected" version appeared in March 1979. William Abbott, Stephen Gerzadowicz, Joseph Lux, and John Osness all provided help with this edition. The USCF rules were written as part of the FIDE rules section, although the pairing rules were separate. Cumulative was listed as the only tiebreak method for Swisses. This edition also introduced the idea that a player should not be assigned the same color three times in a row. Rules for computer participants were added for the first time.

From 1979 through 1986 chess tournaments underwent substantial change, which prompted much demand for a revised rule book. Several committees were appointed to do the job but failed to make progress. Finally, under the aegis of the USCF Policy Board, Jerry Bibuld and Glenn Petersen wrote an initial draft of the new rules for comment by a panel of National Tournament directors.

Meanwhile, FIDE was revising its rule book, with two important changes aimed at making it easier to use. Interpretations were incorporated into the rules themselves, and the rules were reorganized in a manner developed by USCF's Tim Redman and Gerry Dullea. These changes were the basis for the revision drafted at the 1983 Manila Congress.

Tim Redman was appointed by the Doyle Policy Board as editor for the forthcoming USCF rule book. After consulting existing drafts, he completely rewrote the USCF rules and procedures to improve clarity, incorporate recent practice, and allow pairings to be fully computerized. Dullea continued to work as his principal assistant, drafting additional sections while Redman focused on the central game and tournament rules. Both had the benefit of expert advice from directors across the country. George Cunningham provided technical assistance in defining the statistical relation between color allocation and win expectancy.

The Redman edition was the first to include a significant rule change that has made tournaments fairer and easier to run—players with a legitimate reason were no longer prohibited from stopping both clocks. Prior to this change, a player who needed a director when none was in sight had to send a third party to find one. By the time the director arrived at the board, the player's game was sometimes lost or hopeless. Another important change was the separation of FIDE rules from USCF rules. (This current revision goes even further by placing the FIDE rules many chapters after the USCF rules to emphasize the differences between them.)

Redman's book also added sections on the new sudden death time controls, computer memberships, handicapped players, players' rights and responsibilities, USCF Code of Ethics, and the Crenshaw-Berger tables for round robin pairings, which correct a color imbalance caused by a withdrawal in a round robin. Half-point byes, having become popular since the previous edition, were described for the first time. In the case of an ambiguous sealed move, instead of declaring a forfeit, a director finding two or more reasonable interpretations of the move could leave the choice between them to the opponent. Officially put into use May 1, 1987, the book was applauded as being user friendly, providing much more in the way of explanation than previous editions. A much more detailed index was also included.

Since 1987, sudden death time controls have become extremely popular; by 1992 more than 80 percent of Swiss tournaments in the nation used them. Rules for sudden death have been developed and improved through actual practice and are incorporated into the general USCF rules in this edition.

A player need not have a score sheet to win on time in sudden death, but scorekeeping was originally required for players having at least five minutes remaining, as in traditional time limits. Enforcement of this rule proved difficult; there were continual complaints about players with over five minutes not keeping score in an effort to "blitz" opponents with under five minutes. This was not a problem in conventional time controls, as a player who stopped keeping score could not win on time. A new sudden-death rule providing that if either player has less than five minutes remaining, neither is required to keep score, was first used at the 1988 New York State Action Championship and met with such immediate success that it has since been adopted by both FIDE and the USCF (Rule 15C).

The revised 1992 FIDE rules are included in this edition. Several have also been adopted as USCF rules; however, the U.S. continues to be the world's Swiss system pioneer, and new ideas are more likely to start with the USCF and eventually to be adopted by FIDE than vice versa.

The Swiss System

The invention of the Swiss system has been credited to Dr. J. Muller of Brugg, Switzerland. The first Swiss system tournament is believed to have been held at Zurich in 1895.

The original Swiss tournaments around the turn of the century usually ran for four or five rounds over two days and averaged about ten participants. By 1904 the number of entries had greatly increased, and the system was being attacked by contributors to the *Swiss Chess Magazine,* who claimed that the method was too dependent on chance factors. "This all sounds very familiar," said Harkness of these attacks, recalling that his innovations designed to expand the popularity of chess had also come under fire from the old guard within the USCF.

The Swiss system achieved little popularity outside its native land until its introduction into the United States in the 1940s. Occasionally, an unimportant central European tournament was conducted under the method. Brief descriptions of the system were sometimes included in the German yearbooks, in which it would be mentioned one year but ignored the next; apparently this system was considered of little significance.

Grandmaster George Koltanowski, the "Dean of American Chess," is given credit for introducing the Swiss system into this country and strenuously advocating its widespread use. In 1942 Koltanowski visited Texas and persuaded the Texas Chess Association to try the Swiss instead of the then prevailing Holland system (Rule 30H). The 1943 Pennsylvania Championship, directed by Koltanowski, is the first known Swiss tournament in America. During the next few years, many state and regional tournaments adopted the system. It answered the problem that had long seemed unsolvable—how to handle many participants in a limited time.

The 1945 U.S. Intercollegiate was the first national tournament to use the Swiss, and its success led the USCF to consider using the same method for the U.S. Open. But instead, there was a compromise with tradition. The 1946 U.S. Open in Pittsburgh had 58 entrants, and an 8-round Swiss preliminary was used in place of the old round robin prelims. The top ten from the Swiss qualified for a round robin final for a total of 17 games, too long by today's standards.

When the 1947 U.S. Open in Corpus Christi produced a record 86 entries, it was believed that an 8-round Swiss prelim would have little meaning with such a large field. This fear now seems unjustified, but it did result in the USCF's taking the fateful step of holding the entire event as a 13-round Swiss. Every U.S. Open since, and almost all other major events, have used only the Swiss system, with some turnouts far beyond what other methods could have attracted or handled. The U.S. Open drew substantial new highs of 181 players at Milwaukee in 1953, 266 at Chicago in 1963, 400 at Ventura in 1971, 778 at Chicago in 1973, and 836 at Pasadena in 1983, all playing in one section. Some multi-section events such as the National Scholastics, National Open, World Open, and New York Open have drawn even larger totals; the 1986 World Open had 1,506 players, more than the total membership of the USCF in 1953.

This edition of the rule book, like its predecessor, has major changes in pairing methods for the ratings-driven Swiss system tournament. The United States has led the way in the adoption of the Swiss, which continues to gain world-wide acceptance. The development of the Swiss system, along with the invention and refinement of the rating system by Kenneth Harkness and Arpad Elo, have been the two major contributions by the USCF to the popularization of chess throughout the world.

Major Changes in This Edition

In addition to elaborations on both new and old topics, this book has many rules changes and matters addressed for the first time. We believe that Tim Redman was right to devote more of his 1987 rule book to explanation and discussion than past rule books, and our edition continues this trend.

We realize that some experienced tournament directors might prefer a shorter book with rules only, but reactions at the annual

USCF Rules Committee workshops have convinced us that the majority of directors will welcome the expanded explanations. We also believe that the discussion of a rule is most comprehensible when it appears together with the rule, and thus have rejected suggestions that all such material be placed in a separate chapter.

And a rule book is not only for directors. Many players, including beginners, will read this book, and they, too, can learn from the rule explanations. Even material not relating to rules, such as the last two paragraphs of 3D on the three meanings of "piece," may help new players feel more at home at a chess club or tournament and facilitate their understanding of chess literature.

Following is a summary of this book's more significant changes and additions. "Change" indicates a change in the rules; "supplementary," an addition to the rules reflecting how most experienced tournament directors have handled the situation in practice; and "explanation," an addition or change intended to promote comprehension. Some "supplementary" rules will be changes for some directors, as not all have followed the common practices mentioned in previous rule books.

5C (change): This reflects the new USCF Quick Chess rating system, which began in 1991.

5F (change): The Allegro Clock material anticipates availability of an exciting new product. Without the Allegro's being declared the standard timer for sudden death controls in this book, its production would be less likely. To learn if the clock is available, contact the USCF office.

8C1 (explanation): Castling restrictions for the king that do not apply to the rook are specified, addressing one of the most frequently asked beginner's questions.

9 (explanation): Even experienced players are confused by the question of when a move is completed. The old term "completed" and the new "determined" are used in a precise manner in an attempt to clear up the confusion.

10C (change): If a player touches pieces of both colors and it cannot be established which was touched first, the director shall rule that the player's own piece was touched first. This is also a new FIDE rule.

10E, 10F (supplementary): These elaborate substantially upon the old touch-move rules.

10G (supplementary): This states for the first time the existing practice that if a player accidentally releases a piece on a legal square, the move is determined and cannot be changed.

11A, 16R (change): When an illegal move is corrected, the players do not recover the time used between the illegality and its discovery.

11D (change): In sudden death, the opponent of a player who completes an illegal move and punches the clock is given two additional minutes. This compensation previously applied only to sudden death time pressure.

11D1, 16D3 (change): The rules for sudden death time pressure have been changed to allow the opponent two moves rather than one to correct an illegal move. This change should cause few problems reconstructing the position, but may be enough to correct many illegal moves. In particular, the "trick" of illegally moving the king alongside the opposing queen and then capturing the queen with it on the next move will be impossible.

13A3, 14A3, 14G1 (change): If it cannot be established whether checkmate or stalemate occurred before or after a flag fall, the director shall rule the checkmate or stalemate valid.

13C2 (change): A player may call his or her own flag down to protect against an opponent's updating the score sheet. This rule was adopted by the USCF in 1990.

13C4 (supplementary): A player who fills in moves after the flag is down does not automatically lose the right to win on time, though the moves filled in do not count. A director who is unsure how many were filled in should give the benefit of the doubt to the opponent.

13C6 (change): If both flags are down, neither player may win on time in that control, even if a claim was made before the claimant's flag fell.

13C11, 14C6, 14F2 (change): The penalty for an incorrect claim of a win on time or a draw by triple occurrence of position or the 50-move rule is now the addition of two minutes to the opponent's clock. The old penalty was five minutes subtracted from the claimant's clock, with no penalty specified for a 50-move rule claim. Especially in fast time limits the loss of minutes lost was often disastrous. Also, the rules are now simplified so that all specified time penalties (11D, 13C11, 14C6, 14F2) are the same, with the single exception of 14H4b.

14B2, 14B3, 14C4 (explanation): The consequences of improper draw offers and irregular triple occurrence of position claims are discussed in much greater detail than previously.

14C7 (change): A claim of a draw by triple occurrence of position is transformed into a draw offer if the claimant moves (or has moved) and punches the clock.

14C8 (change): In sudden death time pressure, a player with under five minutes remaining may be awarded a draw by triple occurrence of position based on the observation of a director or witness.

14E2, 14E3 (change): A player may not win on time with only king and bishop, king and knight, or (vs. no pawns) king and two knights unless having a forced win.

14F1 (change): The 50-move rule is now standard under both USCF and FIDE rules. Exceptions for special positions are irregular and must be posted before round one.

14F3 (explanation): The 50-move rule is to be applied literally, even if the claimant's opponent can mate on move 51.

14F4 (change): In sudden death, if a player with less than five minutes remaining requests it, the director or a deputy may count moves and award a draw under the 50-move rule.

14G2 (change): In sudden death, if the game continues for at least five minutes with both flags down and neither player claims the draw, the director may rule a draw.

14H, 14I (change): Possibly the most controversial area considered by the editors was that of the claim of insufficient losing chances in sudden death.

The 1987 rule book, written in the infancy of sudden death, presented king and knight vs. king and knight (a position that is now an automatic draw unless there is a forced mate) as an example of a position in which the draw would be upheld. To make the draw so difficult to obtain was unpopular with many players; some were extremely upset when opponents played on in hopelessly drawn positions in order to win on time.

Many directors used a far more liberal standard than that of the rule book. A popular variation was that if the director thought a Class C player would probably at least draw the position against a Grandmaster with both having ample time, the draw was awarded. This variation generally worked better than the published rule, but there were complaints from players who believed that too many claims were being upheld and from directors who felt that too many claims without merit were being made.

An early draft of this book presented the Class C player vs. the Grandmaster as the main rule, along with two variations for directors wanting fewer claims upheld. However, experienced directors reacted that having one standard rule was of paramount importance, to reduce the substantial confusion now existing among players.

Therefore, the new rule is a compromise between the extremes of previous practice. The draw now should be awarded if the director believes that a Class C player would have little chance to lose the position against a Master, with both having ample time. A director seeking a more precise standard may consider "little" to mean less than 10 percent.

A director who is unsure whether or not a position meets this standard should employ a new option—to temporarily deny the claim with no time penalty and to observe the game with the intent of upholding the claim if the opponent is making no progress. A director who does not have time to be stationed at the game may instead watch it intermittently for lack of progress, inviting a repeat claim if warranted.

Such claims are now allowed only to players with under five minutes remaining, and in order to reduce those without merit, the penalty for a clearly incorrect claim is the loss of one minute on the claimant's clock. This subtraction is the only exception to this book's policy that all specified time penalties are the addition of two minutes to the opponent's time.

14I provides guidelines on how to rule in certain simplified positions. To give an example of a position handled three different ways under the new compromise rule and the two earlier extremes, a player claiming a draw with king and knight together in the middle of the board vs. king and rook would have the claim denied under the 1987 rule book, upheld under the "C player would probably draw a Grandmaster" rule (according to all Grandmasters asked!), and temporarily denied pending observation for progress under the new rule in this book.

14J (change): The director may now rule any disputed game a draw if this ruling is more equitable than any other possible.

14K (change): If an Allegro Clock is used, the game is drawn after 175 moves.

15A1 (supplementary): The treatment of players who do not keep score for religious reasons, or have not learned to keep score, is addressed for the first time.

15C (change): In sudden death, if either player has less than five minutes remaining, neither is required to keep score. This rule was approved by both the USCF and FIDE between rule books.

15F1 (change): A player may not ask to borrow the opponent's score sheet unless both players have at least five minutes remaining in the current time control.

16C (change): The rule requiring players to keep their hands off the clock while the opponent's side is running now applies to all games, not just sudden death time pressure.

16K (change): If both players are late for a game, the first to arrive must split the elapsed time between the players.

16P (supplementary): The problem of erroneously set clocks is addressed.

16X (change): An extra minute should no longer be added to each side of the clock. This change was approved by the USCF between rule books.

20 (supplementary): Extensive elaboration and examples are given regarding the conduct of players and spectators.

21I1 (change): An appeals committee of two is sufficient if both are certified at the senior director level or higher.

21I5 (supplementary): The function of an appeals committee is not to substitute its judgment for that of the director, but rather to overrule the director only if it is clear the latter's ruling is incorrect.

21I6 (supplementary): In the event of a tie vote by an appeals committee, the director's decision shall stand.

21J (change): The new position of special referee is created as an alternative to the appeals committee.

23A1 (change): If extraordinary circumstances such as extreme weather conditions or civil unrest prevent most potential entrants from playing in a tournament, the organizer may appeal to the USCF executive director for permission to limit the prizes to 100 percent of entry fees collected.

23A2 (supplementary): The USCF's existing rule on tournament cancellations, with minor modifications, appears in the rule book for the first time.

22C, 28K4 (supplementary): Half-point byes are discussed in greatly expanded detail, reflecting existing practice.

28C1 (supplementary): Treatment of players with erroneously assigned multiple USCF ratings is discussed.

28C2 (change): The circumstances under which a player is required to disclose a foreign or FIDE rating are listed.

28D through 28I (supplementary): Described in detail are when and how the director should assign a rating, how to treat a claimed old rating that cannot be verified, and the consequences of finding in mid-tournament that a player is ineligible for his or her section.

28L3 (supplementary): A player who has won an unplayed game due to the opponent's failure to appear should not be assigned a full-point bye.

28L5 (change): Assigning the full-point bye to a score group other than the lowest in order to allow a new player to achieve a published rating should be considered only in events of exactly four rounds.

28M3 (supplementary): Cross-section pairings are described as an additional bye alternative.

28N1 (change): For combined individual-team tournaments, a new pairing method addresses the problem of teammates' obtaining an unfair advantage for individual awards if they cannot face each other.

28Q1 (change): An improved version of the Kashdan system for pairing adjourned games is presented.

28S (supplementary): Reentries are discussed and pairing rules for them listed.

29J (change): Pairing priorities in the area of colors vs. ratings are modified. The most significant changes are:

The 100-point rule for color switches is replaced by an 80-point rule for alternation or extra-white situations and a 200-point rule for the more significant extra-black situations.

All transpositions should be evaluated based on the smaller of the two rating differences involved, not only on the difference in the lower half as in the past.

A transposition involving a switch of no more than 80 points should be preferred to any interchange.

A player who has already played more blacks than whites should not be assigned black in the last round, unless there is no other way to pair the score group without players facing each other for a second time. Note that this procedure may result in some very odd pairings (such as dropping the top-rated player in a group with an odd number), which will provoke complaints. This is why the same rule is not justified for avoiding excess whites.

29K (change): Discussed for the first time is the fact that the order in which pairings are switched to improve colors can be significant. The two methods commonly used are assigned names, and the "Look Ahead Method" endorsed as standard. The less effective "Top Down Method" is listed as a variation since many directors, especially those with less experience, have been using it.

29N2 (change): If pairings are redone due to an error or late withdrawal, it is recommended that no game be canceled in which Black's fourth move has been determined.

29N3 (supplementary): Selective re-pairing is described for situations in which pairings need to be redone when some games have started.

29O (supplementary): How the director may handle unreported results in Swisses is described in detail.

29Q (change): Unrateds with plus scores may be paired against each other in class tournaments.

29S (supplementary): Round robin tables may be used to help pair a small Swiss, in order to avoid players having to meet twice.

30G (supplementary): Advice is offered on how the director should treat a quad with an odd number of players.

30H (supplementary): The Holland system of round robins, mentioned but not described in the previous rule book, is explained.

30I (change): The new Unbalanced Holland system is described.

31G4 (supplementary): A team captain should advise a team member about a draw only if asked, and must respond without first looking at the position.

33D (supplementary): The "prizes based on points" system is discussed.

34E (change): The standard tie-break order is now Modified Median, followed by Solkoff, Cumulative, and Cumulative of Opposition.

34E1 (change): A system is now specified for scoring the unplayed games of tied players involved in tie breaking; previously only the unplayed games of the opponents of tied players were mentioned. Also, a player who scores in actual play now wins on tie break automatically over one whose entire point total is due to unplayed games.

36E (change): Reflecting existing practice, computers may not be paired against each other.

36I9 (supplementary): The operator of a computer may consult players of any strength regarding offering or accepting a draw, or resigning, for the computer.

36I13 (change): A new FIDE rule has made necessary a warning to organizers who allow computers and also are interested in humans being FIDE-rated.

39, 40, 41 (change): The definitions of standard sets and boards have been tightened somewhat to encourage the use of commonly seen equipment, keeping in mind that some tournament players are annoyed by equipment they are not used to. Equipment not meeting these standards may still be used if both players agree, or if standard equipment is not available. For non-USCF play, somewhat different equipment is likely to be acceptable.

43, 44, 45, 46 (supplementary): A new chapter, "The Well-Run

Tournament," discusses in detail subjects mostly new to this rule book, including starting rounds on time, efficient pairing procedures, pairing sheets, reporting methods, wall charts, table numbers, table setup, location of headquarters and skittles (analysis) rooms, announcements, lighting, and noise.

U.S. CHESS FEDERATION'S

OFFICIAL

RULES OF CHESS

FOURTH EDITION

OFFICIAL RULES OF CHESS

USCF SECTION

1. INTRODUCTION

1A. Scope. Most problems concerning rules that may arise during a chess game are covered in this book. However, the rules of chess cannot and should not regulate all possible situations. In situations not explicitly covered, the tournament director can usually reach a fair decision by considering similar cases and applying their principles analogously. The United States Chess Federation (USCF) presumes that its tournament directors have the competence, sound judgment, and absolute objectivity needed to arrive at fair and logical solutions to problems not specifically treated by these rules.

1B. Validity. USCF play shall be governed by these rules of chess and by all USCF procedures and policies. World Chess Federation (Fédération Internationale des Echecs, or FIDE) rules shall not be used unless specifically announced in advance. For FIDE matches, championships, or other events that use FIDE rather than USCF rules, see Chapters 20, 21, and 22.

1C. Types of events.

1C1. Major events. While the basic laws of chess do not vary from event to event, some material in this book is designed principally for major tournaments and is unlikely to be relevant otherwise. For example, unethical behavior is rare in chess; many players reading this book will play virtually all their games as friendly encounters in the spirit of good sportsmanship. But there are rare occasions, especially when large prizes or important titles are at stake, when a player steps beyond the bounds of friendly competition. Rules are needed to cover these situations.

1C2. Director discretion. In areas in which the director has discretion, it is appropriate to be strictest with rules enforcement and penalties in events that are stronger or offer larger prizes. Losing a game due to an inadvertent rules violation can be sufficiently upsetting to deter a beginner from future chess participation.

2. THE CHESSBOARD

2A. Explanation. The game is played by two opponents moving pieces on a square board called a "chessboard."

2B. Description. The chessboard is composed of sixty-four squares of identical size, eight squares by eight squares, alternately light and dark. The light squares are referred to as "white squares" and the dark squares "black squares," even though other colors are frequently used. (For instance, in tournament play "black squares" are often green.)

2C. Placement. The chessboard is placed between the players in such a way that the nearer corner to the right of each player is white.

2D. Files. The eight vertical rows of squares are called "files."

2E. Ranks. The eight horizontal rows of squares are called "ranks."

2F. Diagonals. The lines of squares of the same color, touching from one edge of the board to another, are called "diagonals"; those touching from one corner of the board to another are called "long diagonals."

3. THE PIECES

3A. Each player's pieces. At the beginning of the game, one player ("white") has sixteen light-colored pieces (the white pieces), the other ("black") has sixteen dark-colored pieces (the black pieces).

3B. Description of the pieces. These pieces are as follows:

a white king, usually indicated by the symbol:

a white queen, usually indicated by the symbol:

two white rooks, usually indicated by the symbol:

two white bishops, usually indicated by the symbol:

two white knights, usually indicated by the symbol:

eight white pawns, usually indicated by the symbol:

a black king, usually indicated by the symbol:

a black queen, usually indicated by the symbol:

two black rooks, usually indicated by the symbol:

two black bishops, usually indicated by the symbol:

two black knights, usually indicated by the symbol:

eight black pawns, usually indicated by the symbol:

3C. Initial position. The initial position of the pieces on the chessboard is as follows:

3D. Meaning of "piece." The word "piece" has acquired various meanings in chess jargon. When used in a rules context, a "piece"

is anything on the chessboard—a king, queen, rook, bishop, knight, or pawn. This book will not subsequently use the alternate connotations of "piece," which follow for informational purposes only.

A second meaning of "piece" excludes pawns. For instance, a chess player referring to "passive pieces" or "an attack by pieces" or "forking my pieces" is referring to pieces other than pawns.

A third and even more limited meaning: If a player is said to win, lose, or sacrifice a piece, the meaning is only bishop or knight. If a queen, rook, or pawn is won, lost, or sacrificed, it is referred to by name—"winning the queen, winning a pawn," etc. A bishop or knight is also known as a "minor piece," a queen or rook as a "major piece."

3E. Other expressions involving pieces. These are presented for informational purposes only.

3E1. Castling long. Castling on the queenside (using a rook on a1 or a8). See 8A2 for castling.

3E2. Castling short. Castling on the kingside (using a rook on h1 or h8).

3E3. Discovered check, double check. See Rule 12, Check.

3E4. Exchange.

a. "The exchange" or "an exchange" refers to the difference between one player's rook and the other's bishop or knight. A player giving up a rook for a bishop or knight is said to "lose the exchange" and that player's opponent to "win the exchange."

b. "The exchange of queens" indicates the capture of each player's queen by the other player. The same language may be used regarding rooks, bishops, knights, or pawns.

3E5. Fork. A simultaneous attack on two or more pieces.

3E6. Interpose. To place a piece between one's king and an opponent's checking piece. See 12A.

3E7. Material. Pieces other than the king.

3E8. Pin. A piece is said to be "pinned" if it either cannot legally move because such a move would expose its king to check, or moving it would be unwise because this would allow the opponent to advantageously capture a shielded piece.

3E9. Sacrifice. To deliberately allow the capture of a piece or pieces, receiving in immediate return no pieces, or a piece or pieces usually considered to have less value. The ultimate objective of a sacrifice is often to expose the opponent's king to attack, or to recover the sacrificed material and more.

3E10. Zugzwang. A situation in which moving any piece is disadvantageous. The player "in zugzwang" would be better off declining to move (passing), but this is not permitted.

4. OBJECTIVE AND SCORING

4A. Checkmate. The objective of each of the two players in a game of chess is to win the game by checkmating the opponent's king. A player's king is checkmated when the square it occupies is attacked by one or more of the opponent's pieces (see Rule 12, Check) and the player has no move that escapes such attack.

4B. Other decisive outcomes. A common way for a player to win the game is the resignation of the opponent, conceding inevitable checkmate. A player may also win in other ways, such as the opponent's exceeding of the time limit. See Rule 13, The Decisive Game.

4C. Draws. An indecisive result or draw may be agreed upon, usually indicating that neither player expects to be able to checkmate the other. See Rule 14, The Drawn Game, for details of this and other types of drawn games.

4D. Scoring. For a won game, the winner gets one (1) point and the loser zero (0); for a draw, each player gets a half point (½). See Rule 22 for the scoring of unplayed games.

5. THE CHESS CLOCK

5A. Time controls and time limits. Each player must make either a certain number of moves, all moves, or all remaining moves in an allotted period of time, these factors being specified in advance. If both players complete the required moves in the allotted time, a new period begins. Each such time period is called a "time control" or "control."

The phrase "time limit" is inclusive of all time controls, but also is sometimes used to indicate only the present control. Time controls appear in tournament publicity as, from left to right, number of moves, slash, time. For instance, if each player must make 40 moves in 1½ hours, this is abbreviated 40/1½ or 40/90 (for 90 minutes).

5B. Sudden death time controls. If the final or only time control requires all moves to be made in a specified time, this is considered a "sudden death" or "allegro" control. The abbreviation "SD" is generally used for a final such control, the abbreviation "G" for an only such control. For example, "40/2, SD/1" indicates 40 moves in two hours followed by the rest of the game in an hour, while "G/30" means each player has 30 minutes for the entire game.

5C. Quick Chess. The USCF maintains a separate rating system for Quick Chess games in which players have less than thirty minutes to complete all their moves. As of this writing, Quick Chess includes only time limits from G/10 through G/29. This range may be expanded in the future. All Quick Chess rules are identical to the regular USCF sudden death rules herein except that scorekeeping is not required, so all provisions relating to chess notation are irrelevant.

5D. Accumulation of time. The time unused by a player during one control accumulates and is added to the player's available time for the next control.

5E. Standard timer for non–sudden death. The standard timer for games not concluded by a sudden death control is a mechanical apparatus consisting of two clocks that tell time by means of hands moving on a dial (analog clocks). Other types of clocks, such as digital, may be used if both players agree, or if an analog clock is not available. See Chapter 4, "Equipment Standards," for further discussion of clocks.

5F. Standard timer for sudden death. *This section applies once the Allegro Clock is commercially available.* If the Allegro Clock or a similar clock is not available, 5E applies. See also Chapter 4, "Equipment Standards."

The USCF Allegro Clock, a clock with time delay and, possibly, move-counting capabilities, is the standard timer for sudden death time controls. This clock allows games to be decided entirely by the players, with no need for directors to consider insufficient losing chances or count for the 50-move rule (see 14H7). Games are drawn after 175 moves are completed (see 14K).

If using an Allegro Clock without a move counter, the draw after

175 moves can still be achieved as a result of the claimant's score sheet or a count by the director or another acceptable witness. (For other options of declaring the game a draw, see adjudication of ridiculous positions.)

The Allegro Clock may be set to allow each player a small amount of reaction time for each move before starting to consume reflection time. The standard delay is five seconds per move. For Quick Chess (G/10 to G/29) the standard delay is three seconds, and for Blitz Chess (G/5) two seconds. The Allegro Clock may also be used for non–sudden death play by setting the delay to zero.

5G. The flag. Control of each player's time is effected by means of a clock equipped with a flag or other special device used to signal the end of the hour; the flag falls to indicate the player's time has been used up. Some digital clocks have a beep, a light, or a display of all zeros to indicate that the player's time has been exhausted. References in this book to a flag falling or being down also apply to such "flag substitutes."

5H. Punching the clock. After moving, a player presses the button on his or her side of the clock, which stops that side from running and starts the opponent's side. This book refers to such action as "punching the clock."

5I. Stopping the clock. A player who wishes to make a claim of any sort or see a director for any legitimate reason may stop both sides of the clock before claiming and/or finding a director. This book refers to such action as "stopping the clock" or "stopping both clocks." If the opponent's clock is accidentally started when a player tries to stop both clocks, the director will determine whether the claim is still in order.

5J. Further details. See Rule 16, Use of the Chess Clock.

6. THE RIGHT TO MOVE

6A. The first move. White makes the first move. The players then alternate in making one move at a time until the game is over.

6B. A player on move. A player is said to "be on move" or to "have the move" when the opponent's move has been completed.

7. DEFINITION OF THE MOVE

7A. Basic definition. With the exception of castling (8A2) and promotion of a pawn (8F6), a move is the transfer of a piece from one square to another square that is either vacant or occupied by an opponent's piece.

7B. Crossing an occupied square. With the exception of the king and rook in castling, no piece except the knight may cross a square occupied by another piece.

7C. Capturing. A piece played to a square occupied by an opponent's piece captures the latter as part of the move. The captured piece is removed immediately from the chessboard by the player making the capture. (See 8F5 for capturing en passant.)

8. THE MOVES OF THE PIECES

8A. The king.

8A1. The king's move. Except when castling, the king moves to any adjoining square that is not attacked by one or more of the opponent's pieces.

8A2. Castling. Castling is a move of the king and either rook, counting as a single move and executed as follows: the king is transferred from its original square two squares toward either rook on the same rank; then, that rook is transferred over the king to the square adjacent to the king on the same rank.

8A3. Castling permanently illegal. Castling is illegal for the duration of the game:

   a. if the king has already moved, or

   b. with a rook that has already moved.

8A4. Castling temporarily illegal. Castling is not presently possible if:

   a. the king's original square, the square which the king must cross over, or the square the king is to occupy is attacked by an opponent's piece, or

   b. there is any piece between the king and the rook with which it castles.

8B. The queen. The queen moves to any square (except as limited by 7B) on the file, rank, or diagonal(s) on which it stands.

8C. The rook. The rook moves to any square (except as limited by 7B) on the file or rank on which it stands.

8C1. Castling. Several restrictions on the king in castling do not apply to the rook:

   a. A player may castle with a rook whose original square is under attack.

b. A player may castle with a rook that crosses over a square under attack by an opponent's piece.

c. There is no prohibition against the rook occupying a square attacked by an opponent's piece at the conclusion of castling, but this is impossible as the king would have to illegally cross an attacked square to bring it about.

8D. The bishop. The bishop moves to any square (except as limited by 7B) on the diagonal(s) on which it stands.

8E. The knight. The knight's move is composed of two different steps. First, it makes one step of one single square along the rank or file on which it stands. It does not land on that square, as its move is not complete. Then, still moving away from the square of departure, it moves one step of one single square on a diagonal. It does not matter if the square of the first step is occupied.

This move is sometimes called an "L" move, as it is equivalent to moving the knight two squares vertically, the one square horizontally (or two squares horizontally, then one square vertically). Note that the knight always moves to a square different in color than that of its starting square.

8F. The pawn.

8F1. The pawn's move. The pawn may only move forward.

8F2. The first move of each pawn. On its first move, it may advance either one or two vacant squares along its file.

8F3. Subsequent moves of each pawn. On its subsequent moves, it advances one vacant square along its file.

8F4. Pawns move vertically but capture diagonally. The pawn is unique among chess pieces in that it captures differently than it moves. When capturing, it advances one square along either of the diagonals on which it stands.

8F5. Capturing en passant. A pawn, attacking a square by-passed by an opponent's pawn, the latter having advanced two squares in one move from its original square, may capture the opponent's pawn as though the latter had moved only one square.

This capture may only be made in immediate reply to such advance and is called an en passant ("in passing") capture. Note that only a pawn that has advanced a total of exactly three squares from its original square is in position to make such a capture.

8F6. Pawn promotion. On reaching the last rank, a pawn must immediately be exchanged, as part of the same move, for a queen, a rook, a bishop, or a knight of the same color as the pawn, at the player's choice. This exchange of the pawn for another piece is called "promotion," and the effect of the new piece is immediate. For instance, it may give check.

Note that promotion is in no way related to other pieces remaining on the chessboard; for example, a player may have two or more queens or three or more knights. The choice of the piece is not final until it has been placed on the board and released.

8F7. Promoted piece not available. If the desired piece is not available to replace a promoted pawn, the player may stop both clocks in order to locate that piece and place it on the board. A player who cannot quickly find such a piece may request the assistance of the director. It is improper to punch the clock with the pawn still on the last rank. If this is done, the opponent may immediately restart the player's clock without moving.

As soon as the new piece is placed on the board, either player should restart the clock. It is common practice, however, to play using an upside-down rook for a second queen. In the absence of the player's announcement to the contrary, an upside-down rook shall be considered a queen.

9. DETERMINATION AND COMPLETION OF THE MOVE

9A. Transfer to a vacant square. In the case of the transfer of a piece to a vacant square, the move is determined with no possibility of change when the player's hand has released the piece, and completed when that player punches the clock.

9B. Capture. In the case of a capture, the move is determined with no possibility of change when the captured piece has been removed from the chessboard and the player's hand has released the capturing piece, and completed when that player punches the clock.

9C. Castling. In the case of castling, the move is determined with no possibility of change when the player's hand has released the king, which has moved two squares toward a rook, and completed when that player, having transferred the rook to its new square, punches the clock.

9D. Pawn promotion. In the case of the promotion of a pawn, the move is determined with no possibility of change when the pawn has been removed from the chessboard and the player's hand has released the new piece on the promotion square, and completed when that player punches the clock. If the player has released the pawn on the last rank, the move is not yet determined, but the player no longer has the right to play the pawn to another square.

9E. Checkmate or stalemate. In the case of a move which produces checkmate or stalemate, the move is determined with no possibility of change upon release as described in 9A, 9B, 9C, or 9D, whichever applies. The move is completed simultaneously with its determination.

9F. Last move of the time control. When determining whether the prescribed number of moves has been made in the allotted time, the last move is considered complete only after the player punches the clock. The player's flag may be up after releasing the piece, it may be up while hitting the clock, but if it is down after the move and the opponent has not yet handled the clock, the player has failed to make the time control.

Except for 9E, there should never be a dispute about whether the final move of a time control or a flag fall occurred first, because a player's task is to punch the clock in time to prevent the flag fall. If the flag is down, the player has not accomplished this task, and the director must rule that the move was not completed in time.

Note that if the final move of the time control produces checkmate or stalemate, punching or stopping the clock, while recommended, is not required (see 9E, 13A, and 14A).

9G. "Determined" moves and "completed" moves. As described in 9A through 9D above, there is a period between the release of a piece and the punch of the clock during which the move is determined but not completed. The significance of this period is as follows:

9G1. Player still on move for claims. Claims of triple repetition of position (see 14C), the 50-move rule (see 14F), or insufficient losing chances in sudden death time pressure (see 14H) remain in order during the period between determination and completion of the move. As soon as the player completes the move, it is the opponent's move, and the right to make such claims belongs exclusively to the opponent.

9G2. Determination irrelevant to time control. In the case of 9F (last move of the time control), whether or not the player has determined the move is of no significance in deciding whether the player has made the prescribed number of moves in the allotted time. The player's flag must remain up after the final move has been completed, not just determined.

9G3. Draw offers. The interval between determination and completion of the move is the proper time to offer a draw (see 14B1).

9H. Stopping the clock. If a player determines a move and then stops the clock to see a director for any reason, rather than punching it the determined move is not yet completed and the player retains the options of 9G1.

10. THE TOUCHED PIECE

10A. Adjustment of pieces. A player who is on the move and first expresses the intention to adjust (e.g., by saying *"j'adoube"* or "I adjust") may adjust one or more pieces on his or her squares.

10B. Touch-move rule. Except for 10A, a player on the move who deliberately touches one or more pieces of the same color, in a manner which may reasonably be interpreted as the beginning of a move, must move or capture the first piece touched that can be moved or captured.

10C. Touching pieces of both colors. Except for 10A, a player on the move who deliberately touches one or more pieces of each color, or who moves the player's piece and intentionally displaces an opponent's piece with it, must capture the opponent's piece with the player's piece, or, if this is illegal, must move or capture the first piece touched that can be moved or captured. If it is impossible to establish which piece was touched first, the player's piece shall be considered the touched piece.

10D. Piece touched cannot move. If no piece touched has a legal move, and no opponent's piece touched can be legally captured, the player is free to make any legal move.

10E. Accidental touch of piece. A director who believes a player touched a piece by accident should not require the player to move that piece. For example, a player's hand reaching across the board may inadvertently brush the top of a nearby king or queen, or a player may hit a piece with an elbow. See also 10F.

10F. Appearance of adjustment. Sometimes it is clear that a player is adjusting, even when that player improperly fails to say *"j'adoube"* or "I adjust." For instance, a player who uses one finger to slide a piece to the center of its square is not acting in a manner usual to the beginning of a move, and probably should not be required to move the piece. Players are warned, though, that it is wise to announce one is adjusting in advance, as a safeguard against being forced to make an unwanted move.

10G. Accidental release of piece. A player who deliberately touches a piece and then accidentally releases it on an unintended but legal square is required to leave it on that square.

10H. Piece touched off the board. There is no penalty for touching a piece that is off the board. A player who advances a pawn to the last rank and then touches a piece off the board is not obligated to promote the pawn to the piece touched until that piece has been released on the promotion square. For explanation of pawn promotion, see 8F6.

10I. Castling. For description of castling, see 8A2, 8A3, 8A4.

10I1. King touched first, or king and rook simultaneously. If a player intending to castle touches the king first, or king and rook at the same time, and then realizes that castling is illegal, the player may choose either to move the king or to castle on the other side if legal. If the king has no legal move, the player is free to choose any move.

10I2. Rook touched first. If a player intending to castle touches the rook first, there is no penalty except if castling is illegal, the player must move the rook if legal.

10J. When to claim touch-move. To claim the opponent has violated 10B or 10C, a player must do so before deliberately touching a piece.

11. ILLEGAL POSITIONS

11A. Illegal move during last ten moves. If, during a game, it is found that one of either player's last ten moves was illegal, the position shall be reinstated to what it was before the illegal move. The game shall then continue by applying Rule 10 (touch-move) to the move replacing the illegal move. If the position cannot be reinstated, then the illegal move shall stand. Except in sudden death, the clocks shall not be adjusted (see 16R). 11A is not in effect during sudden death time pressure (see 11D1).

11B. Illegal move prior to last ten moves. If it is found that an illegal move was made prior to each player's last ten moves, the illegal move shall stand and the game shall continue.

11C. Accidental piece displacement. If, during a game, one or more pieces have been accidentally displaced and incorrectly replaced, then the displacement shall be treated as an illegal move. If, during the course of a move, a player inadvertently knocks over one or more pieces, the player must not punch the clock until the position has been reestablished. The opponent may punch the clock without moving, if necessary, to force the player who knocked over the piece(s) to restore the position on his or her own time.

11D. Illegal move in sudden death. If, in a sudden death control, a player completes an illegal move by punching the clock, in addition to the usual obligation to make a legal move with the touched piece if possible two minutes shall be added to the remaining time of the opponent of the player who made the illegal move.

11D1. Illegal move in sudden death time pressure. A director should not call illegal moves in sudden death time pressure. If either player has under five minutes remaining in a sudden death time control and the illegal move is not corrected before the opponent of the player who made the illegal move completes two moves, the illegal move stands and there is no time adjustment. See 16D3.

11E. Incorrect adjourned position. If, after an adjournment, the position is incorrectly set up, then the position as it was at adjournment must be set up again and the game continued, subject to the provisions of Rule 11A (the ten-move rule). The clocks shall not be adjusted.

11F. Incorrect initial position. If, before the completion of black's 10th move, it is found that the initial position of the pieces was incorrect, or that the game began with the colors reversed, then the game shall be annulled and a new game played. However, the players shall begin the new game with their clocks still reflecting the elapsed time each player used in the annulled game. If the error is discovered after the completion of black's 10th move, the game shall continue.

11G. Incorrect placement of chessboard. If, during a game, it is found that the board has been placed contrary to 3C, which requires a white square in the nearer corner to the right of each player, then the position reached shall be transferred to a board correctly placed and the game continued.

11H. Director witnessing illegal move. Except in sudden death time pressure (see 11D1), a director who witnesses an illegal move being made shall require the player to replace that move with a legal one in accordance with 10B, the touch-move rule.

Variation 11H1. In an event in which most games are not watched by directors, the director may refrain from correcting all illegal moves he or she may notice but simply serve as a witness should one of the players point out the illegal move before ten more moves have been made.

11I. Spectators. Spectators must not point out illegal moves, except to the director in a manner neither heard nor noticed by the players. See 20M regarding behavior of spectators.

11J. Deliberate illegal moves. If a player intentionally makes illegal moves, the director may impose penalties.

12. CHECK

12A. Definition. The king is "in check" when the square it occupies is attacked by one or more of the opponent's pieces; such pieces are said to be "checking the king." Check is parried by capturing the opposing piece, interposing one of the player's own pieces between the checking piece and the king (not possible if checking piece is a knight), or moving the king.

12B. Double check. If the square the king occupies is attacked by two opposing pieces, this is also known as "double check," and may be parried only by moving the king.

12C. Responding to check. Check must be parried on the move immediately following. If a player's king is unable to escape check, it is "checkmated" and the player loses the game (see 13A).

12D. Check by interposing piece. A piece blocking a check to the king of its own color, commonly referred to as "interposing," can itself give check to the enemy king.

12E. Moving into check. A player may not move the king to a square attacked by one or more opponent's pieces.

12F. Calling check not mandatory. Announcing check is not required, and is rare in high-level tournaments. It is the responsibility of the opponent to notice the check, and a player who does not may suffer serious consequences (see Rule 10, The Touched Piece).

13. THE DECISIVE GAME

13A. Checkmate. The game is won by the player who checkmates the opponent's king, providing the mating move is legal. This immediately ends the game.

13A1. The clock after checkmate. A player who checkmates the opponent is not obligated to then punch or stop the clock, as checkmate takes priority over a subsequent flag fall. A player delivering checkmate may choose to punch the clock to minimize the possibility of dispute.

13A2. Flag fall before checkmate. If a player claims a win by time forfeit before the opponent determines a move delivering checkmate, the time forfeit claim is proper.

13A3. Unclear if checkmate or flag fall came first. After considering all available evidence, including testimony by the players and any witnesses, a director who is still unable to decide whether the claim of the flag fall occurred first shall deny the time claim and rule the checkmate valid.

13B. Resignation. The game is won by the player whose opponent resigns. This immediately ends the game. Saying "I resign" or tipping over the king are relatively clear ways to resign.

Stopping both clocks does not necessarily indicate a resignation. Since a player may be making a claim or seeing a director, the opponent should not assume a player who stops both clocks has resigned without further evidence.

Likewise, the offer of a handshake is not necessarily a resignation. On occasion, one player believes the handshake agrees to a draw while the other interprets it as a resignation.

13C. Time forfeit. The game is won by the player who properly claims that the opponent has not completed the prescribed number of moves in the allotted time, provided that the claimant has a reasonably complete score sheet when the flag falls (see 13C7) and mating material (see 14E).

13C1. Only players may call flag. Only the players in a game may call attention to the fall of a flag; it is considered to have fallen only when this is pointed out by either player. A director must never initiate a time-forfeit claim.

Spectators, including players of other games, who point out the fall of a flag in any manner may be disciplined by the tournament director to the point of expulsion from the playing room, loss of their own games, or expulsion from the tournament. See 20M, Behavior of spectators. The recipient of such assistance may also be penalized; see 20E.

13C2. Player may call own flag for protection. A player may call attention to the fall of his or her own flag. This initiates the time forfeiture procedure, the same as if the opponent had made a claim. A player will likely exercise this option in order to make it clear that any moves the opponent may subsequently fill in or correct on the score sheet are invalid for the purpose of having an adequate score. See 13C3.

13C3. Filling in moves with flag down. Once the fallen flag is pointed out by either player, neither is permitted to fill in or correct any previous moves missing from the score sheet. It is especially important that a player who expects to win on time not fill in missing moves. Such additions or corrections are not considered for the purpose of determining whether the score sheet is reasonably complete, and may obscure a valid claim.

13C4. Consequence of filling in moves. A player who improperly fills in missing moves after a fallen flag has been pointed out may not win by time forfeit unless the director is certain that the player's score sheet would have been sufficient to win on time without the improper additions. A director who is unsure on this point should give the benefit of the doubt to the opponent of the claimant.

13C5. How to claim. To claim a win by time forfeit, a player should stop both clocks and state the claim. If the opponent accepts the claim, the game is over. If the opponent does not accept the claim, the claimant must present the claim to a director.

13C6. Claimant's clock. If a player who claims a time forfeit states the claim with claimant's flag still up, but then fails to stop the clock in time to avoid also exceeding the time limit, the claim will be void (see 13C13 and 16T). A director who is aware that a claimant has neglected to stop the clock should instruct such a player to do so.

13C7. Definition of reasonably complete score sheet. Unless otherwise posted or announced in advance at the site, a reasonably complete score sheet is one that has no more than three missing or incomplete move pairs (consecutive moves, white and black or black and white). The absence of three consecutive individual moves, e.g. white-black-white, counts as two incomplete move pairs.

The move pair is considered incomplete if either side's move is omitted or incomplete. No move pair is ever considered to be "half complete."

Minor ambiguities in scorekeeping or errors involving no more than one symbol are of no consequence. The common error of omitting one move by one player and subsequently putting moves in the wrong columns counts as only one error. Moves that are indecipherable or recorded only with check marks are considered missing.

13C8. Use of opponent's score sheet. The director may use the score sheet of the claimant's opponent to determine that the requisite number of moves has been made or that the claimant's score sheet is in error. The director may also use the opponent's score sheet to assist in playing over the game. No player, however, may be forfeited based solely on the evidence of his or her own score sheet.

13C9. Player may demonstrate making time control. If the opponent of the claimant demonstrates that the required number of moves must have been made in order to reach the position on the board, the director shall deny the claim.

13C10. Director not obligated to play over game. If the claimant's score sheet appears to be sufficiently complete and both score sheets appear to be substantially identical and agree on the number of moves made, the director need not play over those moves but may instead require the player whose flag has fallen to demonstrate why the opponent's score sheet is not sufficient to win on time.

13C11. Time forfeit claim denied. If a flag is down but a claimant's score sheet is insufficient to win on time, two minutes shall be added to the claimant's opponent's remaining time and the game shall continue. No further time forfeit claims on that time control period are allowed; the following time period shall be in effect.

13C12. Both score sheets inadequate. If both players agree that sufficient moves have been made or that both score sheets are inadequate for time forfeit claims, and it is impossible to establish the exact number of moves, no further claims on that time control are permitted. The subsequent time control period is in effect. The players should diagram the position to serve as a reference point for future claims.

13C13. Player out of time cannot claim. A player whose own flag has fallen may not win on time during that control.

13C14. Role of director during time trouble. It is beneficial for a director to be present in an area with games in which the players are in time trouble, to observe the players and safeguard against disturbance, such as spectators or players talking or crowding too close to a game. However, it is not recommended that directors concentrate on watching clocks. This would accomplish little, as only players may call flags down, and a fallen flag constitutes evidence equal in value to the witnessing of a falling flag.

13C15. Variations. Any variations on these procedures, such as use of FIDE methods that require a director or deputy to be present at each board, must be clearly announced before the start of the tournament.

13D. Late arrival for game. The game is lost by the player who arrives at the chessboard more than one hour late for the beginning of the game or arrives after the expiration of the first time control period, whichever comes first. The absence countdown begins at the actual starting time of the round, which is not always the scheduled starting time. A director who learns that a player is unavoidably delayed may waive the one-hour forfeit rule.

Variation 13D1. To win under 13D, a player must set up board, set, and clock, start opponent's clock, and run clock until opponent has one hour of elapsed time. If both players are late, the first to arrive must split the elapsed time before starting opponent's clock (see 16K, Both players late). For example, if the first player to arrive is 40 minutes late, each player would start with 20 minutes elapsed, and the second player would not lose on time until 80 minutes late.

13E. Late arrival for adjournment resumption. The game is lost by the player who arrives at the chessboard more than one hour late for the resumption of an adjourned game or arrives after the expiration of the existing time period, whichever comes first. A director who learns that a player is unavoidably delayed may waive the one-hour forfeit rule. However, if the player who sealed the move is the late player, the game is decided otherwise if either of the following conditions exist:

13E1. Checkmate. The absent player has won the game by virtue of the fact that the sealed move produces checkmate.

13E2. Stalemate or insufficient material. The absent player has produced a drawn game by virtue of the fact that the sealed move has caused a stalemate, or if one of the positions in 14D has arisen.

13F. Late arrival by both players. If both players arrive at the chessboard more than one hour late, the director may declare the game lost by both players.

13G. Players must give notice if withdrawing or skipping a round. A player who does not notify the tournament director well in advance of the inability to play in any round and then defaults the game under 13D should be ejected from the tournament, and may be fined a sum up to the amount of the entry fee, payable to the organizer. The player may be barred from any of the organizer's tournaments until the fine is paid. On request, the player may be retained in or readmitted to the tournament at the director's discretion.

13H. Sealing of invalid move. The game is lost by a player who has sealed a move that the director finds has no reasonable interpretation (see 19G). However, a director who finds there are two or more reasonable interpretations of an ambiguous sealed move may allow sealer's opponent to choose between the possibilities (see 19F).

13I. Refusal to obey rules. The director may declare a game lost by a player who refuses to comply with the rules. If both players refuse to comply with the rules, the director may declare the game lost by both players.

14. THE DRAWN GAME

14A. Stalemate. The game is drawn when the king of the player on the move is not in check and that player has no legal move. This type of draw is called "stalemate." Providing that the stalemating move is legal, this immediately ends the game. Note that it is incorrect to refer to all drawn games as "stalemate." The draws described in 14B through 14K are not stalemates.

14A1. The clock after stalemate. Just as with a checkmate, a player who stalemates the opponent is not obligated to then punch the clock, as stalemate takes priority over a subsequent flag fall. A player delivering stalemate may choose to punch the clock to minimize the possibility of dispute.

14A2. Flag fall before stalemate. If a player claims a win on time before the opponent releases a piece that will deliver stalemate, the time forfeit claim is proper.

14A3. Unclear if stalemate or flag came first. After considering all available evidence, including testimony by the players and any witnesses, a director who is unable to determine whether the flag fall occurred first shall deny the time claim and uphold the stalemate.

14B. Agreement. The game is drawn upon agreement between the two players. This immediately ends the game.

14B1. Proper timing of draw offer. A proposal of a draw should be made by a player only after determining a move and before punching the clock. The opponent may accept the proposal or may reject it either orally or by deliberately touching a piece (see 10B). In the interim, the player who made the offer cannot withdraw it.

14B2. Improper offer with opponent on move. If a player improperly offers a draw while the opponent's clock is running, the opponent may accept or reject the offer. A player who offers a draw in this manner may be warned or penalized for annoying the opponent (see 20G).

14B3. Improper offer before moving. If a player improperly proposes a draw before moving, the offer stands until the opponent either accepts or rejects it. Such a proposal, while unlikely to annoy the opponent, can be disadvantageous, as the player may subsequently notice a strong move and regret the inability to withdraw the offer.

The opponent of a player offered a draw in this manner has the right to require the player who offered the draw to move before deciding whether to accept the offer, and may respond, "Make your move first," or words to that effect, or remain silent. In any case, the offer may not be withdrawn.

14B4. Flag fall during pending draw offer. A player who offers a draw may claim a win on time if the opponent oversteps the time limit while considering the proposal unless the offer is accepted before the flag fall is claimed.

14B5. Repeated offers. Repeated draw offers may be construed as annoying the opponent, and penalties are possible (see 20G). If the first offer has been declined, it is improper to offer another draw unless the opponent has since offered a draw or the position has changed substantially.

14B6. Premature or prearranged draws. It is unethical and unsporting to agree to a draw before a serious contest has begun. The same is true of all arrangements to prearrange game results (see 20L). In case of clear violations of the moral principles of the game, penalties should be imposed at the director's discretion.

14C. Triple occurrence of position. The game is drawn upon a claim by the player on the move when the same position is about to appear for at least the third time or has just appeared for at least the third time, the same player being on move each time. In both cases, the position is considered the same if pieces of the same kind and color occupy the same squares and if the possible moves of all the pieces are the same, including the right to castle or to capture a pawn en passant.

14C1. No "repetition of moves" or "perpetual check" draw. There is no rule regarding a draw by "repetition of moves." The draw is based on repetition of *position,* the three positions need not be consecutive, and the intervening moves do not matter. There is also no rule regarding "perpetual check." It is irrelevant whether the claimant of 14C is delivering check.

14C2. How to claim. If a move is required to complete the third occurrence of the position, the player claiming the draw under 14C should write this move on the score sheet, not play the move on the board, stop both clocks, and state the claim. If no move is required to complete the repetition, the player should stop both clocks without moving and state the claim.

In both cases, if the opponent agrees, the game is drawn. If a director denies the claim, the claimant is still obligated to play any announced or recorded move.

14C3. Player must be on move. Only a player on the move may claim a draw under 14C. If the opponent is on move, a player may not claim, and any claim the player may have made before punching the clock is invalid (see 14C7). The right to claim is restored to that player, however, if the same position appears again with the same player on move, or if any other position appears for at least the third time with the same player on move.

14C4. Claim after moving without punching clock. A player who moves and then does not punch the clock, but either allows it to run or stops both clocks, retains the right to claim a draw under 14C. However, these procedures are not recommended. The player who moves and allows the clock to run will lose the time that elapses before a ruling if the claim is not upheld, and the player who moves and stops both clocks runs the risk of accidentally starting the opponent's side. See 5I, Stopping the clock.

14C5. Claimant's clock continues to run. If a player who claims a draw under 14C fails to stop the clocks, the director should instruct the player to stop them.

14C6. Resolution of claim. If the claim is found to be correct, the game is drawn. If the claim is found to be incorrect, two minutes shall be added to the opponent's remaining time.

14C7. Irrevocability of claim. A player who makes a draw claim under 14C cannot withdraw it, but it may be transformed into a draw offer. If a player moves, then claims a draw and punches the clock, or claims a draw, then moves and punches the clock, the move stands, and this is considered an offer of a draw.

14C8. Sudden death time pressure. In sudden death, a player with less than five minutes remaining may be awarded a draw by triple occurrence of position based on the observation of a director, deputy, or impartial witness(es). A player may stop both clocks to see a director in order to demonstrate the ability to force a triple occurrence of position.

14C9. Claimant's score sheet. Except for 14C8, the claimant must have a score sheet adequate to demonstrate the validity of the claim.

14D. Insufficient material to continue. The game is drawn when one of the following endings arises, in which the possibility of a win is excluded for either side:

14D1. King vs. king.

14D2. King vs. king with bishop or knight.

14D3. King and bishop vs. king and bishop, with both bishops on diagonals of the same color.

14D4. There are no legal moves that could lead to the player being checkmated by the opponent.

14E. Insufficient material to win on time. The game is drawn when a player exceeds the time limit if one of the following conditions exists:

14E1. Opponent has only a lone king.

14E2. Opponent has only king and bishop or king and knight, and does not have a forced win.

14E3. Opponent has only king and two knights, the player has no pawns, and opponent does not have a forced win.

14F. The 50-move rule.

14F1. Explanation. The game is drawn when the player on the move claims a draw and demonstrates that the last 50 consecutive moves have been made by each side without any capture or pawn move. If the director wishes to allow more than 50 moves for certain positions, details must be posted at the tournament before the first round.

14F2. Resolution. If the claim is found to be correct, the game is drawn. If it is found to be incorrect, two minutes shall be added to the opponent's remaining time.

14F3. Winning position irrelevant. If a valid claim exists, the game is drawn regardless of the position. Even if the opponent can show an immediate mate, the game is drawn.

14F4. Director may count moves in sudden death. In sudden death, a player with less than five minutes remaining and a simplified position in which no pawn moves or captures seem likely may stop both clocks, declare to a director an intention to invoke the 50-move rule when possible, and ask for assistance in counting moves. A director who agrees this is appropriate may count moves or use a deputy or a clock with a move counter to do so.

a. If director or deputy will count moves, the count should begin by crediting moves already made and listed on the score sheet of the player intending to claim. An opponent who believes a different number of moves has been made should present this case if and when the count reaches 50.

b. The director or deputy may either keep score, make check marks, or combine the two.

c. After the count by the director or deputy begins, neither player has a right to know the count until 50 moves are reached. At that point the game is declared drawn unless the opponent successfully challenges the move count.

d. The opponent may challenge either the moves on the claimant's score sheet before the director/deputy count, the count itself, or both, but must have a score sheet adequate to support the challenge.

e. If the challenge is upheld, the game shall continue with the director or deputy resuming from the corrected count. If the claimant's score sheet is responsible for the wrong count, two minutes shall be added to the remaining time of the claimant's opponent. If the director/deputy count was wrong, there shall be no time adjustment.

f. The director may insert a clock with a move counter and ask the claimant to stop both clocks and point out when the clock indicates that both sides have completed 50 moves. If this method is used, the director should inform the players that if a move is erroneously not counted or double counted, the players should stop the clock and notify the director.

14G. Both flags down in sudden death. The game is drawn if both flags are down in a sudden death time control and this is pointed out by either player. If a player whose flag is still up claims a win on time but does not stop the clock in time to prevent the flag from falling, the game is drawn.

14G1. Checkmate and both flags down. In a sudden death control, if a player points out that both flags are down prior to a checkmate, the game is drawn. After considering all available evidence, including testimony by the players and any witnesses, a director who is unable to determine whether the claim of both flags down occurred first shall deny the time claim and rule the checkmate valid.

14G2. Players apparently unaware of situation. If a sudden death game with both flags down continues for at least five minutes, the director may rule it a draw. This exception to the standard rule that only players may call flags down is justified by the need to avoid delaying the tournament.

14H. Claim of insufficient losing chances in sudden death.

14H1. Explanation. In a sudden death time control, a player with less than five minutes of remaining time may stop the clock and ask the director to declare the game a draw on the grounds that the player has insufficient losing chances.

The draw shall be awarded if the director believes that a Class C player would have little chance to lose the position against a Master with both having ample time. The exact losing chances of any position cannot be calculated, but a director wishing a more precise standard may consider "little" to mean less than 10 percent. A director unsure whether a position meets the above standard should temporarily defer a ruling by using option 14H4c or 14H4d.

14H2. Ratings of players irrelevant. The director should not consider the ratings of those playing in making the decision. A low-rated player who claims a draw vs. a Master should obtain the same ruling as a Master with the same position who claims a draw vs. a low-rated player. However, see 14H5, which may allow a player's ability to be of assistance.

14H3. Times on clocks irrelevant. The director should not consider the times on the clocks in making a decision. If the draw is awarded, this may save a player with a few seconds left from an otherwise inevitable time forfeit, but it is precisely the intention of this rule to protect players from losing on time when they are very unlikely to lose otherwise.

14H4. Resolution. The director has four possible ways to resolve the claim:

a. A director who believes the claim is clearly correct should declare the game drawn.

b. A director who believes the claim is clearly incorrect should deny the claim and subtract one minute from the claimant's remaining time.

c. A director who is uncertain regarding the validity of the claim may temporarily deny it, make no adjustment of claimant's remaining time, and watch the game with the intent of upholding the claim if the opponent is making no progress.

d. A director uncertain regarding the validity of the claim also has the option of temporarily denying the claim, making no adjustment of claimant's remaining time, and inviting a later re-claim if the opponent is making no progress.

This option is especially useful when the claimant's opponent has substantial time remaining and the director cannot commit to lengthy viewing of the game. The director should attempt to view the game on occasion and may rule a draw if appropriate, even without a re-claim. To resolve a "no progress" re-claim, the director has the same four options listed above, 14H4a through 14H4d.

14H5. Conferring with players. A director who is unsure how to rule may confer privately with either player or with both players separately regarding the player's plans. The director should be careful not to say anything which might assist the player if the game is resumed.

14H6. Player with fallen flag may not claim. A player whose flag is down may not claim insufficient losing chances.

14H7. USCF Allegro Clock. If a USCF Allegro Clock is used and set for the required time delay on each move, 14H and 14I are not in effect. The reaction time provided for each move is likely to be sufficient for a player with insufficient losing chances to hold the position.

14I. Advice on claims of insufficient losing chances in sudden death under Rule 14H.

14I1. Consulting strong players. If unsure how to rule, the director may consult a Master or near-Master who has no stake in the outcome. The director should be careful to explain the conditions of 14H1 to such a player.

14I2. Types of positions. In complex positions often neither side has a valid claim, while in simple positions both sides may have one. For instance, with much material on the board a Master may be down a piece without compensation but still have better than a small chance to beat a C player. But in endings such as described in 14I3, even a player behind in material should sometimes be awarded the draw.

14I3. Opposite bishop endings. Some opposite bishop endings with most or all pawns fixed may offer a Master, even if a pawn or two ahead, little chance to outplay a C player and should be ruled draws.

14I4. Queen vs. queen, rook vs. rook. With no pawns and queen vs. queen or rook vs. rook the draw should be awarded unless it is one of the rare positions in which there is a quick forced win. If claimant has additional material and opponent does not, the ruling should still ordinarily be a draw.

14I5. Bishop or knight vs. rook, rook vs. rook and knight, queen vs. queen and bishop or knight. With no pawns the player behind in material should not be awarded a draw, but it may be appropriate for the director to watch for progress under 14H4c or 14H4d.

In such positions another option for the claimant is to ask the director to begin a move count for the purpose of enabling a 50-move rule claim (see 14F4). Whether or not to start such a count is at the director's discretion. A director who so chooses may observe for lack of progress and count for the 50-move rule simultaneously.

14I6. King vs. king, rook pawn and possibly bishop. A player with a lone king should be awarded a draw vs. king and rook pawn or king, rook pawn, and bishop of different color than the queening square if claimant's king can stop the pawn from queening. As in 14I4 and all other such cases, if claimant has additional material, the ruling should still ordinarily be a draw.

14I7. Rook vs. rook and bishop. With no pawns, unless there is an immediate win of material or an unusual problem position, a draw claim with a rook vs. opponent's rook and bishop should be denied and one minute subtracted from the claimant's clock. This is, however, an appropriate position for a 50-move rule count.

14J. Draw declared by director. On rare occasions the director may encounter a situation in which a ruling is required and deciding in favor of either player would be unfair to the opponent (for example, see 20E2d and 20E2h). In such situations the director may rule a draw on the grounds that this is more equitable than any other possible ruling. A draw may also be ruled in cases like 19E (sealed move envelope missing) if the director recalls that the position was about equal but does not remember it.

14K. Allegro clock 175-move rule. If an Allegro Clock (see 5F) with a time-delay feature or a similar clock is used, the game is drawn after the completion of black's 175th move.

15. THE RECORDING OF GAMES

15A. Manner of keeping score. In the course of play each player is required to record the game (both player's and opponent's moves), move after move, as clearly and legibly as possible, on the score sheet prescribed for the competition. Algebraic notation is standard, but descriptive or computer notation is permitted. The player may first make the move, then write it on the score sheet, or vice versa. See Chapter 3 for an explanation of these notation systems.

15A1. Players unable to keep score. Players unable to keep score due to physical handicaps may have assistance in scorekeeping as described in 35F, and should be excused from scorekeeping if such assistance is unavailable. Players unable to keep score for religious reasons may be excused from scorekeeping or permitted to have assistance as in 35F, at the director's discretion. Beginners who have not learned to keep score may be excused from scorekeeping, at the director's discretion. Players excused from scorekeeping are not entitled to make claims which require score sheets; those permitted to have assistance retain such rights.

15B. Scorekeeping in time pressure, non–sudden death. A player with less than five minutes on the clock until the time control may stop keeping score until the end of the time control period. Doing so, however, may make it impossible to claim a draw by triple repetition of position or the 50-move rule or a win on time forfeit.

15C. Scorekeeping in time pressure, sudden death. If either player has less than five minutes remaining, both players are excused from the obligation to keep score. A score sheet is not required to win on time in a sudden death control.

15D. Reconstruction after time control. Upon making the time control, if the next control is not sudden death, the player(s) must make all efforts to fill in the missing moves.

15E. Reconstruction before sudden death. Upon making the time control, if the next control is sudden death, it is less important to fill in the missing moves. The director has the option of waiving this requirement.

15F. Use of opponent's score sheet for assistance. A player who has an incomplete score sheet and wishes to consult the opponent's score sheet for assistance may ask to borrow it from the opponent under the following conditions:

15F1. Clock times. Both players have at least five minutes remaining in the current time control.

15F2. Borrower's clock runs. The clock of the player making such a request is running and shall continue to run until the score sheet has been returned.

15F3. Compliance. The opponent is urged to comply with such a request, but this is not mandatory. If the opponent denies the request, the player may stop both clocks and see a director. A director who agrees that the request is appropriate shall instruct the opponent to lend the player the score sheet. The opponent may not refuse as all score sheets belong to the organizers. See 15L.

15F4. Excessive requests. Repeated requests of this type may be deemed by the director to be inappropriate, and the offender may be penalized under 20G, which prohibits distracting or annoying the opponent.

15G. Borrowing not needed. A player who is able to read the opponent's score sheet without borrowing it is free to use the information gained for assistance in keeping score.

15H. Reconstruction of score sheet by one player. After the completion of a time control, a player who alone has to complete the score sheet must do so before making another move, and with that player's clock running if the opponent has made a move. An additional set and board may be used.

15I. Reconstruction of score sheets by both players. After the completion of a time control, if both players need to complete their score sheets, the clocks should be stopped until they are completed. An additional chess set and board may be used. This does not apply if the director rules that it is unnecessary. See 15E.

15J. Reconstruction impossible or unnecessary. If it is impossible or unnecessary to reconstruct the moves as prescribed above, the game shall continue. The players should make a clear diagram of the position reached, and the next move played will be considered the first one of the following time control unless the players agree that a later move number has been reached.

15K. Reporting of results. When a game is completed, the result must be immediately reported in the manner required by the director. Both players, not just the winner, are responsible for registering the result. If they do not do so, they may each be penalized. See 29O.

15L. Ownership of score sheets. The score sheets of all games in a tournament are the property of the sponsoring organization(s). If the organizer requires that a copy of each game score be submitted by the players, duplicate score sheets must be provided, and players who fail to submit score sheets may be penalized.

16. USE OF THE CHESS CLOCK

16A. Allowable time controls. The USCF office maintains a list, available on request, of the currently allowable time limits for different types of tournaments.

16B. How to set clocks. Mechanical clocks should be set so that each unit will register six o'clock when the first time-control period expires. If there is a second time control of one hour per player, this expires at seven o'clock, a third such control at eight o'clock, etc.

16C. Removing a player's hand from clock. Each player must remove his or her hand from the clock button after depressing the button and must keep the hand off the clock until it is time to press it again.

16D. Special rules for sudden death time pressure. In a sudden death time control, if either player has less than five minutes remaining, the following rules are in effect.

16D1. Using the clock. Each player must operate the clock with the same hand that moves the pieces.

16D2. Picking up clock. Each player is forbidden to pick up the clock.

16D3. Illegal moves. If an illegal move is not corrected before the opponent of the player who made the illegal move completes two more moves, then the illegal move stands, and there is no time adjustment. See 11D.

16E. When flag is considered down. The flag is considered to have fallen when this is pointed out by either player. See 13C1.

16F. Evidence provided by flag. In the absence of an evident defect in the clock or flag mechanism, the fallen flag is considered as proof that the time-control period has ended. See 16G and 16H.

16G. Premature flag fall. If a clear white space shows between the right side of the minute hand of the clock and the left side of the 12 marker on the clock's face, the flag is considered to have fallen prematurely. The director should deny the claim of a time forfeit and the game be continued with a different clock if possible. A later time-forfeit claim in that control by either player is still allowed.

16H. Flag fall without white space can cause forfeit. Even though it may seem that the flag fell early, if the clear white space described in 16G is not apparent, the player's time has expired. For instance, if the right side of the minute hand is touching the left side of the hour marker, even though it may not reach to the center of that marker, the time has been used up. Players should realize that this possibility exists and should refrain from using all their apparent time if not essential.

16I. Starting the clock. At the time determined for the start of the game, the clock of the player with the white pieces is started by the player with the black pieces. During the game, each of the players, having moved, stops the player's clock and starts that of the opponent.

16J. White's first move optional if black absent. If the player with the black pieces is late, white may either make the first move and start black's clock, or may start black's clock without making a move.

16K. Both players late. If both players arrive late, the first to arrive must split the elapsed time before starting the opponent's clock. For example, if the first player to arrive is 40 minutes late, the clocks should be set to reflect 20 minutes of elapsed time on each side.

16K1. Elapsed time not reflected. If the first late player to arrive fails to do this and instead sets the clocks to reflect no elapsed time on either side, this setting stands unless corrected by a director or changed by agreement between the two players.

16K2. Elapsed time incorrectly reflected. If the first late player to arrive sets the clocks to give the opponent a disadvantage, such as charging the opponent with all the elapsed time, and this is noticed by or pointed out to the director, the improper times shall be corrected and the player responsible for them penalized at the director's discretion.

16L. Possible stipulations. The director may require that clocks face a certain direction or that black or white sit on a particular side of the table. In the absence of such a requirement, black determines which side of the board the clock is on, and the player arriving at the chessboard first may choose either side of the table to sit on.

16M. Equipment needed to start clock. Except for splitting the elapsed time if both players are late or lack equipment, no player may subtract time from a late opponent except by starting a clock. A late opponent's clock may not be started until the board and pieces are in place. If equipment becomes available only after the beginning of the round, the elapsed time from the beginning shall be divided equally between the two players. See also 13D, Late arrival for game.

16N. Beginning the round. With the exception of games rescheduled by the director, all clocks should start promptly at the time specified for the round. If feasible, the director should give a warning and then announce that play must begin. In a tournament where it is impractical for the director to announce that play should start, players should be urged in advance to begin games promptly and informed that no permission is needed to start clocks at the specified time if the pairings are posted.

16O. Defective clocks. Every indication given by a clock is considered to be conclusive in the absence of evident defects. A player who wishes to claim any such defect must do so as soon as aware of it. A clock with an obvious defect should be replaced, and the time used by each player up to that time should be indicated on the new clock as accurately as possible.

The director should use judgment in determining what times shall be shown on the new clock. A director who decides to subtract time from one or both players shall leave that player(s) with the greater of either five minutes to the time control or at least one minute for each move the player still needs to meet the time control.

16P. Erroneously set clocks. An erroneously set clock should be handled in the same fashion as a defective clock. As in 16O, the director should use judgment in deciding whether to make time adjustments. The most common situation of this type involves a clock set to expire at 7:00 rather than the correct 6:00. This is best handled by simply deducting an hour from the remaining time.

Sometimes this hour difference is not pointed out and there is an eventual time claim. Even though the clock may show 6:00 with a flag down, if the total elapsed time shown for both players is about an hour more than possible, considering when the game started, the player should not be forfeited, and should be given the hour in question.

16Q. Interruption of game. If the game is to be interrupted for some reason beyond the control of the players, such as a defective clock, the clock should be stopped by one of the players. When doing so, the player must state the reason for stopping the clock and see the director if necessary to resolve the situation.

16R. No time adjustment for reinstated position. If an illegal move is noticed within 10 moves (11A, 11E, or 11F), the position before the illegal move is reinstated. Both clocks should be stopped while the position is being reset; however, the game should then continue with no time adjustment. The players do not recover the time they used after the illegal move.

16S. Priority of agreed result over time-forfeit claim. A resignation or an agreement to draw remains valid even when it is found later that the flag of one side had fallen.

16T. Both players exceed time control. If both players exceed the time control, no claim of time forfeit is possible. In a non–sudden death control, the game continues. In a sudden death control, the game is drawn.

16U. Avoiding the need to reset clocks. It is recommended that secondary and subsequent time controls allow one hour per player so that the minute hand will be at twelve and the flag will fall when the player's time expires. This avoids the need to reset clocks and the problems sometimes caused by resetting. The latter include questions or disputes about player resetting, directors being diverted from other duties to reset, time shortage situations with no flags when players forget to reset, and players whose flags have just fallen resetting the clock before their opponents claim forfeit wins.

16V. One vs. two controls when time is limited. If there is not enough time for a second control of an hour per player, it is recommended the tournament have only one control unless the organizer believes the players would prefer otherwise. For instance, if games must end in two hours, G/60 should be preferred to 30/30 followed by SD/30 unless players have indicated a preference for the latter.

16W. Resetting clocks when necessary. If a period of less than one hour is used for a second or later control period, when both players complete the number of moves required of the previous time-control period, the players should reset both clocks by moving them forward one hour minus the length of the next time-control period. The director may specify alternate procedures.

16X Extra minute not added. The old rule permitting an extra minute on each side of a mechanical clock to compensate for possible inaccuracies is no longer in effect.

16Y. Assisting players with time management prohibited. No one, except a player's opponent, may call that player's attention to the fact that a flag is down, the opponent has moved, or the player has forgotten to punch the clock after moving. These prohibitions also apply to the director. For a rare exception regarding calling flags in sudden death, see 14G2.

17. SCHEDULING

17A. Determination of game times. All games must be played in the tournament rooms at the times designated by the organizers unless the director specifies otherwise. For example, a player whose game ends late or is adjourned may be granted additional time to eat or rest (a half hour is common), or a first-round game may be scheduled for play before the start of the tournament.

17B. Delayed games. If a player is granted a late start by the director, the opponent may not start the player's clock until the time specified by the director.

17B1. Informing opponent of new time. The director should inform the opponent of a player allowed a delayed start of the revised starting time, either by writing the new time on the pairing sheet or by telling the player involved.

17B2. Opponent not informed of new time. If the director fails to provide the notice described in 17B1, the opponent presumably will start the player's clock at the originally scheduled time. In such cases, the opponent will eventually be required to reset the clocks to reflect the revised starting time and grant the player the time promised by the director.

17C. Changes in round times. Changes in starting times of rounds should be made only in the event of an emergency. It is especially undesirable to make rounds earlier than previously scheduled, as players may forfeit or lose time as a result.

18. THE ADJOURNMENT OF THE GAME

18A. Description. If a game is not finished at the end of the time prescribed for play, the director may indicate that it is time for adjournment or accept the request of either player to adjourn. At that point the player on move, after deciding which move to make, does not play that move on the board but instead writes it in unambiguous notation on the score sheet, puts the score sheet and that of the opponent in the sealed move envelope, seals the envelope, and then stops both clocks.

Until stopping both clocks, the player retains the right to change the sealed move. If the player who is told to adjourn makes the move on the chessboard, for whatever reason, that move becomes the sealed move.

If a player is recording the game in a score book, the director may either take possession of the entire score book or allow the sealed move to be written on a separate piece of paper and sealed in the envelope.

18B. Sealing a move early. In tournaments in which the adjournment time is fixed beforehand, normally after the full period of the first time control, a player who has completed the number of moves required may ask the director for permission to seal early. Such a player absorbs the time remaining before the scheduled adjournment by having his or her clock advanced by the amount of time remaining in the session. Such requests are ordinarily granted during the last hour of the session.

18C. When to adjourn. Unless announcing in advance that all games will adjourn at a specific time, the director has discretion as to when to adjourn any game after the first time control. The duration of all playing sessions shall be controlled by the wall clock, but the director should refrain from adjourning a game in which one or both players are in serious time trouble. This situation could arise, for example, if the game was started late and half the elapsed time before the start was not deducted from each clock.

18C1. Adjournment despite time pressure. If it is necessary for the start of the next round, a game may be adjourned in a secondary time-control period in which one player is short of time but the other has a large amount. The director should be aware that despite the time pressure of one player, the game may not end soon, delaying the start of the next round.

18C2. Allowing breaks. In tournaments with more than one round per day, it is customary to allow a player whose game has just been adjourned a standard amount of time to eat or rest (a half hour is common) before beginning the next game. On occasion, this may require the next round opponent to start that game after the regularly scheduled starting time. See 17A, Determination of game times.

18D. The sealed move envelope. The following should be indicated on the sealed move envelope: names and colors of the players, position immediately before the sealed move, time used by each player, name or color of the player who sealed the move and number of that move, date and time for resumption, and the signatures of both players, indicating they verify and understand the information written on the envelope.

18E. Custody of sealed move envelope. The director is responsible for custody of the envelope.

THE POSITION
IMMEDIATELY BEFORE THE SEALED MOVE
(circle the initials of the black pieces)

	Clock Shows	Time Consumed
WHITE	_____ : _____	_____ : _____
BLACK	_____ : _____	_____ : _____

U S C F SEALED MOVE ENVELOPE

"The player having the move must write his move in unambiguous notation on his scoresheet, put this scoresheet and that of his opponent in an envelope *(carbon copies of the scoresheets need not be enclosed)*, seal the envelope, and then stop the clocks." *(FIDE Article 15.1)*

WHITE *(printed)* _____

   (signature) _____

BLACK *(printed)* _____

   (signature) _____

NUMBER OF SEALED MOVE _____

   SEALED IN ROUND _____ SECTION _____

   BY _____

GAME TO BE RESUMED AT _____ M.

   ON _____ 19 _____

US CHESS FEDERATION

BLACK

WHITE

18F. Problems of the next-to-last round.

Substantial effort should be made to complete all unfinished games, especially those involving prize contenders, from previous rounds before the last round begins. This must, however, be balanced by the need to start the final round as close to the scheduled time as possible.

18F1. Considerations.

When deciding whether to adjourn games in such cases, the director must weigh the harm to other contenders that might ensue if one of the players loses the final game and then decides to resign the adjourned game, either because a long delay in resumption seems likely or for unethical reasons. On the other hand, delaying the last round for many hours can cause immense player dissatisfaction; some in contention may even withdraw rather than wait.

18F2. Pairing players unaffected by result.

A director who does

not wish to adjourn a long game may seek private assurances from both players that they will not withdraw and will play the last round regardless of the result of the long game. This would allow all players to be paired except those whose pairings would be affected by the result of that game.

18F3. Sudden death. Widespread use of sudden death time controls has minimized the problems associated with last round pairings.

See also 28Q (Pairing unfinished games) and 29M (Last round pairings with unfinished games).

18G. Adjudications. Only under emergency circumstances may a director permanently adjudicate a game, that is, declare a result based upon best play by both sides. When used in other than emergency situations, this fact must be clearly specified in all tournament publicity and posted and announced at the site.

18G1. Example of emergency. An "emergency" situation could arise, for example, if a player with substantial time remaining and a poor position disappears for more than 15 minutes or is present but shows little interest in considering the position. Such behavior is unsportsmanlike and the director is encouraged to adjudicate, possibly after a warning. See 20H.

18G2. Director declares game over. 18G does not prevent a director from declaring the result of a game that has ended without the players noticing this. For example, if the game has been decided by 13A (Checkmate), 13D or 13E (Late arrival), 14A (Stalemate), or 14D (Insufficient material to continue), the director may declare the game over.

19. RESUMPTION OF THE ADJOURNED GAME

19A. Setup. When the game is resumed, the position immediately before the sealed move shall be set up on the chessboard, and the times at adjournment shall be indicated on the clocks.

19B. Opening the envelope. The envelope shall be opened only when the player who must reply to the sealed move is present. The director then opens the envelope, makes the sealed move on the chessboard, and starts the player's clock.

19C. Opponent of sealing player absent. The clock of an absent player who must respond to the sealed move shall be started at the beginning of the adjournment session, but the envelope containing the sealed move shall be opened only when the player arrives.

19D. Sealing player absent. If the player who has sealed the move is absent, the player responding to the sealed move is not obliged to play a move on the chessboard. Such a player has the right to record the move in reply on the score sheet, seal it in an envelope, and punch the clock. The envelope should then be given to the director and opened on the opponent's arrival.

19E. Sealed move envelope missing. If the envelope containing the move recorded in accordance with Rule 18D has disappeared, the game shall be resumed from the position at the time of adjournment with the clock times as they were at the time of adjournment.

If it is impossible to reestablish the position, the game is annulled, and a new game must be played unless the director determines it is impractical to do so or another solution offers greater equity. If the time used cannot be reestablished, the director must decide how to reset the clocks.

19F. Sealed move ambiguous. A director who feels an ambiguous sealed move has two or more reasonable interpretations may allow the sealer's opponent to choose among the possibilities. The sealer's opponent's clock will run while considering which to choose.

19G. Sealed move invalid. If the envelope contains no sealed move or the sealed move is illegal and the director finds there is no reasonable interpretation of it, the player who sealed the move loses the game.

19G1. Agreed draw and invalid move. If the players agree to draw and then find that an invalid move was sealed, the draw stands.

19G2. Resignation and invalid move. If a player resigns and then finds that the opponent sealed an invalid move, the resignation stands.

19G3. Loss on time and invalid move. If the opponent of the player who sealed loses the game due to failure to appear in time for its resumption and then finds that the sealed move was invalid, the loss on time stands.

19H. Game resumed with wrong times on clock. If, upon resumption, the times have been incorrectly indicated on either clock, the error must be corrected if either player points this out before making a move. If the error is not so established, the game continues without any correction unless the director determines that another solution offers greater equity.

19I. Game resumed with incorrect position. If, upon resumption, the position is set up incorrectly, this is considered an illegal move. See 11E.

19J. Agreed result of adjourned game. If both players agree on the result of an adjourned game before resumption, both players must notify the director.

20. CONDUCT OF PLAYERS AND SPECTATORS

20A. Conduct of players. Players shall participate in the spirit of fair play and good sportsmanship, and must observe the USCF Code of Ethics. See Chapter 8.

20B. Use of recorded matter prohibited. During play, players are forbidden to make use of handwritten, printed, or otherwise recorded matter. While the penalty is at the discretion of the director, a forfeit loss is usually ruled if the material is relevant to the game while a lesser penalty or warning is common otherwise. For example, a player on move five of a King's Indian Defense would usually be forfeited for reading a book on the King's Indian but given a warning or time penalty for reading one on rook endings.

20C. Use of notes prohibited. The use of notes made during the game as an aid to memory is forbidden, aside from the actual recording of the moves and clock times. This is a much less serious offense than 20B; a warning or minor time penalty is common, with more severe punishment if the offense is repeated.

20D. Use of additional chessboard or computer prohibited. A player who analyzes a game in progress on another chessboard or consults a computer about the position is guilty of a serious violation of the rules. Though the director still has discretion, the usual penalty is loss of the game.

20E. Soliciting or using advice prohibited. Players are forbidden to have recourse to the advice or opinion of a third party, whether solicited or not.

20E1. Solicited advice. This is a serious violation and a forfeit loss is often ruled.

20E2. Unsolicited advice. Ruling on unsolicited advice can be difficult. The giver deserves a penalty, but what of the recipient? The director's task is to prevent a player from benefiting from advice but also not unduly penalize the player for another's offense. There is sometimes no good solution to this problem, but here are a few examples of possible rulings:

a. A Class D player suggests a winning move to a Master. If, as is likely, the director feels the Master would probably find the move without recourse to the advice, no penalty should be imposed.

b. A Master suggests a winning move to a Class D player. If the director feels the D player would probably not find the move without help, the ruling may be that the D player is prohibited from making the move.

c. A move is suggested, and the director is not sure if it is a good one. The recipient seems to have other acceptable moves. The ruling might be that the player must play a different move, as this seems least likely to cause injustice.

d. A winning move is suggested. All other moves seem to lose and the director believes it unclear whether the player would have likely found the move without help. This situation is especially difficult. If the move is allowed, the opponent will feel cheated by the spectator. If it is not permitted, the player will feel cheated, claiming he or she would have found it without help.

Neither ruling is incorrect, but perhaps fairer would be to rule the game a draw (see 14J) or to show the position to several players of similar rating to the one involved, who are unaware of and have no stake in the dispute, to help determine whether a player of that strength is likely to find the move.

e. A weak move is suggested. No need to penalize the recipient.

f. A player with five moves to make in ten minutes and an unclear position forgets to punch the clock and this is pointed out by a spectator 30 seconds later. The director may only guess whether the player would have noticed the clock before the flag fell, and if so, how much time would have elapsed. A time penalty of a few minutes might be appropriate.

g. The situation is identical to f above except that nine of the ten minutes have elapsed before the spectator's intervention. The director must consider that having not noticed for nine minutes, the player may well not have punched the clock in the last minute either. A forfeit is unfair as the player might have noticed in the final minute, but not taking strong action may be even more unfair to the opponent.

Imposing a time penalty on a player already surprised to have only a minute left may be reasonable. It is unclear whether the player would be helped or hurt by the spectator's intervention and a subsequent decision by the director to take away most of the last minute.

h. The situation is the same as g above except that the player who forgot to punch the clock has an easy win and will have no problem making the last five moves in a few seconds if necessary. To give the player even a few seconds would mean defeat for an opponent who had good chances to win on time before the spectator interfered.

Leaving any time for the negligent player would be unfair to the opponent, but ruling a time forfeit would be unfair to the negligent player. The "lesser of evils" solution might be to declare the game a draw in accordance with 14J.

i. In all such situations, if the unsolicited advice comes from a relative, close friend, teammate, or coach, the director may impose a more severe penalty than otherwise and may consider the advice solicited.

j. In a team or individual/team event, if unsolicited advice is given by a teammate or coach, the director has the option of forfeiting the game for team purposes but allowing it to continue for individual purposes and USCF rating, possibly with a further penalty.

20F. Analysis in the playing room prohibited. No analysis is permitted in the playing room during play or during adjourned sessions.

20F1. Adjournment help outside playing room allowed. While a game is adjourned, a player may receive help outside the playing room from any source, including other players, books, or computers. A prohibition on such help would be unenforceable and would penalize only those honest enough to observe it.

20G. Annoying behavior prohibited. It is forbidden to distract or annoy the opponent in any manner whatsoever. A director, upon a complaint by the opponent, has discretion to determine whether any particular behavior is in violation of this rule and to impose penalties.

20G1. Inadvertent annoying behavior. Sometimes a player's actions, though annoying to the opponent and possibly others, are clearly unintentional. For instance, a player may occasionally cough. While the director has the right to invoke rule 20G, this is quite harsh if the player's actions are involuntary. A partial solution is to assign such a player to a board in another room or far away from other games.

20H. Long absence during play. Players with games in progress should not leave the playing room for more than 15 minutes without permission from the director. A first offense usually does not warrant a forfeit unless there is additional evidence suggesting a further rules violation during the absence.

20H1. Quitting without resigning. It is rude and unsportsmanlike to abandon a lost position without resigning. Any player with a bad position who is absent without permission for over 15 minutes risks having the game adjudicated. See 18G and 20H.

20I. Discussion of games. Players should not discuss their games in progress with anyone; this may lead to penalties under 20E. The director has the option of banning all talking in the tournament room, even if not loud enough to be disturbing.

20J. Last round discussion. Especially in the last round, it is improper for contenders paired against each other to engage in secret discussion before or during the game.

20K. Penalties. Infractions of these rules may incur penalties, including time penalties, loss of the game, expulsion from the tournament, or other penalties or combinations of penalties.

20L. Manipulating results. Collusion to fix or throw games, whether before or during the game, in order to manipulate prize money, title norms, ratings, or for any other purpose is illegal and may result in severe sanctions, including revocation of USCF membership. Such agreements include arrangements to split prize money no matter what the result of the game.

20M. Behavior of spectators.

20M1. Spectators have no special privileges. Spectators not playing in the tournament have no special privileges. For instance, if a player complains that a particular spectator's presence near his or her game is disturbing, rather than investigate the complaint to determine its validity, it may be correct for the director to simply require the spectator to move away from that game. If more complaints are received about the same person, the director may ask that spectator to leave the premises. If the spectator has paid an admission fee, it may be appropriate to refund this fee.

If a player repeatedly complains about various spectators for no apparent reason, the director may choose to disregard such complaints, informing the player that spectators are allowed at the tournament.

20M2. Spectator is player with game in progress. If the offending spectator is a player in the tournament, especially one with a game in progress close to the complaining player, the situation is less clear. More consideration should now be given to the merits of the complaint, as it is reasonable for an entrant to expect to be able to watch nearby games while playing his or her own game, and this may be impossible without provoking the complaint. But if in doubt, the director should still consider the rights of players to be preeminent over those of spectators.

20M3. Ongoing problems. Occasionally there may be an ongoing situation in which a player complains that another player's presence is disturbing, or each complains that the other is disturbing. One way to deal with this problem in future rounds is to assign the players to special boards far away from each other or in different rooms.

20M4. Prohibitions. It is highly improper, and warrants ejection from the premises, for any spectator to discuss a player's position or time management with that player, to point out that it is the player's move, or to talk in a loud enough voice to be heard by a player with a game in progress.

20M5. Spectators cannot make claims. Spectators, including parents and coaches, may point out irregularities to the director in a manner neither heard nor noticed by the players, but have no right to make claims of any kind on behalf of players. If a problem arises during play, a player of any age should understand that he or she should promptly stop both clocks and see a director. A spectator who makes a claim may be ejected.

20M6. Spectator visibility. To minimize claims of illegal assistance, if a relative, close friend, or coach of a player is permitted to stand near that player during play, that spectator should stand behind that player rather than in front, so the spectator is not visible to the player.

21. THE TOURNAMENT DIRECTOR

21A. The chief tournament director. Responsible for all play, the tournament director must see that the rules are observed. The director is bound by the official rules of chess, by USCF tournament rules, and by all USCF procedures and policies.

21B. Duties and powers. The chief tournament director's duties and powers normally include the following: to appoint assistants as required to help in the performance of his or her duties; to accept and list entries; to provide suitable conditions of play; to familiarize players with the playing facility and other tournament conditions; to prepare pairings; to display wall charts; to rule on disputes and enforce such rulings; and to collect scores, report results, and forward membership applications and fees to the sponsoring organization and the USCF for the official record.

21C. Delegation of duties. The chief director may delegate any duties to assistants but is not thereby relieved of responsibility for their performance.

21D. Intervening in games. The director's intervention in a chess game shall generally be limited to the following:

21D1. Answering rules and procedural questions.

21D2. Correcting any illegal moves observed, unless sudden death time pressure exists (see 11D) or Variation 11H1 is used.

21D3. Warning about or penalizing players for disruptive, unethical, or unsportsmanlike behavior.

21D4. Settling disputes, including those regarding time forfeits and claims of draws.

21D5. Informing players about opponents' late arrivals or about opponents' leaving the room for an extended period.

21E. The playing director. A tournament director must not only be absolutely objective, but must also be able to devote full attention to directing duties. For this reason, a director, on principle, should not direct and play in the same tournament.

However, in club events and others that do not involve substantial prizes, it is common practice for the director to play. A director may also serve as a houseman. (See 28M1.) Those who choose this double role should be especially careful to maintain objectivity. If possible, a playing director should appoint another director to make rulings involving his or her own games.

A player director who must devote time to a dispute in another game may stop his or her own clock during this period. While the clock is stopped, the director should not look at the position of his or her own game, but the director's opponent is permitted to do so.

21F. Player requests for rulings. A player has the right to stop both clocks to ask the director to rule upon a point of law, procedure, or conduct. The director must first establish the facts without disturbing other games. Extended discussion between director and player(s) is inappropriate in the tournament room; a hallway or headquarters room is more desirable.

21F1. Timing of requests. A player with a valid claim or complaint of any type should immediately stop both clocks and see a director. In most cases, the player who defers such a claim waives the right to make the claim. However, a delayed claim may still be in order if it is based on evidence not previously available, such as the testimony of a witness, or if the situation causing the claim remains in existence.

21F2. Facts are agreed upon. If the facts are agreed upon, the director should rule as follows:

a. If no penalty is prescribed by the rules and there is no occasion to exercise the director's discretionary power to penalize, the players should be directed to proceed with play.

b. If a case is clearly covered by a rule that specifies a penalty, the director should enforce that penalty.

c. If an infraction has occurred for which no penalty is prescribed, the director's discretionary power to penalize may be exercised.

21F3. Facts are not agreed upon. If the facts are not agreed upon, the director should proceed as follows:

a. A director who is satisfied that the facts have been ascertained should rule accordingly.

b. A director who is unable to satisfactorily determine the facts must make a ruling that will permit play to continue.

21G. Evidence. Unbiased evidence is required to support any claim by a player that the opponent violated a rule.

21H. Appeals. A director who believes that an appeal of a ruling on a point of fact or the exercise of a discretionary power to penalize might be in order should advise the player of the right to appeal.

21H1. How to appeal. A player may appeal any ruling made by the chief director or an assistant director, provided that the appeal is made within one-half hour and before the player resumes play, unless additional time is granted by the director. The director may require that the appeal be made in writing. Frivolous appeals may be penalized by the appeals committee. See 21I7.

21H2. Director may reserve decision. The director may reserve a decision temporarily and direct that play continue before the appeal is heard. In this case, the appellant must continue play "under protest," that is, without prejudice to the appeal, regardless of the outcome of further play. If the appellant wins that game, the appeal will be considered moot.

21H3. Response of chief director. A chief tournament director who believes that the appeal is justified may reverse or modify any decision made by the chief director or another director. A chief director who believes that the appeal has some merit, but not enough to be upheld, should advise the appellant of the right to pursue the appeal further.

21H4. Appointment of committee or referee. If a player notifies the director of intent to pursue the appeal further, the director shall appoint a committee or a special referee to hear the appeal, unless the orderly progress of the tournament would be disturbed by such action. If the director determines that either appointment would be disruptive, the player may reserve the right to share in the prize fund by requesting to be paired for future rounds as if the appeal were upheld. The player has the same right in the case of intending to appeal a local decision to USCF.

21I. Appeals committee and special referees.

21I1. Composition. An appeals committee should consist of at least three persons, preferably USCF-certified tournament directors. A committee of two is sufficient if both are certified at the senior director level or higher.

21I2. Procedure. When a committee hears an appeal, all persons except committee members, the director, and both players shall be excluded from the hearing. Witnesses may be called, but only to answer questions from the parties concerned, after which they will be dismissed. The director shall furnish the committee with the current edition of the *Official Rules of Chess* and shall call attention to the rules applicable to the dispute.

21I3. Witnesses. The committee shall elicit the testimony of witnesses as it sees fit. In hearing the appeal, the committee must give preeminent weight to the director's testimony as to anything said or done in his or her presence.

21I4. Consultation. The committee may consult a special referee (see 21J) by phone for advice, or may vote to refer the dispute to a special referee.

21I5. Function of committee. The function of an appeals committee is not to substitute its judgment for that of the director, but rather to overrule the director only if it is clear the latter's ruling is incorrect. The committee should not overrule a proper decision simply because it prefers an alternate proper decision.

21I6. Decision. After hearing the testimony, the committee members shall deliberate among themselves to reach a decision, which shall be put in writing, signed by all the members, and given to the chief director. In the event of a tie vote, the director's decision shall stand.

21I7. Groundless appeals. If the committee finds that the appeal is clearly groundless, it may penalize the player for that reason, or leave the penalty to the director's discretion. In ruling on an appeal, the committee may exercise all powers accorded to the chief director by the rules and other USCF procedures.

21J. The Special Referee. A special referee is a director with substantial experience who is available to provide advice or make a ruling by telephone. Phone numbers of special referees appear in USCF rating lists.

21J1. Usage. The director may refer any appeal to a special referee, but should keep in mind that unless the facts are agreed upon, or the players' differences easily summarized, substantial delay and phone cost may result. Use of a special referee is most appropriate when the tournament director is certified at a lower level than the referee, and when a director of comparable certification to the referee is not immediately available to serve on an appeals committee.

21J2. Selection. When selecting the referee to call, and the alternates to call if the original selection cannot be promptly reached, the director should be sensitive to any reasonable objection by either player against the use of a particular referee.

21J3. The phone call. When placing any call to the referee, the director should invite both players to be present. The director should not inform the referee of the players' names, but refer to them as "white" and "black."

21J4. Player contact with referee. Neither player has an automatic right to speak to the referee. A director who finds such discussion unnecessary may choose not to allow it. It is desirable that both players know in advance what the director will say and agree that it will correctly reflect their viewpoints.

21J5. Validity of referee's decision. The decision of a special referee carries weight equal to that of an appeals committee. No decision of a special referee may be appealed to an appeals committee, nor may any decision of an appeals committee be appealed to a special referee. However, a special referee who believes the dispute can best be settled on-site may refer it to an appeals committee, which then should be appointed.

21K. Use of director's power.

21K1. Conciliation. The director should make every effort to resolve a dispute by informal, conciliatory means before resorting to the exercise of the director's formal discretionary power to penalize.

21K2. Beware abuse of power. Tournament directors should realize that the powers given to them under these rules should be used sparingly, to restore equity or to penalize a serious infraction so as to discourage its recurrence. No one's interests are served by what appears to be the arbitrary or high-handed exercise of authority.

21L. Appeal to USCF. Any decision of an appeals committee or special referee, or of the director when an appeals committee or special referee is not appointed, may be appealed to the USCF.

21L1. Procedure. Appeals in writing must be mailed within seven days of the end of the tournament to the USCF office, which may immediately reject obviously groundless appeals, but will refer others to an appropriate committee. The latter will most often be the Rules Committee, but some appeals may be more appropriate for the Tournament Director Certification Committee or the Ethics Committee. A good-faith deposit of $25 must be included, which will be returned if the appeal has serious grounds. The USCF reserves the right to make final decisions concerning the rules and procedures that govern its competitions.

22. UNPLAYED GAMES

22A. Games forfeited due to nonappearance. A player who does not appear for the game, or appears too late, is given a zero and the opponent a one. On pairing sheets and wall charts, the forfeit is circled or indicated by an "F." Computer wall charts generally use the symbol "X" for the winner and "F" for the loser of an unplayed game.

22B. Full-point byes. If there is an odd number of players for a round, and a suitable houseman (See Rule 28M1) not in the event cannot be found to fill in, one player will receive a full-point (1) bye. For details, see 28L.

22C. Half-point byes. For the convenience of players, the director may allow half-point (½) byes for missed rounds.

22C1. Availability. Half-point byes may be offered during the first half of a tournament or the middle round of a tournament with an odd number of rounds, with or without advance notice. If pre-tournament publicity does not address this subject, players may contact the organizer to inquire about availability.

If half-point byes are allowed for any rounds during the second half of a tournament, they should be mentioned in pre-tournament publicity. An exception may be made in the event of emergency.

22C2. Deadline for bye requests. All requests for half-point byes should be made at least an hour before the bye round unless the director requires otherwise.

22C3. Byes and class prizes. It is recommended that if class prizes that are likely to be won with even or minus scores are offered, half-point byes be unavailable or limited to one for such classes.

22C4. Irrevocable byes. If half-point byes are allowed for the final round, players must give irrevocable notice of such byes before beginning their first game, or if the organizer so announces, their second game. The deadline for claiming such byes should appear in pre-tournament publicity. It is recommended that other byes in the second half of the tournament be treated similarly and that notice of all scheduled irrevocable byes be posted on or near the result charts.

22C5. Cancellation of irrevocable byes. If the director agrees, a player may cancel an irrevocable half-point bye under the condition that if the player wins, the result will be treated as a draw for prize purposes.

22C6. Full-point byes after half-point byes. A full-point bye should not be assigned to a player who has previously taken or committed to a half-point bye unless all others in the score group have already had a bye or a no-show forfeit win. See 28L, Full-point byes.

23. ORGANIZATION AND MEMBERSHIP

23A. Responsibilities of organizer. Tournaments rated by the USCF must be organized by a USCF affiliate or by the USCF itself. This organizer is responsible for all financial matters related to the tournament, and may select an individual or a committee to handle the physical and financial arrangements. These include finding a playing site, setting a date and the times of the rounds, determining the entry fees and prizes, hiring tournament directors, and advertising the event.

The organizing affiliate must select a chief tournament director (also referred to as "director," "TD," or "arbiter") whose USCF certification level is appropriate for the type of tournament anticipated. The tournament director is responsible for all decisions in the tournament regarding rules.

23A1. Obligation to pay guaranteed prizes. An affiliate that guarantees prize money but fails to pay it in full may have its USCF affiliation revoked, and the individual(s) responsible for that affiliate may be denied the right to affiliate under a different name.

If extraordinary circumstances such as extreme weather conditions or civil unrest prevent most potential entrants from playing in a tournament, the organizer may appeal to the USCF executive director for permission to limit the prizes to 100 percent of entry fees collected.

23A2. Tournament cancellations. Tournaments announced in *Chess Life* may be canceled only if one of the following conditions exists:

a. A timely cancellation notice appears in an appropriate issue of *Chess Life*.

b. Physical conditions, such as closure of site or extremely inclement weather, render the site unusable.

A disappointing number of advance entries is never a valid reason for cancellation. Organizers who cancel a tournament in a non-emergency situation without proper notice will be prohibited from announcing tournaments in "Tournament Life" or elsewhere in *Chess Life* for three years. (Additional penalties are also possible.)

23A3. Advance entry refunds. Unless otherwise stated in all advance publicity, advance entry fees are refundable to players who give notice of withdrawal before the close of registration for round one.

23A4. No refunds once event starts. A player who begins play in the first round is not entitled to a refund of the entry fee or any portion of it, even if forced to miss most games due to a medical or other emergency.

23B. Determination of game times. Game times are determined by the organizer unless the director makes or accepts other arrangements. See Rule 17, Scheduling.

23C. USCF membership requirement. For the inclusive dates of the tournament, each player must be a member in good standing of the USCF, unless USCF regulations waive this requirement.

24. INTERPRETATION OF THE RULES

24A. Rules Committee. The USCF shall maintain a standing Rules Committee to review questions pertaining to the rules of play. In case of doubt as to the application or interpretation of these rules, the USCF Rules Committee will examine the case in point and render an official decision.

24B. Appeals to USCF. All appropriate appeals made to the USCF National Office shall be referred to the Rules Committee. A copy of any appeal considered by the committee shall first be furnished to the chief tournament director of the tournament involved, who should respond with a written statement of his or her own position and any other pertinent documentation. A copy of the decision of the Rules Committee shall be sent to all interested parties.

2

USCF TOURNAMENT REGULATIONS AND GUIDELINES

USCF TOURNAMENTS

25. INTRODUCTION

A player entering a competition has a right to know the rules and conditions governing that competition. What follows, therefore, is an exposition of U.S. tournament procedures as they are in practice now. The most significant features of a tournament should be noted in the advance publicity and posted prominently at the tournament site.

These features include round times, speed of play, major pairing variations, prizes, and tie-break procedures. Players should understand, however, that last-minute circumstances can sometimes force revisions of earlier plans, though conscientious organizers and directors do all they can to avoid changes in announced conditions for competition.

The most common types of USCF rated tournaments are the Swiss system and the round robin. Rules for their conduct are discussed below.

26. VARIATIONS AND EXCEPTIONS

26A. Notification. Any variations from these published standards, including variations discussed in this rule book, should be posted and/or announced at the tournament prior to their use, preferably before the first round.

26B. Major variations. A variation sufficiently major so that it might reasonably be expected to deter some players from entering should be mentioned in any *Chess Life* announcement and all other detailed pre-tournament publicity and posted and/or announced at the tournament.

27. THE SWISS SYSTEM TOURNAMENT

The Swiss system can accommodate a large number of players in a relatively short time and has therefore become widespread. Although not as accurate as the round robin in determining a winner unless the latter encounters significant withdrawals, the ratings-controlled Swiss is more precise than earlier versions. Since its methods are complex, novice directors should learn them by working with an experienced director.

A Swiss tournament should ideally have a number of rounds adequate to reduce the number of players with perfect scores to one. This result can be guaranteed by limiting entries to a number no greater than two raised to the power of the number of rounds. For example, a three-round Swiss will produce no more than one perfect score for up to eight players, a four-round Swiss can handle up to sixteen players, a five-round up to thirty-two players.

In practice, however, these numbers are only guides due to the unpredictable number of draws. A properly paired Swiss system usually produces no more than one perfect score from at least double the theoretical number of players. It cannot, however, guarantee a clear winner, nor can it assure that competitors for the same awards will face opposition of similar strength.

It is both a weakness and a strength of the Swiss system that slow starters who achieve a certain final score will tend to have faced weaker fields than players who do well in the early rounds but finish with the same end result. While this situation involves an element of inequity, it tends to keep more players in the running for a longer time, making Swiss tournaments competitive and exciting.

27A. Basic Swiss System Rules. The following rules are listed in order of priority from 27A1 for the highest priority to 27A5 for the lowest. If it is not possible to adhere to all rules in making pairings, the director should generally follow the rule with the higher priority. However, there are cases in which 27A4 or 27A5 have priority over 27A3 (see 29J) and even a variation in which 27A4 can have priority over 27A2 (see 29J6a).

27A1. Avoid players meeting twice. A player may not play the same opponent more than once in a tournament. Even this most basic of all pairing rules must be violated when the number of rounds is greater than or equal to the number of players. If it is necessary for players to play each other twice, then top priority should subsequently be given to having them face each other no more than twice. If two players were paired against each other earlier in the tournament, but the game was forfeited due to the nonappearance of one, they may be paired against each other again.

27A2. Equal scores. Players with equal scores are paired whenever possible. Note that if accelerated pairings (see 28R) are used, many pairings for round two disregard this rule.

27A3. Top half vs. lower half. Within a score group, i.e., all players who have a particular score, the top half by ranking (see 28A) is paired against the bottom half. See 29C1.

27A4. Equalizing colors. Players receive each color the same number of times, and are not assigned the same color more than twice in a row, whenever practical. In odd numbered rounds, the objective is to limit the excess of one color over the other to one. See 29E, 29H, 29I, 29J.

27A5. Alternating colors. Players receive alternating colors whenever practical. See 29E, 29H, 29I, 29J.

28. SWISS SYSTEM PAIRINGS, PROCEDURES

28A. Pairing cards or program. Before the first round, the tournament director prepares a pairing card for each player, or uses a computer program to enter each player. The player's name, rating, and USCF I.D. number are written on the card or entered into the program. For scholastic tournaments, the school is also included. Directors who want states or cities on their wall charts add this information as well.

If cards are used, they are then placed in order of rank, from the highest rated to the lowest. Unrated players and players with the same rating are ranked in random order, with the unrated players being placed at the bottom of the group. The director then numbers the cards, giving the highest-rated player number 1, the second highest number 2, and so on until all the cards are numbered. That number is the player's "pairing number," which will be used throughout the tournament.

Some directors prefer to assign an arbitrary rating of 1200 or 1300 for pairing purposes only to all unrated players. Such assignments usually place them at or near the bottom, causing pairings similar to those that would result if they were paired as unrated. One major difference is that in a score group with an odd number of players the lowest rated player drops, but not an unrated player. An unrated player who is scoring well in the tournament would often be the *highest* rated player in the score group if all games played up to that point had already been rated.

The pairing cards are used to prepare the wall chart and to pair each round. Computer programs also do both and automatically do the sorting and numbering described above.

28B. Numbering late entrants. Players who enter after pairing numbers have been assigned are assigned the next available numbers. These numbers should be accompanied by a symbol such as an asterisk to serve as a reminder that rating and not rank number should be considered when ordering them in their score groups.

Some directors assign an intermediary pairing number such as 12A for a player rated below player 12 but above player 13. This can cause problems or confusion with the wall chart, and the intermediary numbers may not be used in the rating report sent to USCF.

A director using a computer program may be able to insert the late entrants in their proper places with other player numbers being appropriately revised. Care should be taken in doing this if results have been entered into the computer since the records of previous games may not correspond with the revised player numbers.

Other useful information such as address, fees paid, membership expiration date, etc., may also be recorded on the pairing card, if the director prefers this to a permanent record book. The USCF sells standardized pairing cards for Swiss system tournaments. See illustration.

PAIRING NO. _____   RATING _____

Round No.	COLOR		Opponent No.	Circle if unplayed SCORE		TIE BREAK	
	W	B		GAME	TOTAL	A	B
1							
2							
3							
4							
5							
6							
7							
8							

NAME _____

ADDRESS _____

_____

USCF ID No. _____   EXP. DATE _____

OTHER _____

ENTRY FEES $_____   OTHER FEES $ _____

USCF DUES $ _____ OTHER DUES $ _____ TOTAL $ _____

PRIZE: Place _____ AMOUNT $ _____

No. US–12 Swiss Pairing Card (rev. 4/79)
United States Chess Federation, New Windsor, New York 12550

28C. Ratings of players. The rating entered on a player's card is the last published USCF rating in the rating list specified in the "Tournament Life" section of *Chess Life,* unless use of a different rating list was specified in the advance publicity for the tournament, or the director has assigned a player a rating (see 28E). Note that an assigned rating used for a tournament may or may not be used for future tournaments.

28C1. Multiple USCF ratings. If a player is mistakenly assigned more than one USCF rating, the director should try to combine these ratings. Two examples:

a. If the ratings are 1900/5 (1900 based on 5 games) and 1700/4 (1700 based on 4 games), the rating used should be 1811, calculated as follows: 1900 x 5 = 9500, 1700 x 4 = 6800, 9500 + 6800 = 16300, 16300/9 = 1811.

b. If a player with an old established rating of 1900 is erroneously started over as 1700/5 (1700 based on 5 games), the rating used should be that of a 1900 player who draws 5 games vs. 1700 player, or 1860. See Chapter 10, "The USCF Rating System."

28C2. Foreign or FIDE ratings. A foreign or formerly foreign player with a foreign or FIDE rating or category is required to disclose such a rating or category when entering a tournament, if any of the following circumstances exist:

a. The player lacks an established USCF rating.

b. The player's USCF rating has not been published during the past two years.

c. The director requests this information.

If a player fails to disclose such a rating as required, the director may withhold any rating-based prize or unrated prize the player may win.

28D. Players without USCF ratings. Players without official USCF ratings are eligible only for place prizes and prizes for unrated players unless alternate procedures are used to assign ratings, such as the following recommendations:

28D1. Non-USCF ratings verified. Those known to have ratings or categories of other types, such as foreign, FIDE, regional, or USCF Quick (if a Quick tournament, USCF regular).

It is recommended that such players not be considered unrated and that their ratings be used, adjusted if necessary to be consistent with the USCF rating scale. If a player has more than one non-USCF rating, the highest should be used.

Currently (1993), the following adjustments are believed to be roughly appropriate. Changes are likely in the future and will be announced in USCF rating supplements.

Bermuda, USCF Quick (or USCF regular at Quick tournament): No adjustment needed.

Canada (CFC): Add 50 points.

Quebec (FQE): Add 100 points.

FIDE: The following two formulas are provided for guidance:

$$(1)\ USCF = FIDE + 50$$
$$(2)\ USCF = 0.895\ (FIDE) + 367$$

Formula (1) represents an *average* conversion. This means that 50 percent of the time the FIDE-rated player will be stronger than his or her converted USCF rating would indicate. By using formula (2), on the other hand, a tournament director ensures that the FIDE-rated player will be stronger than his or her converted USCF rating only 10 percent of the time, thus providing a greater degree of protection for the players with established USCF ratings. The above is for players with FIDE ratings but no USCF ratings.

England: Multiply the 3-digit rating by 8 and add 700.

Germany (Ingo System): Multiply by 8, and subtract answer from 2940. Lower Ingo numbers reflect greater strength.

Most nations not named: Add 200 points.

Ratings or categories of the former Soviet Union or of the Philippines: Add 300 points. If a category, use the midpoint—for instance, a Russian Candidate Master should be 2100 + 300 or 2400.

Brazil, Peru, or possibly other nations' ratings: These have proved highly unreliable. Players from these countries should not be considered eligible for prizes for classes below 2200 based on such ratings.

28D2. Non-USCF ratings claimed without verification. Players who state they have a rating as listed in 28D1, but this cannot be proved.

Directors may assign ratings, but they should not be under 2200 if this would make the player eligible for a cash class prize.

28D3. USCF label or print out ratings. Players who have unofficial initial USCF ratings on labels or print outs that have not yet appeared in a rating supplement, and who are believed to have no foreign ratings or categories.

Directors are encouraged to use such ratings without adjustment. Players with less than four career games, though, are unrated.

28D4. Director-calculated ratings. Players who have played in one or more USCF-rated events from which their approximate strength may be calculated but do not yet have even unofficial ratings, and who are believed to have no foreign ratings or categories.

Directors may calculate and use such ratings, but if their calculation puts the player within 100 points of a higher prize category, the assignment should be raised to put the player in the higher category. Players with less than four career games are unrated.

28D5. Assignments based on nonrated activity. Players lacking known results in USCF-rated tournaments and believed to have no foreign ratings or categories, but whose strength may reasonably be approximated from other play, such as nonrated club activity, tournaments, or speed games.

Directors may assign ratings, but they should not be under 2200 if this would make the player eligible for a cash class prize.

28D6. No information on player available. Players with no known results, ratings, or categories of any kind.

These players are unrated. They should not be assigned ratings for prize purposes. If assignments are used for pairing purposes, these should not appear on the wall chart.

28D7. Improperly assigned ratings. If a director assigns a player rating that is in violation of any part of 28D, and this is pointed out before prizes are awarded, that player shall not be eligible for prizes based on the assigned rating.

28E. Assigned ratings for rated players. The director may assign a rating to any rated player.

28E1. Rating level. The assigned rating shall not be lower than the player's last published USCF rating, or its foreign or FIDE equivalent, adjusted if necessary, if the player lacks a USCF rating.

28E2. Assignments for unrateds. If the player has no published rating, certain restrictions apply. See 28D.

28E3. Cause for assignment. A rating may be assigned only for reasonable cause, including, but not limited to, the following.

a. The player has shown significant superiority to those in a particular class.

b. The player has demonstrated a tendency to achieve much better results when significant prizes are at stake than when they are not.

c. The player's rating has recently dropped into a lower class due to results that are statistically highly unlikely.

d. The player's moves, time management, statements, or other actions during play in a previous tournament have caused the director to conclude that the player did not make a reasonable effort to avoid losing games.

28E4. Notification. A player assigned a rating should be notified by the director in advance of the tournament if possible, so the player will have this information when deciding whether or not to enter. However, such notification is not always possible since the cause for assignment may not be evident to the director until the late-registration period, or even during the tournament.

28F. Validity of wall-chart ratings. A properly assigned rating that appears on the wall chart without disclaimer is valid for both prizes and pairing purposes unless it is erroneous and a correction appears on a subsequent wall chart.

Directors who wish to use an assigned rating for pairing purposes but not prize eligibility should include a disclaimer on or near the wall chart next to the player's rating to explain that the rating is not valid for prize purposes.

28G. Old ratings. Old ratings of inactive players are still valid. If an old rating cannot be located or confirmed from memory by a reliable person, the director should allow the player to receive a class prize only after confirmation of the old rating.

28H. Revising ratings after tournament begins. The rating of any player may be revised for reasonable cause at any time. If this results in a player being ineligible for the section he or she is playing in, the following procedures shall apply.

28H1. Removal. The player shall be removed from that section.

28H2. Reassignment. The director may offer the player the opportunity to continue in the tournament in an appropriate section, with half-point byes for games missed.

28H3. Entry fee refund.

a. If the erroneous rating assignment is due to false or misleading information or the lack of required information provided by the player, or failure by the player to disclose a rating, the director is not required to refund the entry fee.

b. If the erroneous rating assignment is primarily a mistake by the director or tournament staff, the entry fee should be refunded. If the player is given the option of continuing in a higher section, it is still appropriate to refund the fee if the player has missed sufficient rounds to substantially reduce prize chances.

28I. Opponents of expelled players. If a player is removed from an event or section because he or she is made ineligible by a corrected rating (see 28H), the following adjustments shall be made to such a player's opponent.

28I1. Expulsion before last round paired. If the player is removed before the last round is paired, all former opponents should have their results against that player changed to wins by forfeit.

28I2. Expulsion after last round paired. If the expelled player is not declared ineligible in time to be removed from the last round pairings, that player's opponents in the final two rounds of the tournaments shall have their results against the player scored as wins by forfeit.

Opponents of the expelled player in rounds before the last two shall be scored as follows:

a. Players who lost to the expelled player shall receive half-point byes instead, regardless of whether or not the tournament offers half-point byes.

b. Players who drew against the expelled player shall have their results against the expelled player scored as wins by forfeit.

28I3. Players who won should not have their scores adjusted.

28I4. Games still rated. In both cases 28I1 and 28I2, the actual results shall be transferred to an "extra rated games" section (see 28M4) and reported to USCF for rating.

28J. The first round. The director (or computer) flips a coin to decide who will play white on the first board, the higher- or lower-rated player. After putting all the cards in order of rating, he or she then divides the cards into halves, pairing the highest player in the top half against the highest player in the bottom half, the second highest in the top half against the second highest in the bottom half, etc.

Colors are alternated down through each half. If the coin toss determined that the higher-rated player on board one would receive white, the higher rated on board two receives black, and so on. If there is an odd number of players, the lowest-rated player, but not an unrated player, receives a one-point bye. For bye allocation methods, see 28L.

The boards are numbered in the playing hall and the pairings are posted on pairings sheets, which indicate each player's opponent, board number, and color. It is customary to assign the highest-rated player in the top score group to board one, the second highest in that group to board two, etc. The director may modify the pairings somewhat, especially in the early rounds in order to avoid pairing family members, close friends, or members of the same club against one another.

28K. Late entrants. The director may accept and pair entrants after the announced closing time for registration, but the late entrant shall forfeit any round missed if it is inconvenient or too late to pair the players for play, or may take a half-point bye if the tournament offers them for that round (see 22C, Half-point byes). Late entrants are assigned pairing numbers as described in 28B.

28L. Full-point byes.

28L1. Explanation and display. In any round in which the total number of players in a tournament or section of a tournament is uneven, one player is given a full-point bye. The player's score is posted as a win on the wall chart, but circled to indicate that the game was not played. Wall charts generated by computer generally will print "bye," but will not circle the score.

28L2. Determination. In the first round, the bye is given to the player with the lowest USCF rating but not to an unrated player or a late entrant. In subsequent rounds, it is given to the lowest-rated player in the lowest score group but not to an unrated. If there are no rated players eligible for the bye in the lowest score group, it is given to an unrated player who has played in a USCF-rated tournament too recently to obtain a published rating. If this, too, is impossible, a new player may be assigned the bye.

28L3. Players ineligible for full-point byes. A player must not be given a full-point bye more than once, nor should one be awarded to a player who has won an unplayed game due to the opponent's failure to appear.

28L4. Full-point byes after half-point byes. A full-point bye should not be awarded to a player who has previously taken or committed to a half-point bye unless all others in the score group have already had a bye or a no-show forfeit win. See 22C, Half-point byes.

28L5. New players in four-round events. Directors should try to ensure that new players play at least four games in their first tournament in order to obtain official ratings. In a four-round event, if only new players are available for byes in the bottom score group, the bye may be given to a player one score group above. This should not be done if the player receiving the bye has a substantial chance for a prize. It is preferable to use 28M (alternatives to byes) than to assign a bye to a new player.

NOTE: For half-point byes, see 22C.

28M. Alternatives to byes. Awarding byes may be necessary for the smooth progress of a tournament, but they deprive a player of an expected game. To avoid this, several methods have been used with success. Directors are encouraged to use them to provide games for players who do not want byes. These methods may be combined with one another.

28M1. The houseman. Sometimes a spectator will agree to play a game against a player who would otherwise expect a bye. It is desirable that this spectator has a rating approximately within the range of the lowest score group, but this is not required. The player is voluntarily giving up a free point to play, so no one can legitimately claim the opponent is too weak.

Sometimes the player would rather play an unusually strong opponent than receive a bye. This also is acceptable, but if the strong opponent is rated too high for the section, the director may consider retaining the original bye and listing both players for a rated game in a higher section or an "extra rated games" section. See 28M4.

With the agreement of the opponent, a USCF-rated commercially available computer may be used as a houseman. Such a game shall be rated for the player but not the computer.

It is not required that a houseman be paired against the player who would otherwise receive the bye. Sometimes it is more appropriate to insert a relatively strong houseman into a higher minus score group. In this case, neither the player paired against the houseman nor the one who otherwise would have received the bye has the right to refuse to play.

If a permanent houseman is available, this is the best solution. Such a player is paired normally whenever there is an odd number, not paired when there is an even number, and can even receive half-point byes as the tournament allows them.

Usually, a player whose full-point bye is replaced by a temporary houseman should be assigned no additional full-point byes in the tournament. An exception may be appropriate if the houseman was strong and the player is competing for a class prize against others who have received full-point byes.

28M2. Cross-round pairings. The player who expects the bye is asked to wait until one of the games in the lowest score groups has finished. The loser of that game is then asked to play the next round game early, after a brief rest. The director then pairs the two players and marks the pairing and the result in the appropriate round boxes for each player: for the player who would have received the bye, in the current round; for the opponent, in the next round. This sometimes has the advantage of eliminating the need for a bye in the following round.

Cross-round pairings work best in scholastics and events for low-rated players such as those under 1400, because the bottom boards in such events usually play very quickly. If a cross-round pairing is planned and there is a significant delay before the game starts, the director may offer the option of such a pairing only if both sides start with time elapsed from their clocks. Either player may refuse, which may lead to the cross-round pairing being abandoned and the original bye reinstated.

The use of cross-round pairings should be specially indicated on the USCF rating report.

28M3. Cross-section pairings. In a tournament with multiple sections, there may be more than one section with a bye for a particular round. In this case, a cross-section pairing may be more desirable than a cross-round as the game can begin immediately. The player in the lower of the two sections involved retains the bye but is added to the pairings and wall chart of the higher section for a rated game. The player in the higher section has a game that counts for both score and rating purposes rather than a bye. Such a player should not subsequently be assigned a full-point bye or a bye alternative.

28M4. Extra rated games. Directors may accommodate players who wish to play a rated game without giving up a full-point bye by placing both players on an "extra rated games" wall chart.

28N. Combined individual-team tournaments. Scholastic events are often held as individual Swiss systems with both individual and team awards. Team standings are determined by adding the scores of each school's top scorers, usually the top four. The director should try to avoid pairing teammates, vs. each other, but an absolute prohibition of such pairings can give an unfair advantage in the individual standings to players on strong teams, who may be "paired down" against players with a lower score rather than facing each other.

28N1. Plus-two method.

a. If a score group can be paired among itself without players from the same team facing each other, this should always be done.

b. For score groups of less than plus two (see 28N1c for definition of plus two), if there is no way to pair the score group without players from the same team facing each other, these players should be raised or lowered into the nearest appropriate score group in order to avoid having teammates face each other.

c. For score groups of plus two or greater (at least two more wins than losses), players should not be removed from their score group in order to avoid playing those from the same team.

Variation 28N2. Players from the same team should never be paired against each other unless it is the last round, one is first, and if this leader is not paired against a teammate he or she will have to play someone with a lower score.

Variation 28N3. The basic rule may be modified to use a score other than plus two as the point at which teammates will not be paired out of their score group to avoid facing each other.

Variation 28N4. The director shall decide when it is appropriate to pair players from the same team vs. each other in order to maximize fairness in individual or team standings.

28O. Scoring. The tournament director records the results of the games on the pairing cards or enters them into the computer. These results should also be posted, as quickly as convenient, to wall charts that are prominently displayed. See illustration.

NO.	PLAYER'S FULL NAME — AS SHOWN ON MEMBERSHIP CARD —	RATING	ROUND 1		ROUND 2		ROUND 3		ROUND 4		ROUND 5		ROUND 6		ROUND 7		ROUND 8		
			COL.	OPP.	COL.	OPP.	COL.	OPP.	COL.	OPP.	COL.	OPP.	COL.	OPP.	COL.	OPP.	COL.	OPP.	
1	Attack, Allen A. ID No. 11111111	2000	B 5	1	W 4	2	B 2	2											2
2	Bishop, Barbara B. ID No. 22222222	1950	W 6	1	B 3	2	W 1	3											3
3	Chesser, Curtis C. ID No. 33333333	1900	B 7	1	W 2	1	B 5	1½											1½
4	Defender, Donald D. ID No. 44444444	1850	W 8	1	B 1	1	W 7	2											2
5	Enpassant, Edwin E. ID No. 55555555	1800	W 1	0	B 8	1	W 3	1½											1½
6	Files, Fred F. ID No. 66666666	1750	B 2	0	W 7	0	B 8	0											0
7	Goodplayer, Gordon G. ID No. 77777777	1700	W 3	0	B 6	1	B 4	1											1
8	Helpmate, Harry H. ID No. 88888888	1650	B 4	0	W 5	0	W 6	1											1
9	ID No.																		
0	ID No.																		

– CUMULATIVE SCORES AFTER EACH ROUND –

No. US-18 Swiss Tournament Results Chart (rev. 10/77)   UNITED STATES CHESS FEDERATION • NEW WINDSOR, NEW YORK 12553

28O1. Computer wall charts. One of the major advantages of using a computer is that it can print out updated wall charts each round. In a large event, avoiding the need to enter the color and opponent of each player on the wall chart saves considerable time.

However, it is still recommended that the scores of each player be manually updated as soon as possible. It may be tempting to wait so that the computer can print out all or many scores, but making the players wait for hours to learn results may make the tournament less enjoyable.

28P. Unplayed games. If a player fails to appear within one hour of the start of the round or by the end of the first time control, whichever comes first, the game is scored as a loss for the player and a win for the opponent. That player is then dropped from the tournament unless he or she presents an acceptable excuse to the director. The player's subsequent games are also scored as zero. A player may also withdraw from the tournament, in which case the remaining games are scored as zero.

The scores of unplayed games, including byes, are marked with an "F" or circled on the pairing cards, on the wall chart, and on the rating report (if different from the wall chart). Unplayed games are not USCF rated. Note that a game in which both sides make moves is always rated, even if a player forfeits on time or for an infraction of the rules; this type of forfeit is never marked with an "F" or circled.

See also Rule 22, Unplayed Games.

28Q. Pairing unfinished games. If at all possible, without imposing unreasonable delay in the start of the next round upon the other players, all games from one round should be finished before the next round is paired. If this is not possible, the director has several options:

28Q1. Modified Kashdan system. The director may approach a game in progress, instruct the player on move to seal, and inform both players that either player who offers a draw and so informs the director before pairings for the next round begin will be paired as having drawn, and that either player who does not do so will be paired as having won. The director should stop both clocks before this intervention and restart the clock of the player who is to seal at its conclusion.

This modified method, probably the best way to handle adjournments, has several advantages over the original Kashdan system, in which the director privately asked each player what result he or she was seeking. It is much quicker, does not pressure players to respond immediately, and makes it clearer to the players that the draw offer may be accepted at any time during adjournment.

28Q2. Temporary adjudications. The director can adjourn the unfinished game(s) and either pair the players as having drawn, having won and lost, or having won and drawn. The latter might be appropriate if one player has winning chances and the opponent has drawing chances. If necessary, the director may consult strong players whose own pairings are not affected for help.

See also 18F (Problems of the next-to-last round) and 29M (Last round pairings with unfinished games).

28R. Accelerated pairings in first two rounds. In a tournament where the number of players far exceeds the number two raised to the power of the number of rounds (see Rule 27), more than one perfect score is possible, and top contenders may not play each other. The director has pairing options which in effect "add" an extra round or two to the tournament without any additional games being played.

Accelerated pairings are most effective in a one-section tournament, an Open Section, or a section in which no more than about half the players are in the same 200-point rating class. They may fare poorly in a primarily one-class section as the chances of the lower rated 1–0 defeating the higher rated 0-1 in round two are substantial.

28R2 is more effective but more complicated than 28R1, while the little-tested Variation 28R3 is intended for events with an especially small ratio of rounds to players and large rating differences.

28R1. Added score method. Before the first round, the cards are numbered, put in order of rank, and divided in half. The director notes the top number in the lower half and for the first two rounds mentally adds one point to the scores of all players ranked above that number, for pairing purposes only. He or she divides the cards accordingly and pairs normally.

The effect, in the first round, is to have the top quarter play the second quarter and the third quarter play the fourth quarter. For the most part, the effect in the second round will be to have the top eighth play the second eighth, the second quarter play the third quarter, and the seventh eighth play the last eighth. This method decreases the number of perfect scores.

28R2. Adjusted rating method. Before the first round, after the bye, if any, is issued, the pairing cards are arranged in the normal order, top rated to lowest rated. Then the field is divided from top to bottom into four groups (A1, B1, C1, and D1) as close to the same size as possible and paired as follows:

A1 vs. B1 and C1 vs. D1. These first-round pairings are the same as in Variation 1.

For the second-round pairings, the players are regrouped as follows:

A2: Winners from A1 vs. B1. If there is an odd number of players, the lowest rated drops to the top of C2.

B2: Non-winners from A1 vs. B1, with players who drew having a temporary 100 points added to their ratings. If there are more players in B2 than C2, the lowest-rated losers from B2 are dropped to the top of D2, until B2 has the same number of players as C2. If there are fewer players in B2 than C2, the highest-rated players from D2 are raised to the bottom of B2 until B2 has the same number of players as C2.

C2: Non-losers from C1 vs. D1, with players who drew having a temporary 100 points subtracted from their ratings.

D2: Losers from C1 vs. D1.

Each of these groups is arranged in rating order, including the temporary adjustments for first-round performances. Then each group is paired as follows:

A2: This group is divided in half. The top half plays the bottom half according to basic pairing methods.

B2 and C2: These groups play each other, with the top player in B2 facing the top in C2, etc., according to basic pairing methods. This will result mostly in players with different scores playing—1 vs. 0, 1 vs. ½, or ½ vs. 0—though an occasional ½ vs. ½ is also possible. Whenever the players have different scores, the one with the lower score will be higher rated.

D2: This group is divided in half. The top half plays the bottom half according to basic pairing methods.

For the third and subsequent rounds, the temporary rating adjustments are ignored and the pairings are made according to the basic system.

This variation of accelerated pairings produces only about half the number of perfect scores achieved with the basic system. It therefore decreases the likelihood of multiple perfect scores and causes the final standings to be more dependent on games between the top-rated players.

Variation 28R3. Apply the same principles as 28R2, but divide the field into sixths in the first round and pair the first sixth vs. the second, third vs. fourth, and fifth vs. sixth. In round two, pair the winners of 1 vs. 2 against each other, the non-winners of 1 vs. 2 against the winners of 3 vs. 4, the non-winners of 3 vs. 4 against the winners of 5 vs. 6, and the losers of 5 vs. 6 against each other.

28S. Reentries. Tournaments with alternate schedules allowing players a choice of starting times for the early rounds often permit reentry, in which the player abandons or takes byes in the earlier starting schedule in order to enter the later starting schedule. For example, there may be a three-day schedule with round one at 8:00 P.M. Friday and a two-day schedule with round one at 10:00 A.M. Saturday, with the two schedules merging for round two starting Saturday afternoon. A player who loses or draws on Friday night may choose to "start fresh" by reentering the two-day schedule, in which case the Friday game, while still rated, would not damage the player's chances for prizes.

28S1. Reentry playing opponent twice. If one player has reentered and the other has not, 27A1 applies, and they should not be paired against each other for a second time. Even though the reentry is a new entry, from the standpoint of the opponent who did not reenter, it is the same player.

28S2. Reentries playing each other twice. If two reentries have already faced each other while each was playing his or her original entry, they may be paired against each other for a second time, since neither has faced that player during that entry.

28S3. Reentry colors. Reentries are treated as having no color history; the colors from their original entries are disregarded.

28S4. Reentry with half-point byes. Players sometimes reenter the same schedule with half-point byes replacing games missed. 28S1, 28S2, and 28S3 all apply to such reentries as well.

28T. FIDE title and rating tournaments. In some stronger tournaments, it may be appropriate to make minor variations in normal pairings to maximize the players' opportunities to fulfill the requirements needed to earn international title norms or to gain initial FIDE ratings. However, directors should consider that making irregular pairings to facilitate such title opportunities involves risk of rejection by FIDE of resultant title applications.

29. SWISS SYSTEM PAIRINGS, SUBSEQUENT ROUNDS

29A. Score groups and rank. The words "score group" and "group" refer to players having the same score, even if there is only one player within a group. The players in each such score group are paired against each other (see 27A2) unless they have already faced each other (see 27A1) or are odd players (see 29D) or must play odd players. In a combined individual and team tournament, players are sometimes paired out of their score groups to avoid facing teammates (see 28N). Individual rank is determined first by score (the greater the number of points, the higher the rank within the tournament) and then by rating within a score group (the higher the rating, the higher the rank).

29B. Order of pairing score groups. In general, the director pairs the groups according to rank, starting with the highest and working down. If games within some score groups are still unfinished shortly before the scheduled start of the next round, the director may wish to modify this order and pair around the groups with games still going on, taking care to provide for the "odd players." It may be worthwhile to ask the players involved in a long game to confirm that they are playing the next round, as notice to the contrary after the game will be too late.

It may be helpful to make a quick table beforehand, listing the different score groups in descending order and the number of players in each group, and drawing arrows to show where players must be dropped (in the case of the odd player) to play someone from the group below.

29C. Method of pairing score groups. In the second and subsequent rounds, the players are paired as follows:

29C1. Top half vs. bottom half. If there is an even number of players within a group, they are placed in order of rank, divided in half, and the top half is paired against the bottom half, in as close to consecutive order as possible (e.g., in a group with 20 players, the first ranked would play the eleventh ranked, the second the twelfth, and so on).

29C2. Other adjustments. Transpositions are made in order to avoid pairing players who have already played each other and to give as many players as possible their equalizing or due colors (see 29E). To this end it is also permissible to make an interchange between the bottom of the top half and the top of the bottom half. Rules on transpositions and interchanges are covered below.

29D. The odd player.

29D1. Determination. If there is an odd number of players in a score group, the lowest-rated player, but not an unrated player, is ordinarily treated as the odd player and is paired with the highest-rated player he or she has not met in the next lower group. Care must be taken in doing this that the remaining members of the score group can all be paired with each other, that the odd player has not played all the members of the next lower group, and that the color consequences are acceptable (see 29E and 29H). In any of these cases, the next lowest rated player is treated as the odd player. After determining the odd player, the director pairs as above.

If the entire group is unrated, then an unrated player should be dropped. This player may be selected at random, or the player with the lowest cumulative tie-break points may be dropped. See 34E3.

29D2. Multiple drop downs. It is sometimes necessary to jump over an entire score group to find an appropriate opponent for an odd player. For example, Group 1 has only one player, the only player with a perfect score. This player has already played both members of Group 2, a two-player score group. The player therefore must play the highest-rated player in Group 3 that he or she has not yet played in the tournament.

It is possible that there will be two odd players. In the example above, if the two players in Group 2 had already met, they would both be odd players. They must be paired with the highest-rated players remaining in Group 3 whom they have not played before, the higher-rated player in Group 2 with the highest-rated player in Group 3, and the lower-rated player in Group 2 with the next highest rated in Group 3.

The odd player is normally paired with the highest-rated player he or she has not met from the next lower group. It is acceptable to pair the player against a somewhat lower rated player to equalize or alternate colors, but only within the rules for transposition as explained below.

29E. Color Allocation. The director assigns colors to all players. The objective in a tournament with an even number of rounds is to give white and black the same number of times to as many players as possible; in an event with an odd number of rounds, each player should receive no more than one extra white or black above an even allocation.

In addition to the task of equalizing colors, the director, after the first round, tries to alternate colors, by giving as many players as possible their due ("correct" or expected) color, round by round. The due color is usually the color a player did not have in the previous round, but not always. For example, a player who had white in rounds one and two and black in round three has a due color of black in round four, as equalization has priority over alternation.

29F. Unplayed games. Unplayed games, including byes and forfeits, do not count for color.

29G. First-round colors. In the first round, when the top half of the field plays the bottom half, the director assigns the color to the odd-numbered players in the top half by lot (e.g., by flipping a coin).

The opposite color is given to all the even-numbered players in the top half. This initial assignment by lot governs all further color allocation except in the last-round variation noted below.

It is not necessary for any players to participate in a coin toss for assignment of first-round colors. One toss is sufficient for all sections of a multi-section event, with the same color given to the highest-rated player in each section.

29H. Due colors in succeeding rounds. As many players as possible are given their due colors in each succeeding round, so long as the pairings conform to the basic Swiss system laws. Equalization of colors takes priority over alternation of colors. For example, if a player with WWB in the first three rounds was scheduled to play a player with BBW, the first player would receive black and the second would receive white.

29I. Equalization, alternation, and priority of color. First, as many players as possible are given the color that equalizes the number of times they have played as white and as black. After that is accomplished, as many players as possible should be given alternate colors to those they had the previous round. These are called the "due" colors.

When it is necessary to pair two players who are each due the same color, the higher-ranked player has priority in receiving the due color. When each of these players has the same score in the tournament, the higher ranked is the higher rated; when their tournament scores are unequal, the player with the higher score in the tournament receives priority.

Variation 29I1. The higher-ranked player in plus and even score groups receives priority for color allocation, while the lower-ranked player in minus score groups receives that priority. This variation minimizes color problems in the very low score groups, as well as the very high, sometimes a problem because these are statistically the smallest groups.

Variation 29I2. When two players within a score group are both due the same color, the higher-rated player receives due color. But if several such situations exist within the group, the first higher rated player receives due color, the second does not, the third does, and so on, alternating entitlement from higher- to lower-rated player. This applies both to equalizing and alternating colors.

Variation 29I3. If two players paired against each other are both due for the same color but have not had exactly the same colors for each round of the tournament, priority for assigning color will be based on the latest round in which their colors differed. For example, if a player with WBWB faces one with BWWB in round five, the player with WBWB would be assigned white because he or she played black in round two, the last round in which their colors differed.

Variation 29I4. The last round of a tournament, the director may choose to let opponents with equal entitlement to colors choose their own colors by lot, but only after making all the pairings necessary to come closer to equalized and alternate allocations. For example, if after four rounds both players had received WBWB, for the fifth and final round the director might choose to let the players choose for colors rather than assign them automatically by using one of the procedures outlined above. If this system is adopted, it must be used for all such cases without exception.

29J. Colors vs. ratings. Correct Swiss pairings should consider both colors and ratings, so a tournament director should exercise care not to distort either unduly. To improve colors a director may use either a transposition or an interchange of players.

A transposition is the practice of changing the order of pairing cards within the top half or bottom half of a group. An interchange involves switching a player from the bottom of the top half with a player from the top of the bottom half.

Transpositions and interchanges should be limited as follows:

29J1. The 80-point rule. Transpositions and interchanges for the purpose of maximizing the number of players who receive their due color should be limited to 80 points.

Example: WB vs. WB. To give one of these players a second straight black in round three is only moderately undesirable and does not justify a switch of over 80 points.

29J2. The 200-point rule. Transpositions and interchanges for the purpose of minimizing the number of players who receive black two or more times than white should be limited to 200 points.

Example: BWB vs. BWB. To give one of these players black for the third time in round four is highly undesirable, justifying a higher switch limit (200 points).

NOTE: Extra whites are not included, here or in 29I, because they cause far less player distress. To receive two more blacks than whites in an event is a significant handicap, but to have one of a player's many competitors receive two extra whites is at most a minor disadvantage.

29J3. Evaluating transpositions. All transpositions should be evaluated based on the smaller of the two rating differences involved. For example:

2000 WB vs. 1800 WB

1980 BW vs. 1500 BW

These would be correct third-round pairings were it not for the color problems. Unless a switch is made, there will be a color conflict on each board.

To trade the 1800 for the 1500 is apparently a 300-point switch which would violate 29J1, the 80-point rule. But this is not really the case. The same pairings may be achieved by trading the 2000 for the 1980, only a 20-point switch.

The resulting pairings, 2000 white vs. 1500 and 1800 white vs. 1980, are considered to require only a 20-point switch and thus satisfy the 80-point rule.

In larger groups, the situation is sometimes more complicated, as a permissible transposition may generate numerous additional transpositions, not all of which satisfy the limits for allowable transpositions. This is especially common when some of the otherwise desirable pairings are impossible because the players have already faced each other.

In such situations, the director may strictly observe the limits for transpositions or may be flexible. If colors in the group are substantially improved, it is acceptable for the limits to be exceeded somewhat.

29J4. Evaluating interchanges. For an interchange, the director need only consider one rating difference rather than the smaller of two. The difference between the two players switched is the relevant difference; there is no need to look at the other switch that would produce the same pairings.

While interchanges are theoretically acceptable if the rating difference of the switch is within the limits set forth in 29J1 (80-point rule) and 29J2 (200-point rule), they do violate basic principle 27A3 (top half vs. lower half), and so tend to catch players by surprise, causing questions and complaints. They are sometimes necessary, but should not be used if adequate transpositions are possible. See 29J5.

29J5. Comparing transpositions to interchanges. A transposition which satisfies 29J1 (the 80-point rule) should be preferred to any interchange, provided it is at least as effective in minimizing color conflicts.

If pairing a round in which 29J2 (the 200-point rule) is used because many players have had more blacks than whites, an interchange involving a smaller rating switch than a transposition should be preferred to the latter unless the transposition satisfies the 80-point rule.

Example 1

2050 WBW vs. 1850 WBW
1870 BWB vs. 1780 BWB

These fourth-round "natural pairings" should be switched to improve color allocation. Trading 1870 with 1850 is only a 20-point switch, while switching 1850 with 1780 is a 70-point change, the smaller number of 70 and 180. However, the 20-point switch is an interchange, the 70-point a transposition which meets the requirement of 29J1 (the 80-point rule). Use of the interchange is thus not necessary, and the pairings should be 1780–2050 and 1870–1850.

Example 2

2050 WBW vs. 1850 WBW
1870 BWB vs. 1750 BWB

The same situation as Example 1, except the bottom player of the group is now rated 30 points lower. In this case, trading 1850 with 1750 would be a 100-point switch. This is allowed, as we are trying to avoid assigning two more blacks than whites to someone on board two, so 29J2 (200-point rule) applies. But even though it is permitted, it does not meet the requirement of 29J1 (80-point rule), and thus does not have priority over an interchange.

The interchange of switching 1870 and 1850, a 20-point switch, is preferred, and the pairings should be 1870–2050 and 1750–1850.

29J6. Pairings to avoid. Unless all other possible ways to pair the players in the score group against each other would cause one or more pairings of players who have already faced each other, no player should be assigned either of the following:

a. The same color in more than two successive rounds.

b. Black in the final round when the player has already played more blacks than whites.

Variation 29J6a. Except for the last round, when it may be necessary to pair the tournament or class leaders, players shall not be assigned the same color in three successive rounds.

29J7. Unrateds and color switches. If a player is switched to or from an unrated opponent to improve color allocation, this is not in violation of the 80-point or 200-point rules for transpositions and interchanges.

Variation 29J8. Equalization of colors has priority over rating differences; 29J1 and 29J2 do not apply.

29K. Color adjustment technique. The order in which pairings are switched to improve colors can make a difference, both in the final pairings and in the time it takes to arrive at them. Two methods that have been commonly used are the "Look Ahead" method and the "Top Down" method. The "Look Ahead" method is more accurate and easier to use.

29K1. The "Look Ahead" method. The director counts to see if more than half the group is due for the same color. If not, he or she starts with the top pairing and works down, correcting as many color conflicts (games in which both players are due for the same color) as possible. Unless there is a problem with 29J1 (80-point rule) or 29J2 (200-point rule) or too many players have already faced each other, all colors will balance.

If more than half the group is due for the same color, the objective is to *avoid pairings in which neither player is due for that color.* This will maximize the number of pairings in which both sides receive their due color.

Note that "neither due for a color" is not the same as "both due for the other color." A player may be due no color, for instance, in round two after an unplayed game in round one.

A player may be due based only on alternation while most in the group are due based on equalization. For example, if pairing round four and most in the score group have had two blacks, a player with one of each color and an unplayed game is due for neither color based on equalization. Alternation is not an issue, as equalization has priority, so the player is due for neither color.

Assume most in a group are due for white. The director lays out the pairing cards to examine the "natural pairings." Any pair of players who have already faced each other are changed by the switch involving the minimum rating change, avoiding pairings in which neither player is due for white.

The tentative pairings are checked for games in which neither player is due for white. If there are none, the pairings are final. If such pairings exist, as many as possible are changed by making switches to higher or lower boards, involving the minimum possible rating differences.

Color conflicts are now minimized and pairings stand. While no direct attempt was made to avoid pairings of both players due for white, these were held to a minimum.

Variation 29K2. The "Top Down" method. Using this method, the director, after adjusting to avoid pairing players who have already played, first considers the color situation on board one of the score group, the board involving the top-rated player in the group. If both players are due for the same color, the pairing is changed by moving up the highest-rated player in the bottom half whose color fits, providing the pairing does not violate 29J1 (80-point rule) or 29J2 (200-point rule).

The director then moves down to board two, then board three, etc., correcting any color conflicts encountered in the same manner.

Eventually, the number of color conflicts should be the same as in the "Look Ahead" method. But the pairings are often inferior, and time may be wasted making adjustments that do not reduce the number of color conflicts.

29L. Examples of transpositions and interchanges. See 29J for definitions of these terms. In each case, we start by looking at what the pairings would be were there no color problems.

Example 1

2300 BWB vs. 2040 BWB
2220 BWB vs. 1990 WBW
2180 BBW vs. 1980 WBW
2050 BWB vs. 1950 WBW

Using the "Look Ahead" method, the director finds five players due for white, three due for black. Thus, pairings in which neither player is due for white should be avoided. But there are no such pairings, so the above pairings stand. Note that the 2180 is due for white because equalization has priority over alternation.

The "Top Down" method runs into real problems here. First, the director "corrects" the colors on board one and pairs 2300–1990. Then, he or she does likewise on boards two and three, resulting in 2220–1980 and 2180–1950. This leaves a bizarre pairing on board four: 2050–2040. When the director is asked why two players with ratings so close are playing each other in a group of eight, the response might be "to improve colors." Let's hope no one will notice that the colors for this strange pairing are wrong, too!

The remaining examples will show only the "Look Ahead" method.

Example 2

> 2320 WBWB vs. 1980 WBWB
> 2278 BWBW vs. 1951 WBWB
> 2212 BWBW vs. 1910 BWBW
> 2199 WBWB vs. 1896 BWBW
> 2178 WBWB vs. 1800 WBWB

The director's count shows six players out of ten overall due for white. This means pairings in which neither player is due for white should be avoided.

The only pairing in which neither is due for white is 2212 vs. 1910. There are two options for correcting this.

Option A: The first possibility is 2320–1910. This would require a 70-point switch in the lower half (1980 – 1910 = 70) or a 108-point switch in the upper half (2320 – 2212 = 108), so we count the switch as 70, the smaller number.

Option B: The second option for correcting the colors is 1800–2212. This is a 110-point switch in the lower half (1910 – 1800 = 110) but only a 34-point switch in the top half (2212 – 2178 = 34), and so is preferable to Option A.

The resulting pairings:

White	Black
2320	1980
1951	2278
1800	2212
2199	1910
2178	1896

Example 3

$$2210 \text{ B} \quad \text{vs.} \quad 1900 \text{ B}$$
$$2200 \text{ B} \quad \text{vs.} \quad 1830 \text{ B}$$
$$2150 \text{ W} \quad \text{vs.} \quad 1820 \text{ W}$$
$$2120 \text{ B} \quad \text{vs.} \quad 1790 \text{ B}$$
$$2080 \text{ B} \quad \text{vs.} \quad 1500 \text{ B}$$
$$1920 \text{ W} \quad \text{vs.} \quad 1350 \text{ bye}$$

Eight players are due for white, three for black, and one for neither, so pairings in which neither player is due for white should be corrected. We can quickly see that 2150–1820 and 1920–1350 are the problems. The 1350 player who received a bye in the first round is considered not due for white.

Switching 1820 up a board is a 10-point change (1830 – 1820 = 10) on one side, 50 points (2200 – 2150 = 50) on the other. The lower number is used, so it is a 10-point switch. Moving 1820 down a board is a 30-point switch on both sides (2150 – 2120 or 1820 – 1790 = 30). The 10-point change is selected and board two and three pairings switched.

The two bottom boards may be paired as 2080–1350 and 1500–1920. The smaller of the two switches is 150 points (1500 – 1350 = 150), permissible under the 200-point rule to avoid two extra blacks for a player on the fifth board.

However, there is a better way. An interchange between 1920 and 1900 also corrects the colors, and is a switch of just 20 points (1920 – 1900 = 20). An interchange has priority if it involves a smaller switch than a transposition, and the transposition requires a switch of over 80 points.

The resulting pairings:

White	Black
2210	1920
2200	1820
1830	2150
2120	1790
2080	1500
1900	1350

Example 4

2100 BWB (3 points)   vs. 2080 BWB (3 points)

1990 WBW (3 points)   vs. 2050 WBW (2½ points)

1980 BWB (2½ points) vs. 1800 BWB (2½ points)

Here, an odd player must drop from the 3 group to the 2½ group. The two groups combined will have three pairings, and giving someone three blacks out of four games unfortunately cannot be avoided.

The natural pairings shown above, dropping the low 3 to face the high 2½, are highly undesirable, leaving the colors wrong in all three games.

One way to improve colors would be to switch the 2050 with the second highest 2½, the 1980. This would be a switch of 70 (2050 − 1980 = 70) or 190 (1990 − 1800), which counts as 70.

The alternative would be to switch the 2080 and the 1990 in the 3-point group. This would be 90 (2080 − 1990 = 90) or 50 (2100 − 2050 = 50), counting as 50, and thus slightly preferable.

The resulting pairings:

White	Black
2100	1990
2080	2050
1980	1800

29M. Last-round pairings with unfinished games. Every effort should be made to have all games finished before pairing the last round. If this would unduly delay the start of the last round and inconvenience a large number of people, then last-round pairings can be made and the round begun. In this case, the director must be very watchful of the unfinished games to prevent the results from being arranged to affect the prizes. See 18F (Problems of the next-to-last round) and 28Q (Pairing unfinished games).

29N. Re-pairing a round.

29N1. Round about to start. If a player withdraws without proper notice as the pairings are nearing completion, the director must decide whether time permits a complete revision of the pairings.

If time does not allow this, one solution is to "ladder down" the pairings. For example, if a player with 2 points withdraws, the opponent faces a player with 1½ points, that player's opponent faces a player with 1 point, and so on down until a bye is assigned or the original bye is paired.

In doing this, the director should attempt to find opponents within the same rating range and due for the same color. If the original pairings included any odd players, their pairings may be useful to change. For instance, if a player with 2 points withdraws and another 2 was paired against a 1½, the opponent of the withdrawn player may be paired against the odd player with 2, leaving a 1½ to be "laddered down" rather than a 2.

The use of an appropriately rated houseman should be considered as an alternative to re-pairing.

If a computer pairing program is used, the round can usually be properly re-paired without significant delay, avoiding need for "laddering" or houseman.

29N2. Round already started. The director has the right to make changes in the pairings, if necessary, to correct errors or to handle sudden withdrawals, but it is recommended that no game be canceled in which black's fourth move has been determined.

29N3. Selective re-pairing. If some games have started and others have not, it is often possible to satisfactorily correct the problem by telling those who have started to continue and the others to wait, removing the pairing cards of those who have started, and then pairing those waiting as a separate group, using normal methods.

29O. Unreported results. Occasionally, both players fail to report the result of their game. The result, once learned by the director, counts for rating purposes and (except for 29O3) for prize purposes.

In a Swiss tournament, if it is time to pair the next round and a result is still unreported, the director has several options and should choose the one which offers the greatest equity:

29O1. Ejection. One or both players may be ejected from the tournament. This is appropriate only if there have been prior nonreporting problems with the player(s) involved.

2902. Double forfeit of next round. Both players may be removed from the following round pairings, and forfeited for that round.

2903. Double forfeit of unreported game. Both players may be scored and paired as losses. The real result, when learned, may be recorded as an "extra rated game." See 28M4.

2904. Half-point byes next round. Both players may be removed from the following round pairings and given half-point byes for that round, assuming that half-point byes are available in the event for that round.

2905. Guess the winner. If there is a great rating difference in the unreported game, the director may pair the higher-rated player as a win and the lower-rated as a loss. Such a "guess" is usually right, as not only is an upset statistically unlikely, but players scoring upsets rarely neglect to report results, while those defeating opponents rated well below them tend to have a higher "non-reporting rate" than the average player.

2906. Pair as a win and a draw. A variation of 2905 is to pair the higher player as a win and the lower as a draw. This has the advantage of penalizing someone for non-reporting but also guarantees a wrong pairing. If the director is not sure whether 2905 or 2907 is the better option, this may be an appropriate compromise.

2907. Pair as a double win. The director may pair both players as having won. This has the advantage of generally penalizing the loser, or both players if the game was drawn, with a harder pairing. The disadvantage is that when the loser is paired a full point up in the next round, this may reward the opponent in that round with an inappropriately easy pairing.

This option is more appropriate in a class tournament than one involving mixed classes in the same section; it also works better with even or minus scores than plus scores, and in early rounds rather than late rounds.

2908. Multiple missing results. If more than one game is unreported, all players who failed to report may be omitted from the next round pairings, and paired against each other once the results are known. If this method is used, care must be taken not to allow a player with a chance for prizes an unusually easy pairing, in effect a reward for failing to report the result. This method may also be combined with other methods.

2909. Results reported after pairings done. If the unreported result is reported or discovered after the pairings are posted for the next round, but shortly before the start of that round, and the director used options 2905, 2906, or 2907, it is not generally recommended that the round be delayed by doing all pairings over (but see 29O10). However, the director may consider changing some pairings:

a. If option 2905 was used, and the higher player actually lost, the pairings can usually be quickly improved by transposing the assignments of the two players who failed to report. A further option which can be selected, if the director does not fear significant delay, is to re-pair the entire higher of the two score groups involved.

b. If option 2905 was used, and the game was actually a draw, there may be no simple way to improve the pairings. However, they are probably not that bad (involving just half-point errors, not a full point), and the director may allow them to stand.

c. If option 29O6 was used, and the higher player actually won or drew, the pairings are even better than in b. But if the higher player lost, the situation is similar to a, and the director should consider at least transposing the pairings of the two non-reporters.

d. If option 29O7 was used, the pairings generally should not be changed. If this option has caused a serious problem, then it was incorrect to use it. The director facing this dilemma must choose between letting the pairings stand or doing many pairings over and delaying the round.

29O10. Computer pairings. If pairings are made by computer program, delaying the start of the round to correct all the pairings becomes a more viable option, since the computer may be able to do this in a few minutes.

The director of a large tournament should remember that in addition to pairing delay, there may be significant delay if players must leave their boards, find new pairings, go to new boards, and set up again.

29P. Class pairings. In tournaments with significant class prizes, class pairings may be used in the last round. This allows prizes to be decided by direct encounters between those competing for them. A major benefit is to avoid games in which a player in contention for a large prize faces a higher-rated opponent who is not, a situation which invites collusion to produce a win for the player in contention.

Class pairings should be used only when it is mathematically impossible for any player in that class to win a place prize that is greater than first in the class. If even one player can win more than first in the class, the system should not be used at all, since it would be unfair to pair that player against a Master and have his or her score surpassed by others in the class who were playing each other.

29P1. Full-class pairings. The first common method of class pairings simply treats the class as a separate Swiss system tournament, and pairs accordingly. If there is an odd number of players in the class, the bottom player should be paired as normally as possible outside the class.

29P2. Partial class pairings. Another system pairs players within a rating class who have a chance for class prizes with each other, and then treats the rest of the field normally. This method can be useful when using a computer program that does not do class pairings, since it can greatly reduce the number of pairings that must be made by hand and entered into the computer.

Partial class pairings may unfairly affect special prizes, such as top junior or senior, a factor a director may wish to consider.

29Q. Unrateds in class tournaments. In sections or events restricted to players under a specified rating with unrated players also allowed, if there are two or more unrated players with plus scores in the same score group, the director may pair them against each other. This system is most appropriate in events with meaningful cash prizes; it tends to make it more difficult for players with foreign experience to win undeserved prizes.

29R. Converting small Swiss to round robin. A 5-round Swiss with six entries or 3-round Swiss with four entries may be converted to a round robin format. This may be acceptable for a quick one-day tournament, but often works poorly for a two-day or three-day six-player round robin.

Withdrawals are likely to cause many more unplayed games in a round robin than in a Swiss and to distort the results more. The round robin format is also not compatible with late entries or half-point byes. It is true that the Swiss may pair players against each other twice, usually the two leaders in the last round, but most players prefer such a rematch to not playing at all.

29S. Using round robin table in small Swiss. A better option than 29R is to maintain an event as a Swiss when there is a small turnout, but to use a round robin pairing table to minimize the possibility of players facing the same opponents twice.

For instance, if a 5-round Swiss has six players, pair round one as in a normal Swiss. Then assign round robin pairing numbers, which cause the first-round pairings to have been correct for round one of a six-player round robin, using the pairing table in *USCF's Official Rules of Chess*. Do not announce that the tournament will be a round robin; it may not be.

As long as there are no dropouts or additions, pair each subsequent round using the round robin table by selecting the round from the table in which the top player in the top score group receives the proper Swiss opponent. Do not use the colors from the table, but assign them according to Swiss rules. If three in a row of the same color is inevitable using a pairing line, there is the option of using the next best line.

If everyone completes the tournament, it will in effect be a round robin, but if there are dropouts or late entries it is possible to switch to Swiss methods at any time. For instance, in the last round if only four players are still in the tournament, use Swiss methods and pair them against each other even if one or both encounters are rematches. This is far better than sticking to round robin pairings and awarding two byes.

The above method may also be used with slightly more players to avoid rematches. For instance, it may be appropriate in a 4-round Swiss with five or six players, a 5-round Swiss with six to eight players, a 6-round Swiss with seven to ten players, a 7-round Swiss with eight to twelve players, or an 8-round Swiss with nine to fourteen players.

Note that in such small Swisses it is especially important to recruit an appropriately rated permanent houseman if possible, since otherwise byes will have a more harmful effect than in a larger Swiss. Repeated announcements among spectators offering free entry to such a houseman are warranted, with the condition that such a player will be paired only when there would otherwise be an odd number. It is even possible to allow such a houseman to be eligible for prizes in the event he or she plays sufficient games to be in contention.

29T. Recommendations. Some disparity in color allocation is inevitable in the Swiss system, as score has priority over color. Tournaments with an even number of rounds cause the most problems, because when a disparity exists, it is larger. Tournaments with an odd number of rounds are therefore apt to keep more players happy, and are easier to pair because it is easier to maintain the expected 3-2 or 4-3 color allocations.

30. THE ROUND ROBIN TOURNAMENT

30A. Description. This tournament format is also known as "all-play-all." Formerly the almost exclusive format for chess competitions, the round robin is most often used now for important events where time is not a factor, club events with one game per week, and one-day four-player events known as "quads."

Although it is the fairest-known tournament format when there are no withdrawals, it cannot accommodate many players, and so is used much less than the Swiss system. A round robin tournament is easy to pair. Players are assigned numbers by lot, and the pairings are read from Crenshaw tables. See Chapter 13.

30B. Scoring. Scoring is the usual one/one-half/zero, except that players who withdraw before playing half their scheduled games shall be scored as not having competed at all. Their completed games must still be rated, but they are not considered part of their opponents' records for prize purposes.

30C. Withdrawals. Dropouts cause major problems in round robins. In special invitationals they may be held to a tolerable level, but in open weekend tournaments and weekly club events serious problems are common. Unlike the Swiss, in which a forfeit affects at most one game, a dropout may generate numerous inequities in a round robin, whether notice is given or not.

30D. Penalties for withdrawals. Players who withdraw without sufficient reason or who repeatedly withdraw from round robins may be denied entry in future such events, or may be charged a special deposit, which will be refunded upon completion of all games. The latter is in addition to any deposit the organizer may choose to require of all players in an effort to minimize withdrawals.

30E. Effect of withdrawals on colors. If there is a withdrawal, the Crenshaw-Berger system provides tables for adjustments to equalize colors.

30F. Double round robins. In double round robins, each player or team plays each of the other players or teams twice, the second time reversing the original color assignment.

30G. Quads. Quadrangular tournaments divide the entrants into groups of four in rating order. The four highest-rated players form the first group, etc. These players then play three-game round robins following the Crenshaw tables.

When the total number of entries is not divisible by four, the director may create a 3-round Swiss among the lowest five to seven players. This works well with a field of six, but not with five or seven since a large percentage of the field will receive a bye. The simplest method of evening the field is to seek another player. If more than one player appears, the late players should be informed that only an odd number prepared to enter immediately will be accepted.

A five-player section may be held as a round robin if all players agree. Players should be warned that this may take much longer since each player will have four opponents and a sit-out. This format is most appropriate with lower-rated players.

The preferred pairing table for quads is as follows: (Players' numbers are assigned in order of rating, not randomly as in larger round robins.)

Round 1: 1–4, 2–3
Round 2: 3–1, 4–2
Round 3: 1–2, 3–4
(colors by toss in this round)

30H. Holland system. The Holland system uses round robin preliminaries to qualify players for finals, which are usually also round robins. There is no standard format, but a typical one might be to divide players into groups of similar strength of about eight to twelve players each, with the winner or top two in each prelim qualifying for the championship finals and others possibly for lower finals.

The Holland system, once the standard U.S. tournament format, was surpassed by the more flexible Swiss system in the 1940s and is used today largely for Blitz (G/5) tournaments, in which the lack of delay for pairings is especially advantageous.

30I. Unbalanced Holland. A Holland variant used successfully in Blitz events places the top-rated players in the first preliminary section, the next highest rated in the second, etc., rather than balancing the strength of the sections. Prizes are awarded for each prelim, and all plus scores in the first prelim qualify for the finals, along with the top two players from the second prelim and the winners of each other prelim.

31. TEAM CHESS

Many varieties of team chess exist in the U.S. Different leagues, interclub events, and tournaments have somewhat different rules. The concern here is principally for team tournaments, but the points made may have wider applicability. Except for 31A, all comments apply to events with team vs. team pairings.

31A. Combined individual/team tournaments. As the name suggests, these are not true team tournaments. They are particularly popular as scholastic events because they allow schools to enter any number of players instead of a team with a fixed roster. The tournament is played as a normal Swiss, except that efforts are made to avoid pairing teammates (i.e., players from the same school) with each other. See 28N.

31B. Player rankings. Players on a team are ranked from strongest to weakest according to rating. Alternates must be lower rated than regular team members. Unrated players, unless assigned ratings (see 28D), must play on lower boards than rated players.

If a player is missing from the line-up, lower-rated teammates must move up to fill the chair so that if a team forfeits a game it is always on the last board. Board order must remain the same throughout the event.

31B1. Board prizes. If individual board prizes are offered, players who play on more than one board are eligible only for the lowest board played. The player's points on all boards combined are credited toward the board prize on the lowest board.

Variation 31B2. An unrated player may play on any board.

31C. Team ratings. Teams are ranked in order of the average of individual ratings of the regulars, not alternates. Unrated players (see 28D) do not affect their team's average rating.

Variation 31C1. In calculating the average team rating, an unrated on board four is assigned 50 points below the rating of board three. An unrated on board three is assigned the average of the board two and four ratings. An unrated on board two is assigned the average of the board one and three ratings. An unrated on board one is assigned 50 points above the rating of board two. This system and 31B1 have been used at the Pan-American Intercollegiate.

31D. Pairing cards. Team tournaments use pairing cards similar to those used in individual tournaments, except that there is space to note both match scores and game points. Ideally, a larger pairing card, such as one measuring five-by-eight inches, should be used. These are available from the USCF office.

The front of the pairing card should contain the team name, the team average rating, the results of the team round by round, the colors of the team, and the team's opponents. The reverse side should contain the names of the players, their ratings, their USCF identification numbers, and the name of the team captain, as well as any information about fees and dues paid.

31E. Pairing rules. Swiss team events should be paired in the same manner as individual events. Teams are grouped by their match points and then ranked within the group by their ratings. Rules governing color allocations apply to the color received by board one. If the first board receives white, for example, so do all teammates on odd-numbered boards, while his or her even-numbered teammates play black. Byes, defaults, lateness, and so forth are treated as in individual tournaments. Scoring is based on match points, without regard to the margin of victory.

Note that colors are less important for teams with an even number of boards than they are in an individual tournament since half the team will have each color in every round.

Variation 31E1. Scoring and pairings may be done by game points rather than match points, or by a combination of the two (match points first, then game points if tied).

31F. Wall charts. Swiss team events are unique in that two sets of wall charts are needed, team charts to display team results and individual charts for individual results. These latter charts, in addition to being informative, are needed for tie-break and rating purposes.

The individual charts are set up by team so that the highest-average-rated team's players would appear as numbers 1, 2, 3, 4, etc., the second highest rated team's players would then continue the sequence, and so on down to the lowest-rated team's players. Note that a player on a lower-rated team could have the highest individual rating in the tournament but still be placed far down on the wall charts.

A form that combines individual and team entries on a single wall chart is also a possibility, as is the use of a separate individual wall chart for each board.

31G. Team captain. The role of the team captain is:

31G1. Registration. To register the team with all appropriate information.

31G2. Arrival. To see that the team arrives on time for each match.

31G3. Line-up. To see that the team plays the correct opponent, in the correct board order, with the correct colors.

31G4. Draw consequences. To advise the players if asked what the likely consequences of a draw would be for the team, and to respond to such a request without looking at the game of the player making the request.

31G5. Reporting result. To report the result of the match to the tournament director in the manner required.

31G6. Wall charts. To check the wall charts for accuracy and to report any discrepancies to the director.

32. PRIZES

32A. Announcement. Prizes to be awarded and the methods used to allocate them must be announced in pre-tournament publicity if they vary from the standards below. In all cases, these guidelines apply equally to individual or teams.

32B. Distribution.

32B1. One cash prize per player. No winner shall receive more than one cash award. The award may be one full cash prize if a clear winner, or parts of two or more cash prizes if tied with others. Prizes such as "biggest upset," "best game," or "brilliancy" are standard exceptions from this rule. A clear winner of more than one cash prize must be awarded the greatest prize.

32B2. Ties. Tied winners of place prizes or tied winners in the same class of class prizes shall be awarded all the cash prizes involved, summed and divided equally, but no more than one cash prize shall go into the division for each winner.

32B3. Class winners tie with place winners. If winners of class prizes tie with winners of place prizes, all the cash prizes involved shall be summed and divided equally among the tied winners unless the class prize winner(s) would receive more money by winning or dividing only the class prize(s). No more than one cash prize shall go into the pool for each winner.

32B4. Priority of identical prizes. A player who is eligible for both a place prize and a class prize of an identical amount shall receive the place prize. A player who is eligible for more than one class prize of an identical amount shall receive the prize for the highest class involved. A player who is eligible for prizes of identical amounts, with one being a rating-based class prize and the other being a prize for juniors, seniors, etc., shall receive the rating-based class prize.

32B5. Offering a choice of prizes. No player shall ever be offered a choice of which cash prize to accept, as this would allow that player to determine which prizes are available to be awarded to others.

Example 1

$$
\begin{aligned}
\text{1st prize} &= \$200 \\
\text{2nd prize} &= \$100 \\
\text{3rd prize} &= \$75
\end{aligned}
$$

Players 1 and 2 tie for 1st and 2nd with 4½–½; players 3, 4, and 5 score 4-1.

Players 1 and 2 win $150 each (equal shares of 1st and 2nd).

Players 3, 4, and 5 win $25 each (equal shares of 3rd).

Example 2

$$
\begin{aligned}
\text{1st prize} &= \$400 \\
\text{2nd prize} &= \$200 \\
\text{A prize} &= \$100 \\
\text{B prize} &= \$50
\end{aligned}
$$

Players 1, 2, 3 score 5–0; players 4, 5 (an A), and 6 (a B) are next with 4-1.

Players 1, 2, and 3 win $200 each.

Player 4 wins no money.

Player 5 wins $100 (the A prize).

Player 6 wins $50 (the B prize).

Note: If instead of the A prize of $100 and B prize of $50 an "Under 2000" prize of $100 and "Under 1800" prize of $50 had been advertised, players 5 and 6 would win $75 each.

Example 3

1st prize = $250	1st A = $75
2nd prize = $200	2nd A = $50
3rd prize = $150	1st B = $75
4th prize = $100	

Players 1 and 2 score 5–0. Players 3, 4, 5, 6 score 4½–½, where 4 and 5 are A players and 6 a B. Player 7 (an A) scores 4-1.

Players 1 and 2 each win $225 (equal shares of $250 + $200).

Players 3, 4, 5, 6 each win $100 (equal shares of $150 + $100 + $75 + $75).

Player 7 wins $50.

Example 4

1st prize = $100
2nd prize = $75
A prize = $50 + clock

Player 1 (Expert) scores 5–0; player 2 (A) scores 4½–½, player 3 (A) scores 4-1.

Player 1 wins $100.

Player 2 wins $75 plus clock.

Player 3 wins $50.

32C. Payment. Prizes advertised as guaranteed must be paid promptly and in full. Failure to pay guaranteed prizes may result in penalties, including revocation of affiliation.

32C1. Withdrawals. Unless the director decides otherwise, players who fail to complete the tournament are not entitled to prizes.

32C2. One player in class. An announced class prize must be awarded even if only one player in that class completes the schedule, unless otherwise advertised.

32C3. No players in class. If no players in a class complete their schedule, awarding an advertised prize for that class is not required.

32C4. Minimum prizes in "based-on-entries" tournaments. In tournaments advertising a prize fund of $501 or more, prizes advertised as being based on a certain number of entries are to be paid at a minimum of 50 percent of the advertised fund. Further, the prize fund is not to be reduced by a greater percentage than the entries fell short. No individual prize may be reduced by more than the proportion of the total prize fund's allowed reduction.

Examples

1. A tournament advertises $1,000 in prizes if 100 players enter. Only 30 enter. The organizer is required to pay at least $500, each prize being at least half the original projection.

2. A tournament advertises $1,000 in prizes if 100 players enter. Only 70 enter. The organizer is required to pay at least $700 in prizes, each prize to be at least 70 percent of the amount originally advertised.

32D. Based-on options. If separate based-on goals are announced for different sections of an event, then each section is treated separately. If the based-on goal is announced for any combination of selections, then the sections involved are considered as a group.

32E. Partial guarantees. Sometimes the overall prize fund is based on entries, but some prize(s), most often first overall, is (are) guaranteed. Organizers should realize that they are guaranteeing more than 50 percent of the projected prize fund under these circumstances.

For example, if projected prizes are $2,000 based on 60 entries with $500 guaranteed to first, and 30 players enter, the $500 first prize must be awarded and the remaining $1,500 that was projected cannot be lowered below $750 (as each prize must not be less than half of what was projected. So, the actual total guarantee is $1,200 ($500 + $750), not $1,000.

32F. Trophies. No player should receive more than one individual trophy or plaque, the most desirable to which he or she is entitled. It is recommended that no class, age, or school grade trophy be as desirable as any of the place trophies. A player should not have a choice of trophies, since such a choice would decide which trophies are available to be awarded to others.

32F1. Tie breaking. Unless another method has been announced in advance, tie breaking will be used to resolve ties for trophies.

Variation 32F2. The winner of a school grade or age trophy may also win a place or class trophy. This addresses the common problem of young children who consider any first place better than any lower place regardless of the category. The use of this variation should be posted or announced at the tournament before the first round.

32G. Other non-cash prizes. No player shall receive more than one non-cash, non-trophy prize, the most valuable to which he or she is entitled.

32G1. Tie breaking. Unless another method has been announced in advance, tie breaking will be used to resolve ties for merchandise, memberships, or free entries, to determine which player wins any title at stake or qualifies to advance into another contest, or to serve any purpose other than the award of money prizes.

33. SOME NOTES ABOUT PRIZE FUNDS

These are recommendations rather than rules or mandates but are included since some less experienced organizers may find them useful.

33A. First prize. A ratio of about ten to one between first prize and the entry fee is typical for serious tournaments, as opposed to club events or other tournaments organized to provide experience. This ratio should be even greater in an event designed to attract top players.

33B. Place prizes and class prizes. When there is apt to be a number of players in a rating class competing in an event, it is frequently the case that some sort of class prize is offered. This should be at least as much as the entry fee paid. Generally, place prizes should be higher than class prizes, both to reward the relative excellence of the chess played and to avoid distribution problems.

In major tournaments, the top prizes for classes or rating-based lower sections are often higher than the lower place prizes, but most organizers consider it inappropriate for any class prize or rating-based lower section prize to be as large as the corresponding overall or top section prize.

33C. Classes. A common variation on class prizes is the use of "under" prizes for players below a specified rating. There is a difference between a Class A prize and an Under 2000 prize, since only a Class A player may win the former, while a Class A, B, C, D, or E player can qualify for the latter. If a prize is intended for a restricted group, it should be named by the class or by both ratings boundaries, e.g., Class A or 1800–1999.

33D. Prizes based on points. Some organizers base prizes on points scored rather than place. Such events often award prizes to all plus scores, a popular feature for players who doubt their ability to win the top-place prizes.

For example, in a 5-round Swiss with an entry fee of $25 to $30, it could be announced that 5 points will win $100, 4½ $50, 4 $30, 3½ $20, 3 $10. With a fee of $50 to $60, prizes might be 5 points $300, 4½ $150, 4 $90, 3½ $60, 3 $30. These levels provide relative safety for the organizer, since even with a poor turnout prizes will often be less than entry fees.

Prizes based on points have proven more popular with Experts and below than with Masters, so organizers should consider not using them in top sections. It is desirable to have such events in sections of no more than two 200-point classes each or to offer supplementary prizes for lower classes unlikely to make plus scores. A separate section for each class is ideal if the expected turnout is sufficient.

The based-on-points method has a unique advantage over prizes that are guaranteed or based on entries. The announced prizes are never reduced, but their *total* varies according to the turnout. This protects the organizer against financial loss without the player disappointment sometimes caused by prize reduction.

33E. Unrateds. Note that many players who are playing in their first USCF tournament, although they have no USCF ratings, are by no means beginners. Some have high ratings or categories in other countries, and not all reveal these to directors as required. Unrated players should generally not be eligible for any prizes of value other than place or unrated prizes. Prizes such as "D/E/Unrated" are not recommended.

When substantial cash prizes are offered in sections for lower rated players, unrateds are often ineligible to enter or have a prize limit far below that of rated players.

34. BREAKING TIES

34A. Introduction. There is no perfect tie-break system; each has its faults. In some events, especially large ones, ease and speed of calculation is a concern. In other events where time is not pressing, play-offs provide a better alternative to traditional tie-break systems. Play-offs are often conducted at a faster time control than the tournament; even five-minute games have been used.

34B. Announcement. When used, tie-break systems should be posted at the site before the first round. There are several tie-break systems that provide good and objective methods for directors to break ties for indivisible prizes.

Frequently, one tie-break method alone will not break the tie, and it is necessary to use a secondary and sometimes even a tertiary method to produce a decision. Thus, at least the first two tie-break systems should be posted. The director should be prepared to explain how the tie-break systems work, as time permits.

34C. Cash prizes. Tie breaks are not used for cash prizes, which are divided evenly among the tied players. An exception is a play-off, which may be used to determine cash prizes if notice of this is given in all detailed pre-tournament publicity.

34D. Choice of tie-break methods. Different systems will yield different results, but the systems discussed here are not capricious or random. Each seeks to discover the "first among equals," the player who has a somewhat better claim to a prize than those who earned the same score based on the strength of his or her opposition. Which system to choose depends on the nature of the tournament, its traditions, and the qualities required for the specific situations and conditions at hand.

34E. Calculating Swiss tie breaks. This section deals with various systems that have been used successfully at all levels of play. For team events, see 34G.

Unless a different method has been posted or announced before the start of the first round, players will expect the following sequence of tie-break systems to be employed as the first three tie breakers. Any variation to be used within the various systems should be posted also. These systems (and some additional ones) are explained in detail following the list.

1. Modified Median
2. Solkoff
3. Cumulative
4. Cumulative of Opposition

34E1. Modified Median. The Median system, also known as the

Harkness system for inventor Kenneth Harkness, evaluates the strength of a player's opposition by summing the final scores of his or her opponents and then discarding the highest and lowest of these scores.

The original system is used for players who tie with even scores, but is modified for other scores to disregard only the least significant opponents' scores. The lowest-scoring opponent is discarded for tied players with plus scores and the highest scoring for tied players with minus scores.

For tournaments of nine or more rounds, the top two and bottom two scores are discarded for even score ties, the bottom two scores for plus score ties, and the top two scores for minus score ties.

These scores are adjusted for unplayed games, which count a half point each, regardless of whether they were byes, forfeits, or simply rounds not played after an opponent withdrew. So an opponent who won the first two games, lost the third, withdrew and did not play rounds four or five would have an adjusted score of 3 points.

If the player involved in the tie has any unplayed games, they are credited as follows:

Wins by forfeit count as zero, as do losses by forfeit without giving proper notice to the director.

Half-point byes or forfeit losses with proper notice count as the score of the tied players or a 50 percent score, whichever is less. For example, in a 5-round Swiss, if a player with a half-point bye scores 2 points, the bye counts as 2 tie-break points; if a player scores 4 points, the bye counts as 2½ tie-break points.

If a player who scored in actual play ties with one whose entire point total is due to unplayed games, tie-break points should not be used; the player who scored in actual play wins automatically.

34E2. Solkoff. The Solkoff system is just like the Median except that no opponents' scores are discarded.

34E3. Cumulative. To determine cumulative tie-break score, simply add up the cumulative (running) score for each round. For example, if a player's results were win, loss, win, draw, loss, the wall chart would show a cumulative score round by round as 1, 1, 2, 2½, 2½. The cumulative tie-break total is 9. If another player scored 2½ with a sequence 1, 2, 2½, 2½, 2½, the tie-break points scored would be 10½. The latter player's tie breaks are higher because he or she scored earlier and presumably had tougher opposition for the remainder of the event. One point is subtracted from the sum for each unplayed win or one-point bye.

This system is ideal for large events, since it is very fast and easy to use. It also avoids the problem, common in Median and Solkoff, of having to wait for a lengthy last-round game between two non-contenders to end for top prizes to be decided. Another advantage is that last-round scores need not be included in calculating cumulative tie-break points, since they have no effect on breaking the tie.

34E4. Cumulative scores of opposition. The cumulative tie-break points of each opponent are calculated as in 34E3, and these are added together.

Additional systems:

34E5. Median (not modified). See 34E1.

34E6. Kashdan. This system rewards aggressive play by scoring 4 tie-break points for a win, 2 for a draw, 1 for a loss, and 0 for an unplayed game. Note that if players with no unplayed games tie, the one with fewer draws will come out ahead.

34E7. Result between tied players. Self-explanatory if two tie, but useful only when they were paired and did not draw. If more than two tie, all results among tied players should be considered, with rank according to plus or minus, not percentage (3–1 beats 1–0).

34E8. Most blacks. Also self-explanatory.

34E9. Opposition's performance. This method averages the performance ratings of the players' opposition. Performance ratings are calculated by crediting the player with the opponent's rating plus 400 points for a victory, the opponent's rating minus 400 points for a loss, and the opponent's rating for a draw. Results of each opponent against the tied player should not be included, since this would give the higher-rated tied player an unfair advantage. After the performance rating for each other tied players' opponents has been calculated, they are averaged. Both this system and 34E10 may be difficult to use when unrated players are in the tournament.

34E10. Average opposition. This system averages the ratings of players' opponents, the better tie-break score going to the person who played the highest-rated average field. It sounds fair but has drawbacks. A tied player rated slightly above another will often have a very slightly higher-rated field and win the tie break by a statistically insignificant margin.

34E11. Sonneborn-Berger. See 34F. The disadvantage of using this system in a Swiss is that losses are disregarded, and a player losing to a strong opponent deserves more credit than one losing to a weak opponent. In a round robin, this problem does not exist, since everyone plays the same field.

34E12. Speed play-off game. The speed play-off, an exciting way to wind up a tournament, has been used as the first tie break to determine the title at several major events.

34F. Round robin tie breaks. The most common method is the Sonneborn-Berger system, also known as the partial-score method. For each player in the tie, add the final scores of all the opponents the player defeated and half the final scores of all the opponents with whom the player drew. Nothing is added for the games the player lost, or for unplayed games. If the tie still remains, the results of the games between the players involved in the tie are used.

34G. Team tie breaks.

34G1. Game (or match) points. Since most team events in the United States are scored on match points, the easiest tie break is simply the total game points earned by the teams involved. However, it is of questionable value because the teams that face the weakest opposition are more likely to win their matches by large margins. If game scoring is primary, the number of matches won is a simple and fair tie break.

34G2. U.S. Amateur Team System. For each round, the final score of the opposing team is multiplied by the number of points scored against that team. For example, if Team A scored 2½–1½ against Team B, which finished the tournament with 3 match points, Team A's tie break for that round is 2½ × 3 = 7½. This system awards credit for an extra margin of victory without the drawbacks of using straight game points, and is preferable.

34G3. Other systems. Most of the individual tie-break systems described in 34E are also suitable for team play, but they have the drawback of making the margin of victory meaningless in match-point scoring. Many players find a team event more exciting when every game can affect the team standings, even after a match has been won or lost.

35. RULES FOR DISABLED PLAYERS

35A. Purpose. The purpose of these rules for players with temporary or permanent disabilities is to encourage them to play chess. Bearing in mind that there are many kinds of disabled individuals who meet a wide variety of challenges, the tournament director enjoys considerable discretionary authority to institute special rules.

35B. Equality of treatment. Players with temporary or permanent handicaps that prevent them from fulfilling certain conditions of the Official Rules of Chess shall have special consideration in meeting those rules. Their opponents shall be offered the same consideration. The tournament director is responsible for seeing that both opponents know about and understand any special rules he authorizes. No player may refuse to play a handicapped opponent.

35C. Eligibility for USCF events. To be eligible to compete, a player must be able to communicate in some unambiguous manner his or her selection of moves, in a way that does not require prompting of any kind from any person. An interpreter may be employed.

35D. Analogous situations. When there are doubts concerning provisions to make in the rules for disabled players, the tournament director should consult the following rules for visually impaired players, closely adapted from FIDE's rules for the visually impaired, and apply them analogously. These rules apply when one or both players are impaired.

35E. Access. USCF organizers should make every effort to secure sites for their tournaments that are accessible to disabled players and provided with accessible facilities for their comfort.

35F. Rules for visually impaired (to be applied analogously in the case of other disabilities):

35F1. Special chessboard. A blind player is entitled to use a chessboard with securing apertures even if a sighted opponent prefers to use a normal board simultaneously. In a game between two unsighted players, each is entitled to use his or her own board.

35F2. Announcement of moves. The moves shall be announced clearly, repeated by the opponent, and executed on his or her board.

35F3. Touch-move rule. On the unsighted player's board, a piece shall be deemed "touched" when it has been taken out of the securing aperture. See also Rule 10, The Touched Piece.

35F4. Determination of a move. A move shall be deemed determined (see Rule 9, Determination and Completion of the Move) when all the following have occurred:

a. A piece is placed into a securing aperture.

b. In the case of a capture, the captured piece has been removed from the board of the player who is on move.

c. The move has been announced.

Only after these events shall the opponent's clock be started. The move is completed (see Rule 9, Determination and Completion of the Move) when the clock is punched.

35F5. Special clock. A chess clock with a flag made especially for the visually impaired shall be admissible.

35F6. Scorekeeping options. An unsighted player may keep the score of the game in Braille or on a tape recorder. See also 35F10, Optional assistance.

35F7. Correction of erroneously stated move. A slip of the tongue in announcing a move must be corrected immediately and before starting the clock of the opponent.

35F8. Conflict between two positions. If different positions arise on the two boards during a game, such differences must be corrected with the assistance of the tournament director and with consultation of both players' game scores. In resolving such differences, the player who has recorded the correct move but has made an incorrect one on his or her board may be penalized by the addition of two minutes to the opponent's remaining time.

35F9. Conflict between positions and game scores. If discrepancies such as those described in 35F8 occur, and the two game scores are also found to differ, the game shall be reconstructed up to the last point of agreement, and the tournament director shall adjust the clocks accordingly.

35F10. Optional assistance. A blind player shall have the right to make use of an assistant, who shall have any or all of the following duties:

a. to make the moves of the blind player on the board of the opponent;

b. to announce the moves of the sighted player;

c. to keep score for the blind player and to start the opponent's clock;

d. to inform the blind player, on request, of the number of moves made and the time consumed by either or both players;

e. to claim a win on time for the blind player;

f. to carry out the necessary formalities in cases when the game is to be adjourned.

If the blind player uses such assistance, the sighted player is entitled to parallel assistance should he or she so desire.

35F11. Assistance for sighted player. If the blind player uses a special chessboard and does not require any assistance, the sighted player may make use of an assistant, who shall announce the sighted player's moves and make the blind player's moves on the sighted player's board. Note that if acceptable to both players, they may both use the same assistant.

35F12. Certification of visual impairment. The USCF accepts a state's certification of a person's legal blindness as sufficient evidence of eligibility for tournaments for the visually impaired and for special considerations under these rules except if that person holds a valid driver's license.

36. RULES AND REGULATIONS
FOR COMPUTER PARTICIPANTS

36A. Membership. Computer programs may be registered by the originator or the legal owner of the program as members of the USCF. The dues for computers are the same as for regular members. The rights of computer members are: the right to play in USCF-rated tournaments, subject to possible restrictions; the right to acquire an official USCF rating; and a subscription to *Chess Life* magazine. Specific identification and registration procedures shall be determined administratively.

36B. Purchase of membership. Computer program owners may purchase memberships only directly from the USCF office. Owners are required to sign a statement agreeing to specific rules. The memberships are available only for experimental programs, and owners are required to sign a noncommercial-use agreement.

36C. Tournament participation. Tournament announcements in *Chess Life* may specify that computers are ineligible by including the symbol "NC." If this symbol does not appear, computers may enter, provided such entries are arranged in advance with the director's consent.

36D. Player objections. The director shall announce to the participants the presence of one or more computer entrants in a tournament. Within a reasonable time after this announcement, a player has the right to object to being paired with a computer by signing the "no computers" list. Such players shall be paired as if they had already played each computer in the tournament.

36E. Computer vs. computer. Computers shall not be paired against each other.

36F. Prize eligibility. Computers may win only prizes specifically designated for them. Other prizes shall be distributed as though computers were not entered.

36G. Commercial computers. Commercially available computers may acquire ratings only through USCF's Computer Rating Agency. Interested manufacturers should write for details.

36H. Consultation. A player who consults a computer for advice about his or her game shall be subject to the same penalties that would be imposed for asking advice from another person. See 20D.

36I. Rules for play involving computers. Following are rules for USCF-rated tournaments in which one player is a computer. In matters not governed by these rules, play is governed by applicable human rules, as interpreted by the director. In the following, the term "computer" refers to a chess program running on a computer. The term "opponent" refers to the computer's opponent. The term "operator" refers to the person running the computer.

36I1. Parameter settings. Before play begins, the operator shall do all initial setting up of the computer. At that time, the operator may freely specify any opening parameters, such as rate of play, suggested openings, value of a draw, etc. After play begins, the role of the operator is passive. During the game, the operator is not allowed to alter any parameter settings that might affect the course of the game.

36I2. Communication of moves. During play, the operator is to communicate the opponent's moves to the computer.

36I3. Execution of moves. The operator is to execute the computer's specified move on the chessboard. "Touch" rules do not apply to the operator, but excessive handling of pieces may violate other rules, such as those against distracting the opponent. A piece shall be deemed touched by the computer when a move involving that piece has been communicated by the program to its output device except that displays of moves it is considering shall not be considered communication of a move. A move for the computer shall be deemed completed when it has been executed on the board by the operator, in accordance with the normal rules.

36I4. The clock. After the computer's move is executed, the operator is to start the opponent's clock.

36I5. Reconciliation of positions. If different positions should arise on the playing chessboard and the computer's representation of same, such difference shall be corrected with the assistance of the tournament director. The director may choose either to accept the playing chessboard as official or retrace the moves to the point of departure. If the director chooses to back up the game, then clocks shall be adjusted accordingly. The director shall penalize the computer if the score indicates that the computer or its operator has caused the discrepancy of position.

36I6. Resetting the computer. If the computer is unable to accept a legal move because of discrepancies, communication trouble, or computer trouble, then the operator may set up the current board position and status, along with clock times. Other parameters set must be the same as those in effect at the start of the game. The clocks are not stopped during the resetting of the computer nor for any other "down time" (time when the computer is unable to function despite the efforts of its operator).

36I7. Clock times. There shall be a clock at the chessboard whether or not there is an internal clock in the computer. The operator and the opponent shall use the external clock, which shall be the official timer for the game.

The operator may communicate the clock times to the computer only if the computer initiates the request.

36I8. Memory-unit exchange. The operator may change or insert memory units when the computer requests this and identifies the unit to be inserted, by description or by generating a coded signal or message with a single, predetermined meaning. Diskettes, disk cartridges, tapes, ROM cartridges ("program modules" in commercial machines), and the like are all considered equivalent forms of memory units.

36I9. Draw offers and resignation. The operator may offer a draw, accept a draw, or resign on behalf of the computer, either with or without consulting the computer or humans of any playing strength about the decision.

36I10. Time forfeits. The operator may claim the game if the opponent has exceeded the time limit.

36I11. Adjournments. The operator shall carry out the necessary adjournment formalities.

36I12. Score. The operator and/or the computer must keep a score of the game.

36I13. FIDE warning. An event with a non-FIDE registered computer cannot be FIDE-rated even for humans who are not paired against the computer.

(See "8." under "Computers in FIDE-rated Tournaments" in Chapter 22).

3

CHESS NOTATION

37. INTRODUCTION

Since 1981, the World Chess Federation (FIDE) has recognized only *algebraic notation* for its highest-level tournaments and has vigorously encouraged the universal use of this system. USCF officially supports the use of this single, worldwide notation system, but still recognizes other systems, including the older descriptive notation and the newer computer algebraic. These three systems and some variants are described here, along with international correspondence notation.

38. NOTATION SYSTEMS

38A. Algebraic. This has become the most widely used system. For a simple explanation of algebraic notation and some practice using it, turn to Chapter 16, "How to Read and Write Chess."

38A1. Pieces. Pieces except pawns are identified by an uppercase letter, the first letter of their names. King and knight start with "K", so "N" is used for the knight. Pawn moves are indicated by the absence of such an uppercase letter.

The names of the pieces vary from language to language, of course, so the identifying abbreviations vary also. Here is a table of the symbols for the pieces in some major Western languages:

English	K	Q	R	B	N
German	K	D	T	L	S
Spanish	R	D	T	A	C
French	R	D	T	F	C
Dutch	K	D	T	L	P
Russian	KP	Φ	Л	C	K
Icelandic	K	D	H	B	R

38A2. Squares. Squares are identified by a small letter and a number, signifying the algebra-like coordinates on the board (thus, the name of the system).

38A3. Files. The rows of squares going from one player to the other ("up and down") are files and are labeled with letters "a" through "h," starting with the row to white's left.

38A4. Ranks. The rows of squares going from the left to the right edge of the board are ranks and are labeled with numbers 1 through 8, starting at white's side of the board. At the start of the game, therefore, white's major pieces are on the first rank and pawns on the second; black's are on the eighth and seventh ranks, respectively.

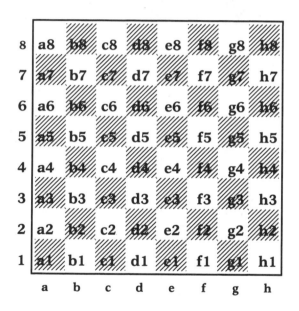

38A5. Moves. Moves are indicated by combining the symbol for the piece and its arrival square, for example, Bg5, Rh6, Nf6. Pawn moves indicate only the arrival square, for example, e4, c5, g3.

38A6. Captures. Captures are indicated by inserting an x or ":" (pronounced "takes") between the piece symbol and the arrival square, for example, Bxe5, N:c6, Rxh6, axb4, Nxf6. Other acceptable forms for indicating capture are Bc6 or ab.

Because there is no abbreviation used for pawns, pawn captures include the original file, the x, and the arrival square, for example, cxd4, exf5, gxh7. In the case of a capture en passant, the arrival square is the one on which the capturing pawn finally rests, and "e.p." is added to the notation, for example, 14 f4 gxf3 e.p.

38A7. Clarification. In cases where these brief notations would be ambiguous, clarification is achieved first by adding the original file of the moving piece or second by adding the rank of the moving piece:

a. If rooks on a1 or f1 can move to d1, such moves are written Rad1 or Rfd1.

b. If rooks on a5 or d1 can move to a1, the notation Raa1 or Rda1 is preferred to R5a1 or R1a1.

c. If knights on f3 or f7 can move to e5, adding the f file would be useless, so the move is N3e5 or N7e5.

d. If knights on f3 or c2 can move to d4, the file is the clarifier: Nfd4 or Ncd4.

e. For a capture, the x goes between the piece identifier and the arrival square: Nfxd4.

38A8. Special symbols.

O-O	castling kingside
O-O-O	castling queenside
x	captures or takes (an earlier version of algebraic notation used a colon instead)
+	check (sometimes "ch")
++	checkmate
=	a pawn promotion, as in f8=Q or d1=N
e.p.	en passant

38B. Figurine algebraic. This system is exactly like regular algebraic, except the abbreviations of the pieces are replaced by internationally recognized symbols: ♚ ♛ ♝ ♞ ♜ This system is obviously advantageous for publications but not practical for players in the tournament hall.

38C. Long algebraic. This system is just like normal algebraic, except that it prevents the possibility of ambiguities by indicating departure as well as arrival square for each move. A sample game might start 1. e2-e4 d7-d5 2. e4xd5 Qd8xd5 3. Nb1-c3 Qd5-a5, etc.

38D. Abbreviated algebraic. This variation of algebraic, designed for quick scorekeeping, omits the capture and check symbols and the rank pawns captured by pawns. For instance, the opening moves of 38C would be written 1. e4 d5 2. ed Qxd5 3. Nc3 Qa5.

38E. Computer notation. This variation of long algebraic, used for play with computers without sensory boards, eliminates the abbreviation of the pieces and capture symbols. Written versions generally use capital letters rather than the small ones otherwise associated with squares.

The sample moves of 38C and 38D would be written 1 E2-E4 D7-D5 2 E4-D5 D8-D5 3 B1-C3 D5-A5. Castling is indicated by the departure and arrival squares of the king: E1-G1, E1-C1, E8-G8, or E8-C8.

38F. English descriptive notation.

38F1. Pieces. Pieces, including pawns, are identified by their initials, as in algebraic. Those that begin the game on the side of the board nearer the king sometimes have a "K" in front of their own initial; those on the queen's side of the board a "Q."

38F2. Files. The files are named for the pieces originally occupying them: QR, QN, QB, Q, K, KB, KN, KR.

38F3. Ranks. The ranks are numbered from each player's point of view, from 1 to 8. White's pieces and pawns begin the game on the first and second ranks from white's point of view, the eighth and seventh ranks respectively from black's point of view.

38F4. Squares. Each square has two names, one from each player's point of view. The white QR, for example, starts the game at white's QR1, which is black's QR8.

38F5. Pawns. When necessary to distinguish it from other pawns, each pawn is named after its file: QRP, QNP, etc.

38F6. Moves. A move to a vacant square is indicated by the piece symbol, a hyphen, and the arrival square. To avoid ambiguity, squares are clarified before pieces. N-KB3 is preferred to KN-B3 unless the QN could also reach the KB3 square, for example, from Q2.

38F7. Captures. A capture is indicated by the abbreviation of the capturing piece, an x, and the abbreviation of the captured piece, for example, BxN, or QRxP (necessary if the KR also attacked a pawn), or NxKBP (necessary if a knight can capture the QBP), etc.

38F8. Further clarification. If the K and Q prefixes do not clarify an ambiguity, or the pieces have made enough moves so that it is no longer obvious which side of the board they started on, clarity is achieved with a slash and rank number after the piece symbol. For example, if either of two knights may capture a bishop, the notation might be N/4xB.

38F9. Check. A check ("ch") may be enough to clarify an ambiguity, for example, B-N5ch even if both bishops could go to N5 squares.

38F10. Other symbols. Castling kingside is O-O, castling queenside O-O-O, and pawn promotion a slash and the new piece (P-B8/Q or PxR/N).

38G. Spanish descriptive. English and Spanish are the two major languages in which descriptive notation is sometimes found. Spanish descriptive notation differs from the English version not only in the piece symbols (see 38A1) but in the order of symbols. For example, the move P-QB4 in English descriptive is written P4AD in Spanish; this would literally translate into P4BQ.

38H. Sample game.

Here, without further comment, is a sample game fragment written in each of the three common notations:

Algebraic		*Computer*		*Descriptive*	
1. e4	e5	E2-E4	E7-E5	P-K4	P-K4
2. Nf3	Nc6	G1-F3	B8-C6	N-KB3	N-QB3
3. Bb5	a6	F1-B5	A7-A6	B-N5	P-QR3
4. Bxc6	dxc6	B5-C6	D7-C6	BxN	QPxB
5. d3	Bb4+	D2-D3	F8-B4	P-Q3	B-N5ch
6. Nc3	Nf6	B1-C3	G8-F6	N-B3	N-B3
7. O-O	Bxc3	E1-G1	B4-C3	O-O	BxN

If you have played through the notation of your choice accurately, you should have reached the following position on your board:

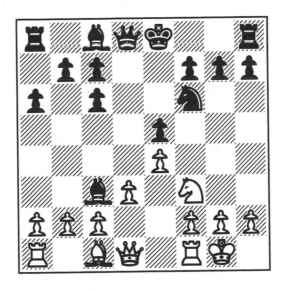

38I. International correspondence notation. To avoid language problems, including different alphabets, international correspondence players use an all-numeric system that is otherwise very similar to computer notation.

38I1. Squares. Each square is designated by a two-digit number, as indicated below. The first digit is a replacement of the a–h files by the numbers 1–8, the second is the conventional rank number.

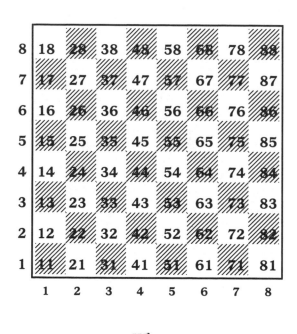

White

38I2. Moves. A move is indicated by a four-digit number that combines the departure and arrival squares without punctuation. For example, 5254 is the same as e4 or P-K4.

38I3. Castling. Castling is noted as a king move: 5171, 5131, 5878, or 5838.

38I4. Pawn promotion. The first two digits indicate the departure square, the third the arrival file, and the fourth the new piece (1=Q, 2=R, 3=B, 4=N). For example, 1714 would be the same as the algebraic a8=N.

38J. Telephone and radio notation. When players or their agents relay moves with their voices, some confusion can arise because b, c, d, e, and g can all sound rather alike. The potential difficulty is solved by using algebraic notation with a variation of the military alphabet: able, baker, charlie, david, easy, fox, george, harry.

4

EQUIPMENT STANDARDS

39. INTRODUCTION

The three elements of chess equipment—pieces, boards, and clocks—are each discussed in detail below. In general, simple, functional designs are preferred for use in tournaments so players, spectators, and directors are not distracted by ornateness, unusual design, or other aesthetic values. The designer and decorator pieces available today serve good purposes other than as suitable equipment for tournament chess.

39A. Choice of equipment. If the organizer of the tournament provides equipment conforming to the following standards, the players should use that equipment. If the organizer does not provide one or more elements of equipment, the players should agree on any that meets the standards or, failing such agreement, play with black's choice if it meets the standards. If black does not provide standard equipment and white does, black does not have the right to delay the start of the game to search for alternative equipment. The director is the final arbiter of whether the equipment in question is standard.

39A1. Black player late. If black is late for the start of a round, the choice of equipment is made by white. Black may not object unless white's choice is for non-standard equipment, in which case black's clock continues to run while substitutions are made. Again, the final decision is up to the director in questionable cases.

39A2. Neither player has standard equipment. If neither player provides standard equipment, the director should rule in favor of the equipment that is the nearest to being standard.

39A3. Non-USCF play. For non-tournament or non-USCF-rated play against opponents not used to popular tournament sets or boards, equipment differing somewhat from these standards is likely to be acceptable.

40. CHESS PIECES

40A. Material. Pieces should be made of plastic, wood, or possibly a material similar in appearance.

40B. Size. The king's height should be 3⅜–4½ inches (8.65–11.54 cm). The diameter of the king's base should be 40–50 percent of the height. The other pieces should be proportionate in height and form. All pieces should be well balanced for stability and comfortable moving.

40C. Form. The conventional Staunton pattern is the standard. The Staunton design was registered in 1849 and first offered for sale to the general public by John Jaques in October of that year. The first 500 sets were hand signed and numbered by Howard Staunton. The design soon became the standard for all serious play. An example of an original Staunton pattern chess set is shown in the accompanying figure. Minor variations in design may be tolerated, especially in sets that are widely used. The king and queen should have clearly different tops, and the bishop's top may have an angled groove. If the bishop's top has a knob of a different color, the set is nonstandard.

40D. Color. Pieces should be the colors of naturally light and dark wood (for example, maple or boxwood and walnut or ebony) or approximations of these colors, such as simply white and black.

40E. Examples. Jaques chess sets are still used for World Championship matches, and are quite expensive. The most commonly used tournament set is the USCF Special, an inexpensive, plastic set with a 3¾-inch king, also sold elsewhere under various names. Also used often are the Player's Choice, a heavily weighted plastic set with a 3½-inch king, an Italian plastic imitation wood set with a 3½-inch king of similar design to the USCF Special, and wooden Staunton sets, very similar in design to the sets mentioned above.

While there is no guarantee of permanent availability, these sets have stood the test of time, and most or all will likely still be available beyond the year 2000. The player wishing assurance that all directors will consider his or her set standard would do well to purchase either one of these sets, a very similar set, or another set that may develop sufficient popularity to be seen on many tournament tables.

41. CHESSBOARDS

41A. Material. The board must be opaque and fabricated from a smooth material that allows the easy movement of pieces. Satisfactory boards have been made from plastic, wood, paper, cardboard, leather, cloth, and marble.

41B. Color. Like the pieces, chessboard colors should offer high

US-665 Closest-Thing-to-Wood Set
Order toll-free 1-800-388-KING (5464)

contrast between the light and dark sections yet remain pleasing to the eye. Good combinations include green or brown with ivory or buff, and walnut or teak with maple or birch. The colors and the finish should allow extended examination without eyestrain.

Squares that do not exactly match the colors of the pieces are popular because they allow ready distinction between empty and occupied squares. For example, the green and buff vinyl roll-up board sold by USCF and others is the most commonly used at tournaments. Shiny vinyl boards, though, should be avoided. Red and black checkerboards are also nonstandard.

41C. Proportions. The pieces should fit comfortably on the board, being neither too crowded nor too isolated on the squares.

US-1416 Ebony Set
Order toll-free 1-800-388-KING (5464)

The king and queen, for example, should be subject to easy placement on a square without touching any edge. Boards for standard sets should have squares of approximately 2–2½ inches (5.08–6.35 cm). One convenient test is that the square formed by the bases of four pawns should be about the same size as any square on their board.

41D. Borders. The width of the border around the squares is a matter of personal taste, so long as it does not affect a player's ability to easily reach the pieces. Some borders include aids to scorekeeping in the form of letters and numbers for algebraic notation and some do not; both designs are acceptable.

US-1425s Player's Special
Order toll-free 1-800-388-KING (5464)

41E. Tables. A table with an inset or otherwise fitted chessboard is very satisfactory. The playing surface should be about 27–30 inches from the ground (normal table height). If the board is not fastened to the table, it should remain stationary. The table should provide ample room for the clock, captured pieces, score sheets, players' elbows or forearms, and water glasses.

42. CHESS CLOCKS

42A. Basic requirements. Chess clocks should be as accurate and silent as possible. They should have a device that clearly signals the end of a time control, such as a "flag" that falls when the minute hand reaches the mark at the figure 12. The flag should be of a size and color so as to be clearly visible to players and directors.

42B. Signaling devices. A clock that calls attention to the fall of the flag with a special noise or light is both legal and highly desirable, providing it causes no disturbance to other players. The prohibition against anyone but the two players calling a flag down does not apply to a clock, which can carry out this function thoroughly and impartially. Likewise, a clock in which the fall of one flag prevents the other flag from falling is both legal and desirable, avoiding the possibility of the both-flags-down draw of 14G or 16T.

42C. Move counters. Clocks with move counters are legal for the above reasons. The counter offers impartial assistance to both players, but its count cannot be used to support or defend against a time-forfeit claim and can sometimes be inaccurate. Players rely on the count at their own risk. Move counters can be useful to a director asked to count moves for the 50-move rule (see 14F4f), and the USCF Allegro Clock may have a move counter to count for the 175-move rule (see 5F and 14K). Players using a counter for these purposes should be aware that if a move is not counted or double counted, and the players cannot easily adjust the clock to reflect this, the clock should be stopped and the director notified.

42D. Digital clocks. Digital clocks are not fully acceptable as tournament equipment in all circumstances, even though most meet the essential demands of accuracy, silence, and a signaling device. (They beep or cease operating instead of having a flag.) Some players have difficulty with the digital readout. Others object to a sound signal (a beep instead of a mechanical click) when one clock stops and the other starts, or have difficulty seeing from a distance which player is on move. Some digital clocks show minutes at times and seconds at other times, which confuses players, and some reset in a confusing way after the first time control, or lose track of hours while counting only minutes during later controls.

Until such objections are overcome, owners and advocates of these devices should not expect to force their use on opponents. If digital clocks are used in competition, the providers should explain all relevant operational facts, such as the signal at the end of the control, a display change from minutes to seconds, and how any clock that resets after each control does so.

42E. Standard clocks. A conventional analog clock is more "standard" than a digital clock and may be used even if black supplies and prefers a digital model.

42F. Allegro Clock. *The following applies once this clock is commercially available.* For games with a final or only sudden death time control, if an Allegro Clock or a similar clock is available it is preferred to any other clock.

The Allegro is a clock with time-delay capability (see 5F). Use of the Allegro promotes higher-quality play and allows the game to be decided entirely by the players, with no need for subjective director rulings on claims of insufficient losing chances.

5

THE WELL-RUN TOURNAMENT

43. INTRODUCTION

It is naturally satisfying to hear compliments from players on a "well-run tournament." It also helps draw more entries next time.

The director who has good knowledge of the rules and pairing procedures, maintains consistent and fair policies, is available to answer questions or settle disputes, and deals tactfully with players is off to a good start. But there are also other matters that contribute to player satisfaction.

Some of these are more important than others, but the less significant items should not be overlooked by the director. Taken together they can make quite a difference. A director should not consider irrelevant any better way of doing something, even if it affects only a few players or saves only a little time each round.

This chapter contains no rules, only advice. Most is intended for directors, but some falls into the domain of the organizer. This is appropriate, since many directors are also organizers and those who are not may influence organizers.

44. STARTING ON TIME

One of the faults that is most noticed and most disliked by players is the failure to start rounds on time. It is at least annoying and an inconvenience to all involved. When a director is chronically late, players will adjust to this by being late, too, and those who would have been late anyway will become later still. Important announcements may not be heard, and it will become more and more difficult to begin subsequent rounds on time.

44A. The first round. Round one is generally the hardest to start on time. Registering late entrants, checking ratings and I.D. numbers, and making out pairing cards are only a few of the frequent distractions.

Most of the following comments are intended for events with a substantial number of entries, in which it is sometimes better to be prompt than precise. For smaller turnouts in which accuracy may be achieved without significant delay, much of this may be irrelevant.

44A. Late fees. If processing late entries is a problem, charge a late fee, or offer a discount for mailed entries (really the same thing), which is adequate to hold down the size of late registration. Late fees are often about 20 percent the size of entry fees, but a difference of $5 or less tends to produce few advance entries.

44A2. Varied schedules. The main reason for alternate schedules in which the first round may be played either Friday night or Saturday morning is to accommodate both players who find Friday rounds inconvenient and those who dislike three games on Saturday. But there is also the side benefit that late registration and round-one pairings are split into two different times, so each is easier to start on time.

If Friday is not available for a weekend Swiss, another possibility is to start one or more sections of a multi-section event about an hour after the others. This works best when separate playing rooms are available, or else there may be a temporary noise problem when the later section starts.

44A3. Attitude. Taking for granted that the first round will start late often produces a leisurely attitude, which can waste more time than some realize. Directors should always be friendly, but shortly before round one is not the time for socializing or spending an unnecessary amount of time answering questions that could be deferred.

44A4. Advance entrants. A list of advance entrants in alphabetical or rating order should be posted so that players will not need to ask if their entries were received.

44A5. Cut-off entries. At some point, it may be necessary to announce that any further entries are not guaranteed a round-one pairing but may have to take a half-point bye instead. If a spare director is available who is not needed to do pairings, have that director continue to accept entries. Meanwhile, start pairing; ask the entry taker for the next name on the list if there is an odd number.

If all directors are needed for pairings, announce that entries are being suspended but will reopen after the round starts, with the late players facing each other. The last player to enter a section with an odd number will have to accept a half-point bye unless an appropriate opponent can be found. Do not award an odd player a full-point bye, but write "wait" on the pairing sheet instead so that player may be paired against a late entrant.

44A6. Looking up ratings and I.D.s. If first round timeliness is a concern, defer checking I.D. numbers until after the round starts. If necessary, even verifying ratings may be deferred; this may slightly affect the pairings, but may be worth it to avoid delay.

44A7. One pairs, the other writes. The director arranges the cards in pairing order while an assistant writes the pairings of those already so arranged. "Pairing order" means the top card of the pile is white on first board, second card black on first board, third card white on second board, etc.

44A8. Ratings on pairing sheet. Even though it takes a little extra time, write each player's rating after his or her name. Players want to know this and do not yet have a wall chart for reference.

44A9. Names on pairing sheet. Speed is of the essence; it usually takes longer to write round-one pairings than to make them. Neatness, first names, or even initials are less important unless the latter two are needed to distinguish players with the same last name.

44A10. Multiple sections. When the first section is paired, post those pairings immediately. Do not wait for all sections to be paired before posting. Even if some pairings are early, remember that it takes time for players to find their names and set up for play. The same applies to large one-section events with multiple-pairing sheets; put the first one up as soon as it is ready.

44A11. Advance entry pairings. When many late entries are anticipated, the advance entries may be paired separately against each other well before late entries close; the late entrants will then be paired against each other. This will slightly change round-one pairings, but is preferable to starting late. Any odd player(s) in the advance-entry pairings should be posted as "wait" rather than bye and then included in the late-entry pairings.

44A12. Player interrupts pairings. Do not allow questions or interruptions to interfere with the pairing procedure. Once all pairings are up, attend to any problems such as an omitted player. This situation may be handled by using a late entrant or houseman or, if not available, giving the player a full-point bye. If the player is anxious to play, another solution may be to find a game in which one player has not yet arrived and substitute the unpaired player. The late player may never arrive, may accept a full-point bye in lieu of a game, or may play a late entrant or houseman.

44A13. Pairings on cards. Never write the pairings on the cards before posting them. Not only will there be more time to do this after the round starts, but some may have to be changed.

44A14. Announcing pairings. Make announcements that pairings are up, but don't announce pairings as a substitute for posting. This may be tempting because speaking is quicker than writing, but player comprehension is often poor and not all are present.

44A15. Announcements in tournament room. Don't delay a late round still further with lengthy announcements. A welcome and a few short announcements of a rules or procedural nature are usually sufficient. Extensive rules discussions are especially inappropriate as rules are best in writing, avoiding confusion and misunderstanding.

44A16. Secluded director. Especially at large tournaments, it is desirable for directors to have a separate room for their work and supplies. This provides the possibility of seclusion when necessary, such as when pairing. An additional director should be available to answer questions and protect the pairing team from interruptions.

44B. Later rounds. Many of the comments of 44A regarding round one also pertain to later rounds. Some, such as registering late entries and looking up ratings, are no longer a problem.

44B1. One pairs, the other writes. This method (44A7) is even more valuable for later rounds, since pairings are more complex and pairing directors have less time to write.

44B2. Necessary interruptions. A player claiming an omission or pairing error should be taken much more seriously than in round one. The chances of a significant error are greater and of correcting it once the round begins less, and the director is more likely to have time to correct it. Nevertheless, if many players are waiting for pairings for a section and a complaint comes from another, it is usually advisable to finish and post the current section first.

44B3. Pairings on cards. As in round one, never write pairings on cards before they are posted.

44B4. Secluded director. Some directors may not need seclusion, but pairings in later rounds are more complex and concentration more necessary. The secluded pairing team is more efficient, provided an assistant is available to answer players' questions and relay important messages to the team.

45. OTHER PROCEDURES

45A. Player numbers on pairing sheets. Beginning with round two, player numbers usually replace ratings on the pairing sheets. This enables players to check opponents on the wall charts for ratings, results, and colors, and makes it easier for the staff to post pairings and results.

The director should beware the possibility, especially in novice or scholastic events, of players going to play at a player number rather than a board number, which often leads to players facing the wrong opponents. This may be avoided by having no numbers in common—for instance, in a scholastic tournament with 250 players, the players may be numbered 1–250, the boards 301–425.

45B. Player reporting of results. The most efficient method is having the player post results directly onto the pairing sheets. If game scores are wanted for publication, duplicate score sheets may be used, but players should still be required to post results on the pairing sheets. Advantages include:

1. Results appear on pairing sheets in board order for easy marking on the pairing cards, which are in that order.

2. If a player neglects to post the result on the pairing sheet or it is posted incorrectly, the players or others may notice the error and correct it.

3. Score sheets have results incorrectly or unclearly marked more often than pairing sheets. Players have better comprehension of how to report on pairing sheets, since they see results already posted when about to post their own.

4. Score sheets or result cards are sometimes submitted by both players showing different results. Pairing sheets allow only one result, and a posting error by one player is likely to be corrected by the other.

45C. Pairing sheets, wall charts, and pairing cards. Some directors transcribe the results from the pairing sheets to the pairing cards, then from the pairing cards to the wall charts. Others first use the pairing sheets to post results on the wall charts, then use the pairing sheets to mark them on the cards. The latter method is more efficient for these reasons:

1. Players find tournaments more enjoyable if wall chart totals are kept up-to-date. Requiring two steps rather than one before a result is marked on the wall chart inevitably delays such updating.

2. Relatively little is gained by early marking of results on pairing cards. Although not difficult, it is more efficient to wait until only a few games are still in progress, then fill in all the results going straight down the pairing sheets with no need to search for unmarked cards. Of course, the director must never wait so long to mark the cards as to delay the next round.

3. There is less chance of pairing cards being dropped or misplaced.

4. It is easy to process withdrawals by writing "out" or "WD" on the pairing sheet, then pulling the card when marking the result on it. This avoids a search through cards marked earlier and helps prevent mistakenly pairing such a player.

5. Some claim that the sheets-to-cards-to-charts method has the advantage that a result incorrectly marked on the pairing cards will also appear on the wall charts, where the error can be pointed out by the players. This does sometimes occur, but such mistakes are often not noticed by the players or not pointed out for several rounds, and without help from the players they will never be noticed by directors.

If mistakes on the cards do not appear on the wall charts, the director or result poster may notice the error when posting the pairing or the result on the wall charts. Another option available to catch errors is to occasionally check every player's score on the card against that score on the wall chart. Using the sheets-to-cards-to-charts method, this will detect wall-chart errors but not the more significant pairing-card errors.

45D. Players writing on wall charts. Players should not write on the wall charts—they should mark results only on the pairing sheets. The directing staff should promptly update the totals on the wall charts. Errors on the charts should be brought to the immediate attention of the staff, not corrected on the charts by the player.

46. TOURNAMENT SETUP

46A. Table setup. It is important to know how many tables can be set up in a room comfortably for a tournament. Assuming the room is rectangular and without significant impediments, this can be calculated from the dimensions. Beware estimates by hotel or meeting hall representatives; they are used to social functions that accommodate more people than chess tournaments.

46A1. Number of rows. Divide the available space by the number of rows of tables to be evaluated. The relevant available space is not the length of each row but the distance from wall to chair to table to chair to chair to table, etc., to the other wall.

If the answer shows an average of at least 10 feet per row, the setup is luxurious. With 9 feet per row it is comfortable. With 8 feet per row it is borderline, though it might be acceptable in a small room (16 feet, 2 rows is better than 64 feet, 8 rows). Eight feet per row is also adequate for many scholastics, because of the smaller size of the players. With 7 feet per row, the setup is totally unacceptable for adults and possibly tolerable only for elementary school students.

For example, if 72 feet are available for an open tournament, 7 rows of tables would be luxurious ($72 \div 7$ is above 10), 8 rows comfortable ($72 \div 8 = 9$), 9 rows borderline ($72 \div 9 = 8$), and 10 rows unacceptable ($72 \div 10 = 7.2$).

Even when space is sufficient and the organizer provides a floor plan drawn to scale, the setup crew may create an uncomfortable setup. The director who requests 8 rows of tables in a 72-foot room will often find something like the rear 5 feet not used and the front 7 feet used for water stations. This leaves $60 \div 8$ or 7½ feet per row, unacceptable when it could be comfortable.

In such a situation the director or organizer should request that the water stations be moved to the hall and the whole room used.

46A2. Number of tables in row. This is a less sensitive subject than the number of rows, since too many tables per row results only in narrow aisles, and players entering and leaving the room are not nearly as annoyed at being bumped as those considering their moves.

Assuming there is at least one 4-foot-wide aisle in the room, if 20 percent of each row is available for aisle space, this is luxurious, 15 percent comfortable, and 10 percent about the minimum acceptable.

So if 60 feet are available to set up 6-foot-long tables, placing 8 tables in each row ($8 \times 6 = 48$) would leave 12 feet left over ($60 - 48 = 12$). This is luxurious, allowing a choice between two 6-foot aisles (4 tables starting at the wall/ aisle/ 4 more tables/ aisle/ 4 more tables) and three 4-foot aisles (aisle/ 4 tables/ aisle/ 4 tables/ aisle).

Placing 9 tables in each row ($9 \times 6 = 54$ feet) would be barely acceptable as total aisle space would be only 6 feet, a bit narrow for two aisles. Probably 5 tables/ aisle/ 4 tables is the best setup, with the 6-foot aisle in the center, enough for players to enter and leave the room without getting in one another's way.

Except for aisles, all tables should touch each other. A five-foot aisle is valuable but five one-foot spaces between tables are useless.

46A3. Which way to face tables. For rooms that are much longer than they are wide, the chess capacity of each is likely to be different depending on whether many short rows of tables or a few long rows are selected. Give some bonus credit for the short rows, as it is desirable that players be able to reach the aisles as quickly as possible.

46A4. Types of tables. Tables measuring 6 feet by 30 inches are ideal for chess, seating four players, two on each side. But many facilities have other sizes which are of varied value.

Tables sized 8 feet by 30 inches give the director the choice between four to a table (comfortable but space consuming) or six to a table (which most players tolerate but some dislike).

Tables sized 6 feet by 18 inches or 8 feet by 18 inches are too narrow for chess but can be used if two are pushed together to make one 36-inch-wide table. This is acceptable though far from ideal.

Round or half-round tables are fairly useless, except in a headquarters or book-sales room, or possibly a skittles room (see 46C2) if space is abundant.

46B. Lighting. It is important to have good lighting in the tournament room; this sometimes justifies a table setup different from that in 46A2 and 46A3. For instance, 46A3 states that 4 tables/aisle/4 tables/aisle/4 tables is a better setup than aisle/8 tables/aisle. But if the lighting is dimmest around the perimeter of the room, aisle/8 tables/aisle may be preferable.

Be skeptical of hotels claiming that lighting is on rheostat and can be turned up as much as desired, since sometimes even the maximum setting is insufficient. Fluorescent lighting is usually better. Best, though, is a room designed to offer a choice between incandescent lighting for social events or fluorescent for meetings, since a chess tournament can use both types simultaneously.

Occasionally even fluorescent lighting is insufficient because the fixtures are too recessed or too few, producing adequate light only directly below but leaving significant dark spots.

A hotel will sometimes offer to install special lighting for the tournament if the permanent lighting is inadequate. If the latter is close to sufficient this may work well, but if the room is very dark without additional lighting it is risky to assume it will be adequate without actually seeing the extra lighting installed.

Supplementary lighting is most effective when it consists either of floodlights shining straight down from a considerable height or tall mercury-vapor or halogen lamps bouncing light off the ceiling. Floodlights pointed at an angle cause glare; table lamps take up much space, since each helps only in a tiny area; lamps of all types take up floor space; electric cords must be taped down or in an area where no one will walk; and extra lighting can cause heat.

46C. Noise. Surveys have indicated that though players like good lighting, they have an even stronger preference for quiet in the tournament room.

46C1. Selection of tournament room. When considering whether a tournament room is suitable, beware of rooms in which the tournament room is on one side of a movable partition and another group on the other side. Most movable partitions are not even sufficient to keep out skittles-room noise (see 46C2). No partition will be adequate if a band is on the other side.

46C2. Skittles room. If at all possible, a separate "skittles room" should be provided for game postmortems, speed chess, discussions, etc. This should be as near to the tournament room(s) as possible without skittles noise being heard by those playing tournament games.

A skittles room set up for at least 15 percent of the total attendance is usually good. One set up for 10 percent is likely to be adequate for all but an occasional peak skittles period. If no skittles room is available, even a table or two in a hall may be helpful. Note that the skittles room can be set up somewhat less comfortably than the tournament room, if need be.

Beware using part of a room for skittles if a movable partition separates it from the tournament room. Some partitions are soundproof, but most are not.

Players should be urged to use only the skittles room for postmortem analysis, speed chess, and other noisy activity. A director who notices such activity in the tournament room should politely request that the players leave. Even though one pair of players may cause insignificant noise, more are likely to join in, and the noise will build. Once many players anticipate being asked to leave and start going to the skittles room on their own, the director's job will be easier.

46C3. Headquarters and wall charts. If possible, avoid setting up the director's table(s) and wall charts in or too close to the tournament room, since they are sources of noise. A nearby room, foyer, or hall is usually better. Even a room which is a considerable distance away from the tournament room may be preferable, if there is nothing else.

46C4. Board numbering. The top boards that will have the most important games should be placed as far from the tournament-room entrance as possible to minimize noise. The lowest boards will be the ones closest to the entrance; these will be used only if necessary. As the tournament progresses, if players withdraw, the least desirable boards should not be used. Of course, if the lighting is not uniform, this should also be considered when numbering boards.

46C5. Doors. Tournament entrances sometimes cause a dilemma. If the doors are kept closed, they may slam with an annoying noise every time a player enters or exits. If they are propped open, noise from the hall may be audible. Doors that close silently are the best solution, but a director who does not have and cannot arrange for these is usually best off propping one door open and trying to keep hall noise down. A sign saying "Silence. You are entering the tournament room" may help.

46C6. Announcements. Except for the beginning of the round, announcements such as "Quiet, please," are not recommended; they disturb some players more than the noise they are intended to avoid. A barely audible "shhhh" is more appropriate, but attempts to quiet groups of players often provide only temporary help. A more lasting solution is to privately ask the noisiest individuals to be quiet or, if their games have ended, to go to the skittles room.

46C7. Top boards. Most major tournaments provide a roped-off area or a stage for the top boards to protect these players from spectators. Without such protection, players may be annoyed by inconsiderate onlookers who hover too closely. When the top boards are isolated in this manner, demonstration boards are often used for spectators. Operators for these "demo boards" and space for both them and seated spectators must be provided. The seated spectators are usually a moderate noise source, so other boards should not play too close to them.

Such demo boards may be necessary in very large and/or important tournaments, but in those somewhat smaller, or in which space or operators are not available, the "barricade system" is an alternative. This involves surrounding the top boards on three sides with rows of 18-inch-wide rectangular tables, one long row and two short rows, with a rear wall serving as the fourth side. The long row is parallel to the rear wall and sufficient space for standing spectators should be provided along it on the outside.

The top board tables should be set up perpendicular to the long row of 18-inch tables and the wall, and each table should touch the long row of 18-inch tables on one side. This allows spectators to stand near the game close enough for good viewing, but not too close.

Some spectators prefer the barricade system, since they can see the game "live" rather than as a re-creation, but others prefer demo boards for the seating comfort or because their eyesight is not good enough to watch live games from the barricade distance.

6

TOURNAMENT DIRECTORS' CHECKLISTS

The following checklists are guides. They may be expanded or contracted, but they are a good starting point for everyone.

PACKING LIST

The following items should be neatly and conveniently arranged in your tournament briefcase or suitcase:

A. General chess stationery

___blank pairing cards
___blank wall charts
___blank pairing sheets
___sufficient score sheets
___sealed move envelopes
___membership forms
   ___USCF

___state association

___local club

___tournament registration forms

___"USCF Rating System" handout

B. Other chess supplies and equipment

___latest edition *Official Rules of Chess*

___TD cap, vest, arm band, or other identifying clothing

___box for receiving score sheets for publication

___time-control signs

___round time signs

___sign and/or handouts about rules and procedures

___no-smoking signs

___signs reminding players to report results

___chess clock and set for emergencies

___board numbers

___rating lists

   ___annuals as far back as possible

   ___the latest cumulative supplement

   ___any supplement(s) since the cumulative

___spare *Chess Life* copies for new players

___sets or boards if supplied

C. General stationery supplies

___loose-leaf notebook or pad for late entries

___electric clock for official tournament time

___unlined paper and poster board for signs

___sticky note-posting pads

__memo pad

__receipt book

__thumbtacks

__masking tape

__duct tape

__rubber bands

__ballpoint pens in different colors

__marking pens for wall charts, possibly in colors

__heavy felt-tip markers for signs

__pens or pencils to lend players

__liquid paper or adhesive labels matching the color of charts

__pencil sharpener

__checkbook

__calculator

__Band-Aids

__aspirin

__antacid

D. Special for this tournament

__advance publicity

   __*Chess Life* issue(s)

   __*School Mates* issue(s)

   __fliers or mail-outs

__list of advance entries

__completed pairing cards of advance entries

__currency/change for registration

__trophies or plaques

__special prizes

___fliers for coming events

___computers/printers/connectors/supplies

PLANNING AND ACTION CHECKLIST

A. Before registration

___meet with organizers and site/hotel staff

    ___learn site facilities

    ___copy machine and access to it

    ___keys to playing room, TD office

    ___phone for incoming calls

    ___is hotel/site transferring calls?

    ___trash cans

    ___water supplies

    ___check (improve) table layout

    ___rope off top boards?

    ___doors slam? to be open or closed?

    ___learn light switches

    ___check for burned-out bulbs

    ___test microphone system

    ___determine key locations (TD table, wall chart and pairing posting, score-sheet receiving, and so forth)

    ___determine any restrictions on posting

    ___prepare for computers and wheelchairs

    ___tape down cords/wires/door bolts with duct tape

___acquire and review advance entries

    ___names

    ___USCF I.D. numbers

    ___players not shown as current USCF members in supplements

    ___ratings

___half-point byes

___planned round forfeits

___meet with TD Staff (see separate list)

___post announcements and signs

___organize for registration

B. During registration

___make sure cash control is working

___review the work of all assistants

___make final decision about acceleration of pairings

C. After first round begins

___put late entry fees in bank or safe-deposit box

___put out box for score sheets or results slips

___lock doors not needed for access

___distribute keys as needed

___complete and post wall charts ASAP

___sign-up sheets (hotel guests, eligibility for special prizes, etc.)

___arrange for management of equipment

___will tablecloths be changed?

___number pairing cards

___check out registration exceptions

    ___memberships

    ___I.D. numbers

    ___ratings

    ___names

    ___addresses

    ___financial questions

D. After last round begins

__assist in preparation of financial report
__prepare prize-list work sheet, filling in as possible

E. After tournament is over

__complete prize-list work sheet
__collect everything posted on walls
__get money for ratings (including cross table)
__get money for expenses and fee
__mail report form and wall-chart copies ASAP
__remind organizer to submit memberships instantly
__remind organizer to report results to media instantly

ANNOUNCEMENT CHECKLIST

__organizer's welcome and other remarks
__introduce TD staff
__thanks to others who deserve it
__introduce titled players/other VIPs
__result-reporting system
__score-sheet submission (including brilliancy notes)
__time controls
__special rules and variations
__smoking rules
__silence in tournament hall
__skittles room
__book and equipment sales

NOTE: Keep it short, sweet, and essential. Save announcements of coming events until before a later round; the players are eager to start the first round.

STAFF MEETING CHECKLIST

__determine experience of everyone unknown
__delegate setup tasks
   __board numbering
   __sets and boards if supplied
   __table rearranging
   __score-sheet/handout distribution
__review locations, general site and tournament
__review supplies
__assign tasks (experience/competence, variety, balance)
   __registration
   __tournament
__assign schedules, including break times
__registration plan
   __money
   __USCF credentials
   __state membership
   __ratings
__hotel rooms or other phone numbers
__review special tournament rules
   __adjournments
   __computers
   __disabled
   __appeals

___pairings

___byes

___other

___TD rules and procedures

    ___visibility

    ___courtesy

    ___covering for meal and other breaks

    ___which pens for wall charts

    ___no playing chess or other games

    ___slow, careful posting on cards

    ___information on pairing sheets

    ___withdrawal procedures

    ___uniform procedures

    ___point-group stacks (highest group on left, lowest pairing number on top)

___round times

___time controls

___time-forfeit procedures

___any questions on rules or other topics?

7

PLAYERS' RIGHTS AND RESPONSIBILITIES

All players have the right to expect:

1. That the tournament director is reliable and has a knowledge of the laws of chess, as per USCF standards.

2. That all prizes shall be awarded as advertised.

3. That the director has this USCF rule book on the premises and available for consultation during the tournament.

4. That any special rules pertinent to that particular tournament shall be announced and/or posted; e.g., time-forfeit procedure, color allocation, tie-break system, smoking policy, etc.

5. That the pairing system used is fair and impartial and that it will be administered fairly.

6. That the starting time of the rounds will be posted and that the rounds will start reasonably on time.

7. That conditions such as lighting, space requirements, noise, etc., be at an acceptable level conducive to good competition.

8. That tournament directors be available at all times in the event of questions or problems.

9. That the round results will be posted in a timely fashion.

10. That upon request, a tournament director will initiate the appeals process.

All players are responsible:

1. To conduct themselves in an orderly fashion.

2. To compete in a spirit of good sportsmanship.

3. To be present at the starting time for each round, if possible.

4. To refrain from analysis of games or audible talking in the tournament room while others are playing.

5. To notify the director well in advance of plans to withdraw from the tournament or miss a round.

6. To promptly report game results in the manner required by the director.

7.   To read pertinent information posted for the players, usually near the wall charts, including the list of times when the rounds are scheduled to start.

8.   To obey the laws of chess.

9.   To conform to the USCF code of ethics. See Chapter 8.

8

USCF CODE OF ETHICS

PURPOSE AND SCOPE

1. The purpose of this code of ethics is to set forth standards to which the conduct of players, tournament directors, sponsors, and other individuals and entities participating in the affairs of the United States Chess Federation, including tournaments and other events sponsored by or sanctioned by the USCF, should conform; to specify sanctions for conduct that does not conform to such standards, and to specify the procedures by which alleged violations are to be investigated, and, if necessary, the appropriate sanctions imposed.

2. The standards, sanctions, and procedures set forth in this code of ethics are not equivalent to criminal laws and procedures. Rather, they concern the rights and privileges of USCF membership, including, but not limited to, the privilege of

participating in tournaments, events, or other activities as a member of the USCF.

3. The standards, sanctions, and procedures set forth in this code of ethics shall apply only to: (A) actions and behavior by members of the USCF that occur in connection with tournaments or other events sponsored by or sanctioned by the USCF; and (B) individuals or entities acting in an official capacity as officers or representatives of the USCF. Each member of the USCF and each participant in a USCF event shall be bound by this code of ethics.

THE USCF ETI IICS COMMITTEE

4. The USCF Ethics Committee is appointed by the Policy Board acting under its powers as set forth in the bylaws of the USCF. The committee exists to consider cases involving unethical conduct at and in connection with events sanctioned by the USCF, and unethical conduct involving the national organization and its activities. It is not within the scope of the committee's charge, nor is it within the scope of this code, to adjudicate local disputes or matters not directly involving the national organization and the events it sponsors or sanctions.

STANDARDS OF CONDUCT

5. The actions and behavior of players, tournament directors, sponsors, and other individuals and entities participating in tournaments or other events sponsored by or sanctioned by the USCF shall be in accordance with the spirit of fair play

and good sportsmanship, as illustrated by the examples below. The following is a list of actions and behavior that are considered unethical. This list is not intended to be exhaustive.

a. Repeated or gross violation of tournament regulations.

b. Cheating in a game of chess by illicitly giving, receiving, offering, or soliciting advice; or by illicitly consulting written sources; or by tampering with clocks; or in any other manner.

c. Deliberately losing a game for payment or in order to lower one's rating, or for any other reason; or attempting to induce another individual to do so.

d. Deliberately misrepresenting one's playing ability in order to compete in a tournament or division of a tournament intended for players of lesser ability; players with foreign ratings are expected to disclose those ratings.

e. Participating in a tournament under a false name.

f. Participating in a tournament while under suspension.

g. A player who suspects another player of cheating should make this accusation only in private to a tournament director or other official. Public accusations of such cheating is itself unacceptable conduct under the terms of this code.

PROCEDURES

6. Any member of the USCF may initiate procedures under this code of ethics by filing a complaint in a timely manner with the USCF Ethics Committee. In the case of any accusation that does not fall clearly under 5a–g above, the Ethics Committee shall have the authority to decide whether the alleged conduct is within the scope of this code of ethics. In the case of each alleged violation that is within the scope of this code of ethics, the following steps shall occur in a timely manner:

a. A factual inquiry shall be made by the Ethics Committee, assisted as necessary by the USCF staff.

b. Appropriate sanctions, if any, shall be imposed by the committee.

c. Such sanctions shall be deemed final unless appealed to the Policy Board by the person or persons upon whom the sanctions have been imposed, or upon the initiative of a member of the Policy Board.

d. Upon appeal a review of the facts and the appropriateness of the sanction shall be undertaken by the Policy Board.

e. The sanctions shall be either continued, modified, or revoked by the Policy Board.

7. In the case of any inquiry pursuant to 6a above, the person accused of unethical conduct shall have the right to examine the evidence against him or her, the right to respond to the accusation, and the right to produce written evidence and documents in his or her own behalf. A person shall be notified of any sanction imposed against him or her. In connection with 6d above, the person upon whom the sanction has been imposed shall be given notice of the time and place the Policy

Board will review his or her case, and shall have the right to appear before the board and present evidence in his or her own behalf.

SANCTIONS

8. The following are some of the sanctions that may be imposed as a result of procedures specified in 6a–e above. In unusual cases other appropriate sanctions may be imposed, or these sanctions may be varied or combined.

    a. *Reprimand.* A determination that a member has committed an offense warranting discipline becomes a matter of record, but no further sanction is imposed at the time. A reprimand automatically carries a probation of at least three months, and possibly longer; if the member is judged guilty of another offense during the probationary period, he or she is then liable to further sanctions for both offenses.

    b. *Censure.* A determination that a member has committed a serious offense warranting discipline becomes a matter of record, but no further sanction is imposed at the time. Censure automatically carries a probation of at least one year, and possibly longer; if the member is judged guilty of another offense during the probationary period, he or she is then liable to further sanctions for both offenses.

    c. *Suspended sentence with probation.* A determination is made that a member has committed an offense warranting discipline. When the discipline is imposed and execution thereof suspended, such suspension shall include probation for at least six months longer than the discipline imposed. If the member is judged guilty of another offense during this period, unless otherwise decreed, the original discipline shall be added to such new discipline as may be imposed for the new offense.

d. *Suspension.* Suspension is a determination that a member has committed an offense warranting abrogation, for a specified period of time, of all membership rights and privileges.

e. *Expulsion.* Expulsion is a determination that a member has committed an offense warranting the permanent abrogation of all membership rights and privileges. An expelled member may be readmitted to membership only by the USCF Policy Board. No application for reinstatement may be considered before two years from the date of expulsion.

f. *Exclusion from events.* This is a more selective determination that a member has committed an offense warranting abrogation of the right to participate in certain specified events or activities.

9. In the case of every sanction that involves suspension or expulsion, a member may not hold any office in the USCF or participate in any capacity in any event or activity sponsored by or sanctioned by the USCF.

10. The effective date of a sanction shall be the date named by the Ethics Committee in its determination or, failing that, five days after written notification of such sanction to the member upon whom the sanction is imposed.

11.   The USCF business office shall be advised of each such notice, in writing, and such notice shall declare the date upon which the sanction becomes effective. The business office shall in turn report each sanction to the Policy Board.

9

TOURNAMENT
DIRECTOR CERTIFICATION

PURPOSE

The USCF certifies tournament directors in order to standardize procedures and ensure a competent tournament director (TD) for each level of USCF-rated tournament.

GENERAL QUALIFICATIONS

1. All certified TDs must be current members of USCF. If a TD allows his or her membership to lapse, his or her TD certification is canceled and is not automatically restored upon payment of membership dues.

2. Except at the club level, all certified TDs must have an established USCF rating as an over-the-board player. TDs are encouraged to remain active as players to maintain proper perspective when directing.

3. All TDs are encouraged to work with and assist other directors with greater experience and expertise to increase directing knowledge and understanding. All TDs are likewise encouraged to provide opportunities for less experienced directors to share in their philosophical understanding of tournament direction.

4. Every TD should own a copy of USCF's *Official Rules of Chess*. TDs should become thoroughly familiar with these rules and administrative procedures regarding the sale of memberships, reporting formats and deadlines, basic rating formulas, and a variety of other subjects.

TD TESTING PROCEDURES

5. Tests are written by the Tournament Director Certification Committee (TDCC) and administered by the technical director designated by the executive director. These tests are generally mailed to qualified applicants to be completed with the assistance of any printed matter, but applicants are bound by honor not to discuss specific questions with other persons. Applicants must return all testing materials within two months.

6. Applicants for promotion of TD certification level shall provide the technical director with the names, dates, and number of entrants of the tournaments that satisfy the experience requirements.

7. Applicants who fail the test for local or senior level of TD certification must wait two months before taking the test a sec-

ond time. Applicants who fail the second attempt must wait six months before taking the test a third or subsequent time.

8. Applicants who fail the test for associate national or national level of TD certification must wait three months before taking the test a second time. Applicants who do not pass the second attempt must wait one year before taking the test a third or subsequent time.

9. All documents, including completed tests, shall be submitted to:
    Technical Director
    U.S. Chess Federation
    186 Route 9W
    New Windsor, NY 12553

CHIEF TDS, ASSISTANT TDS, AND TOURNAMENT AIDES

10. The chief TD has the ultimate authority and responsibility for the tournament. In general, the chief TD must be physically present during play and should not himself be a player in a tournament he or she directs.

11. In unusual circumstances two directors may jointly function as co-chief TDs. Each co-chief receives USCF credit for one tournament with one-half the total number of entries.

12. An assistant TD serves under the chief TD performing assigned tasks relevant to tournament direction. Assistant TDs gain USCF credit for their experience when their duties include pairings and rules enforcement. Such credit is limited

to 1 assistant per 50 players or fraction thereof. Assistant TDs must be certified TDs.

13. Tournament aides serve under the chief TD performing primarily clerical tasks, such as entering results on pairing cards and wall charts. Aides do not possess the authority to make pairings or enforce rules, and they do not need to be certified TDs.

TOURNAMENT CATEGORIES

14. Category I—An international tournament recognized by the World Chess Federation (FIDE) held in the United States. Such tournaments should be directed by an international arbiter who also holds the rank of national TD or associate national or senior TD.

15. Category N—A tournament that awards a national title.

Subcategory N1—A national tournament open to a large group of players. Examples: U.S. Open, U.S. Junior Open, U.S. Senior Open, National Open, U.S. Class, U.S. Amateur, U.S. Amateur Team, U.S. Masters, U.S. Action, U.S. Game/60, Pan-American Intercollegiate Team, National High School, National Junior High School, National School Grade, and National Elementary School Championships. Such tournaments must be directed by national TDs.

Subcategory N2—A national tournament restricted to a small group of players. Examples: U.S. Championship, U.S. Women's Championship, U.S. Junior Championship, U.S.

Cadet, U.S. Blind, U.S. Computer, U.S. Armed Forces Championships, and the Arnold Denker National Tournament of High School Champions. Such tournaments may be directed by associate national TDs.

16. Category A—A USCF-rated Swiss system tournament, except Category I or N, that regularly draws more than 300 entrants and awards $5,000+ in prizes. Examples: World Open, New York Open, American Open, Memorial Day Classic, and Lipkin-Pfefferkorn Open. Such tournaments may be directed by associate national TDs.

17. Category B—A USCF-rated Swiss system tournament, except Category I or N, drawing 100 or more entrants. Such tournaments may be directed by senior TDs.

18. Category C—A USCF-rated Swiss system tournament, except Category I or N, drawing 50 to 99 entrants. Such tournaments may be directed by local TDs.

19. Category D—Any USCF-rated Swiss system tournament, except Category I or N, drawing fewer than 50 entrants. Such tournaments may be directed by club TDs.

20. Category R—A USCF-rated round robin tournament of eight or more rated entrants with a mean rating of at least 1800.

21. Category T—A USCF-rated team-vs.-team Swiss system tournament involving at least twelve teams of four or more players.

THE CLUB DIRECTOR

22.   Experience Requirement: An applicant for club TD accreditation must sign a statement indicating that he or she has read, has access to, and will abide by the rules contained in USCF's *Official Rules of Chess.*

23.   Testing Requirement: None.

24.   Limitations: A club TD may not be the chief TD for USCF Grand Prix or Category N tournaments and should not be the chief TD of Category A, B, or C tournaments.

25.   Expiration: Three-year nonrenewal term. After three years, the club TD must apply for local TD status. The Tournament Director Certification Committee (TDCC) may, at its discretion, reinstate club TD certification for a TD who fails the local TD test after three full years of experience.

THE LOCAL DIRECTOR

26.   Experience Requirements:

a. Satisfactory performance as chief or assistant TD of three or more Category D tournaments of at least three rounds which total 50 or more entrants, or

b. Attendance at a workshop offered by the TDCC at a U.S. Open Championship, or

c. Satisfactory performance for three years as a club TD, but

d. Experience requirements are waived for any applicant who takes the local TD test (closed book) under supervision at a Category N tournament. Applicants must contact the technical director in advance of the tournament to request this option.

27. Testing Requirements: Objective test of moderate difficulty designed to measure the applicant's knowledge of basic rules.

28. Limitations: A local TD may not be the chief TD of Category N tournaments and should not be the chief TD of Category A or B tournaments.

29. Expiration: Four-year renewable term. The testing requirement for re-certification is waived for a local TD with satisfactory performance as the chief or assistant TD of four tournaments during the four-year term.

THE SENIOR DIRECTOR

30. Experience Requirements:

a. Satisfactory performance as chief TD of five Category C tournaments of at least four rounds, and

b. Satisfactory performance as chief TD of five or more additional Swiss system tournaments of at least four rounds, such that the 10 or more tournaments total at least 400 entrants, but

c. Any of the following may be substituted for one of the tournaments in Requirement B (limit, two substitutions):

1. attendance at a workshop offered by the TDCC at U.S. Open Championship;

2. satisfactory performance as assistant TD to a national TD or associate national TD at a Category A or B tournament;

3. satisfactory performance as chief TD of a Category R tournament;

4. double credit is given to a local TD if he or she trains a club TD as his or her assistant at any tournament. "Double credit" refers to two tournaments, not double the number of entrants;

5. double credit, as defined above, is given to the TD of an official state or region open championship; but

d. Experience requirements are reduced to satisfactory performance as chief TD of three Category C tournaments for any applicant who takes the senior TD test (closed book) under supervision at a Category N tournament. Applicants must contact the technical director in advance of the tournament to request this option.

31. Testing Requirement: Difficult objective examination designed to evaluate the applicant's knowledge and judgment in situations not clearly addressed by the rules.

32. Limitations: A senior TD may not be the chief TD of Category N tournaments and should not be the chief TD of Category A tournaments.

33. Expiration: Five-year renewable term. The testing requirement for re-certification is waived for a senior TD with satisfactory performance as a chief or assistant TD of five tournaments during the five-year term.

THE ASSOCIATE NATIONAL DIRECTOR (ANTD)

34. Experience Requirements:

a. Satisfactory performance as chief TD of ten Category B tournaments of which three awarded $1,000+ in prizes, and

b. Satisfactory performance as chief TD or assistant to a national TD at a Category N or A tournament, and

c. Satisfactory performance as chief TD of a Category R tournament, but

d. Allowable substitution for Requirement A is a satisfactory performance as chief TD of six Category B tournaments and an additional 16 Category C tournaments, three of which awarded $1,000+ in prizes.

35. Testing Requirement: Essay examination of substantial difficulty designed to measure the applicant's understanding of the rules as they relate to complex problems. The examination is graded by an experienced national TD.

36. Limitations: An associate national TD may not be the chief TD of Category N1 tournaments.

37. Expiration: Six-year renewable terms. The testing requirement for re-certification is waived for an associate national TD with satisfactory performances as the chief or assistant TD of six tournaments during the six-year term.

THE NATIONAL DIRECTOR (NTD)

38. Experience Requirements:

a. Satisfactory performance as chief TD of 15 Category B tournaments, three of which awarded $1,000+ in prizes, and

b. Satisfactory performance as chief TD of a Category R tournament, and

c. Satisfactory performance as chief TD or assistant to a national, associate national, or senior TD at a Category T tournament of at least four rounds, and

d. Satisfactory performance as assistant to a national TD at a Category N1 tournament, and

e. Satisfactory performance as chief TD or assistant to a national TD at an additional Category N or A tournament, but

f. Allowable substitution for Requirement A is a satisfactory performance as chief TD of ten Category B tournaments and an additional 20 Category C tournaments, three of which awarded $1,000+ in prizes.

39. Testing Requirement: A rigorous essay examination designed to measure the applicant's understanding of the philosophies behind the rules. The examination is graded by an experienced national TD.

40. Limitations: None.

41. Expiration: Life.

THE INTERNATIONAL ARBITER (IA)

42. The title of international arbiter is awarded by the World Chess Federation (FIDE).

43. The USCF will sponsor the international arbiter applications for senior, ANTD, and NTDs who meet all the following requirements:

a. Thorough knowledge of the Laws of Chess and the FIDE Regulations for chess competitions;

b. Absolute objectivity, demonstrated at all times during his or her activity as an arbiter;

c. Sufficient knowledge of at least one official FIDE language;

d. Experience as chief or deputy arbiter in at least four category I events governed by the FIDE Laws of Chess and Rules of Play such as the following:

1. The final of the National Adult Championship (not more than two);

2. All official FIDE tournaments and matches;

3. International title tournaments and matches;

4. International chess festivals with at least 100 contestants.

44. Testing Requirement: An essay examination designed to measure the applicant's understanding of the philosophies behind FIDE rules. The TDCC grades the examination.

45.   Limitations: None.

46.   Expiration: Life.

WAIVERS

47.   The TDCC reserves the right to give special consideration to applicants in extraordinary situations. Requests detailing the extraordinary circumstances must be submitted in writing to the TDCC chairperson through the technical director.

CERTIFICATION RESTRICTIONS

48.   The USCF may impose restrictions on a TD's certification upon documentation of technical incompetence, partiality, professional misconduct, or inefficiency.

49.   Allegations of these offenses will be investigated by the TDCC or the executive director. The accused will be afforded due process. In every investigation the TDCC or executive director will consider the past accomplishments of the TD in service to chess, and other substantiated complaints against the TD.

50.   Imposed restrictions may include warnings, probations, requirements of additional experience or testing to maintain or advance level, demotions of level, limitations on the types of tournaments that may be directed, temporary suspensions of directing certification, or permanent decertifications.

51. Any imposition of TD restrictions made by the executive director may be appealed to the TDCC. Any decision made by the TDCC may be appealed to the Policy Board. Any decision made by the Policy Board may be appealed to the Board of Delegates. All appeals should be filed within 30 days of notice of action taken. Restrictions will generally remain in effect during the appeals process.

Uniform Code of Discipline

52. Technical Incompetence: In cases in which technical incompetence on the part of the TD has been demonstrated, the TDCC will normally impose additional testing requirements for the TD to maintain his or her level of certification. In extreme cases the TDCC may demote the TD's level of certification or suspend his or her certification until greater competence is demonstrated. Technical incompetence is typically demonstrated by gross misapplication of USCF's *Official Rules of Chess.*

53. Partiality: In cases in which partiality on the part of the TD has been demonstrated, the TDCC will normally impose a suspension of directing privileges for a period not less than three months and not greater than three years. In extreme cases the TDCC may recommend permanent decertification to the Policy Board. Partiality is typically demonstrated by bribery, fraudulent reports, deliberately unfair pairing or scoring practices, deliberately inconsistent rules enforcement, and even minor irregularities that benefit the TD as a player in an event in which he or she is eligible for a prize.

54. Professional Misconduct: In cases in which professional misconduct on the part of the TD has been demonstrated and reconciliation between the complainant and the TD cannot be achieved, the TDCC will normally issue a warning to the TD. Extreme cases of professional misconduct, especially when representing the USCF at a national tournament, may warrant certification demotion or suspension. Professional misconduct is typically demonstrated by denigration of a player, arrogance, rude behavior, and failure to respond to official inquiries by the executive director, his or her designee, or the TDCC.

55. Inefficiency: In cases in which inefficiency has been demonstrated as the cause of a poorly directed tournament, the TDCC will normally issue a warning to the TD. In extreme cases certification may be suspended until the TD demonstrates improved procedural techniques. Inefficiency is typically demonstrated by lack of adherence to an announced tournament schedule, untimely or inaccurate posting of pairings and results, and untimely or inaccurate calculation of tournament-prize distributions.

10

THE USCF RATING SYSTEM

INTRODUCTION

Tournament results, pairing rules, and ratings are so interdependent that each player should have at least an idea of how chess ratings operate; more detailed knowledge is appropriate for a director. The details of the rating system are complicated, but available from USCF.

Every player in a USCF-rated tournament obtains a rating upon playing a total of at least four games. This rating goes up or down with nearly every game played, because it is a measure of the player's results against his or her particular opposition.

USCF maintains two separate rating systems, one for time controls of G/30 or slower and the other for Quick Chess games faster than G/30. As of this writing, the only ratable Quick Chess time limits are from G/10 to G/29. The two rating systems are identical, except that each game affects an established Quick Chess rating less than it does a regular rating, and the "regular" or "slow" rating is given substantial weight in establishing a player's initial Quick Chess rating.

Example 1. In the regular rating system, a previously unrated player plays six games against opponents whose ratings average 1500, winning three and losing three. The player starts with a "provisional" rating of 1500, the average of his or her opponents, because the player's even score against them indicates ability equal to the average of the group. The player's first rating would be the same if he or she had drawn all six games or had any other combination of results leading to a 3–3 score.

Expected score. The rating system is based on the theory that the rating difference between two players corresponds to their expected score against each other. For example, in an extended series of games of either regular or Quick Chess between two players, the higher rated is expected to score approximately:

Rating difference	Scoring probability
0 points	50%
50 points	57%
100 points	64%
150 points	70%
200 points	76%
250 points	81%
300 points	85%
350 points	88%
400 points	91%
450 points	93%
500 points	95%
550 points	96%
600 points	97%
675 points	98%
800 points	99%

Initial ratings. A player's initial rating may be approximated with the following formula. The actual calculation method may be slightly different, and opponents' ratings may have changed since last published, so any calculation is likely to be slightly different than the official rating the USCF computer will ultimately assign. For Quick Chess any regular rating the player may have is given substantial weight, so the following method will work for Quick Chess only if the player lacks a regular rating.

$$R = A + \frac{400\,(W - L)}{N}$$

where R is the rating, A the average rating of the opponents, W wins, L losses, and N the number of games.

Although this formula works well for all games at once, many players find it easier to apply it to each game and then average the results. This may be done by adding 400 to the opponent's rating for a win, subtracting 400 for a loss, and making no adjustment for a draw, as in example 2.

Example 2. In a player's first tournament, he or she defeats a 1212, loses to a 1610, loses to a 1340, and draws with a 1438.

$$1212 + 400 = 1612$$
$$1610 - 400 = 1210$$
$$1340 - 400 = 940$$
$$1438 \qquad = 1438$$

Total   5200

5200 divided by 4 (number of games) equals 1300, so the player's initial rating is 1300. It will be published as 1300/4, indicating that it is based on only four games. The fewer games played, the less reliable the rating.

Provisional ratings. For a player's first 20 games, he or she is considered "provisional," and has a rating based on the overall average of all individual performances.

Provisionally rated players are not unrated. Almost all USCF-rated tournaments use provisional ratings and allow players to compete for prizes based on the rating classes they indicate.

Example 3. The player with a 1300/4 rating enters another tournament, of three rounds, and beats a 1220, loses to a 1380, and beats a 1440. We now must weight the old rating of 1300 by multiplying it by the four games played, and average a total of seven games:

$$1300 \times 4 \quad = 5200 \text{ (old rating)}$$
$$1220 + 400 = 1620$$
$$1380 - 400 = 980$$
$$1440 + 400 = 1840$$
$$\text{Total} \qquad\quad 9640$$

9640/7 = 1377.14, so the player's new rating is 1377/7, meaning 1377 based on seven games.

Established ratings. The formula for players with "established" ratings, based on 20 or more games, is different and more complicated, but the principles remain similar.

Basic change. If equally rated players draw, there is no rating change. If one wins, that player goes up 16 points and the loser down 16.

Handicap effect. Additionally, there is a handicap effect of up to another 16 points for rating differences, which increases or decreases the exchange described in the above paragraph. This works approximately as follows. On the table below, find the rating difference in question. The corresponding number of adjustment points are listed, rounded to the nearest whole number, and should be added to the basic change when rating the lower-rated player and subtracted from the basic change when rating the higher-rated player.

Note that the USCF computer does not round the adjustment points to the nearest whole number, so a rating difference of 11 or 12 is really about one-half adjustment point, etc. But such minor differences tend to cancel each other out, so a player using this table should not be too far off.

Rating difference	Adjustment points
0–11	0
12–33	1
34–55	2
56–77	3
78–100	4
101–125	5
126–150	6
151–176	7
177–205	8
206–238	9
239–272	10
273–314	11
315–365	12

366–445	13
446–470	14
471–715	15
over 715	16

Let us consider the outcome if two players rated 340 points apart meet:

If the higher rated wins, the rating change is 16 minus 12, or 4 points gained by the higher player and lost by the lower.

If the game is a draw, the lower player gains, and the higher player loses, 12 points.

If the lower player wins, the lower player gains 16 plus 12 or 28 points, and the higher loses the same number.

Quick Chess changes. To determine a Quick Chess rating change, use the above methods but multiply the calculated change by 60 percent. So a result which gains or loses 20 points in the regular rating system will gain or lose 12 points (60 percent of 20) in the Quick Chess system. The 60 percent ratio is subject to future change.

Higher ratings change more slowly. For players rated 2100–2399, the final rating change is multiplied by three quarters, and for those rated 2400 and above, by one half. These adjustments have no effect on their opponents, so if a player over 2100 plays one under, the player gaining points will have a rating increase not equal to the other player's decrease.

Rating floors. To stabilize established ratings, 100-point rating floors exist, currently every 100 points between 1400 and 2300. A player who achieves an established rating of 2300 cannot drop below 2200, one who reaches 2200 cannot drop below 2100, etc. However, a player with poor results over a long period of time may write to the USCF office and request consideration of lowering his or her rating floor by 100 points.

Rating classes. For purposes of general identification and often for the awarding of tournament prizes, rated players are grouped as follows:

Name	Rating range
Senior Master	2400 and above
Master	2200–2399
Expert	2000–2199
Class A	1800–1999
Class B	1600–1799
Class C	1400–1599
Class D	1200–1399
Class E	under 1200

International ratings. International (FIDE) ratings are calculated somewhat differently. They are published only for players rated over 1999.

FIDE Masters earn their titles by ratings, but the higher titles of International Master and International Grandmaster also require outstanding performances in a number of high-level events. These titles, unlike ratings, are lifetime awards.

USCF lifetime titles. The long-standing success of FIDE's lifetime titles led in 1991 to the establishment of similar lifetime titles by USCF for all classes of players.

Significance of titles. Unlike ratings, which show *current strength*, USCF lifetime titles indicate *lifetime achievement*. USCF lifetime titles are as follows:

Title level	Title	Abbreviation
2900	5-Star Master	✩✩✩✩✩
2800	4-Star Master	✩✩✩✩
2700	3-Star Master	✩✩✩
2600	2-Star Master	✩✩
2500	Star Master	S
2400	Senior Life Master	s
2300	Advanced Life Master	M
2200	Life Master	m
2100	Advanced Expert	X
2000	Certified Expert	x
1900	Advanced Class A	A
1800	Certified Class A	a
1700	Advanced Class B	B
1600	Certified Class B	b
1500	Advanced Class C	C
1400	Certified Class C	c
1300	Advanced Class D	D
1200	Certified Class D	d
1100	Advanced Class E	E
1000	Certified Class E	e

The USCF system of lifetime titles is similar to the FIDE system for GM and IM titles. There is no time limit to earn a title; norm points remain on file until a player achieves the next higher title. The titles do not affect players' USCF ratings.

Display of titles and norms. USCF rating supplements and address labels currently display, after each player's rating, that player's title and the number of norm points the player has toward the title 100 points higher. For example, "1660°B2" in a rating supplement indicates that the player is rated 1660, has the Advanced B (1700 level) lifetime title, and has two norm points toward the next highest title, Certified Class A (1800 level).

Display of points for title two levels up. The rating supplements and address labels indirectly display norm points toward the title two levels above the present title. A player with an *odd number* of points toward the title one level higher than present has *two points* toward the title two levels above, while one with an even number one level up has no points two levels up.

Norm point requirements. Ten norm points are required to obtain a title. A player who achieves a norm for a title one level above the present level earns two norm points toward that title.

Achieving a norm two levels up. A player who achieves a norm for a title two levels above the present title earns two norm points toward that title and five points toward the title one level above the present title. For example, a player with the 1600 title who achieves an 1800 norm earns two points toward the 1800 title and five points toward the 1700 title.

Achieving a norm three levels up. A player who achieves a norm for a title three levels above the present title is awarded the title one level above the current title (two levels below that of the new norm), obtains five norm points toward the title two levels above, and obtains two points toward the title three levels above. Likewise, a player making a norm four or more levels above the existing title obtains the title two levels below that of the new norm. For example, a player with the 1600 title who achieves a 1900 norm earns the 1700 title, five points toward the 1800 title, and two points toward the 1900 title.

Norm point requirements. Norm points are earned by exceeding the expected score of a player with the minimum rating of that level by the following number of game points, which is called the Delta:

Rounds	Delta
4	0.7
5	0.6
6	0.5
7	0.4
8	0.3
9 or more	0.2

For example, in a 6-round event, an 1800 player is expected to score 3–3 with all opponents rated 1800. Therefore a 3½–2½ score, 0.5 points above this expected score, would achieve an 1800 norm.

A 1900 player with all opponents rated 1800 is expected to score 3.84 points out of six games so a minimum score of 4.34, or in this case 4½ points, is needed to achieve a 1900 norm. A 5½–½ score would earn a 2000 norm.

Four-round minimum. Norms can be earned only in events of four rounds or more, not counting unplayed games.

Two-point minimum. A minimum score of two points is needed to achieve a norm, not counting unplayed games.

Ratings and titles. While titles do not affect ratings, ratings may affect titles. A player who achieves an established rating but not the title corresponding to 100 points below that rating is awarded that title.

Matches. Norm points are not available in matches.

Life Master titles. Through 1996 the Life Master title is available either through the norms method or the old way, which required a rating of 2200 or over to be maintained for 300 games. After 1996, these titles will be available only via norms.

Quick titles. Lifetime titles are available in both the regular and Quick Chess rating systems, but each system is separate, so separate norms are required.

Demotion. Ordinarily, a player's title is never lowered. However, a player with a long period of poor results may ask USCF to consider lowering a title one level. A player might wish to make such a request if certain events do not allow those above a specified title level.

11

CORRESPONDENCE CHESS

Correspondence chess, though often identified with its most popular form, postal chess, actually embraces all the forms of chess competition that do not involve a face-to-face, over-the-board contest between the contestants. Its roots are allegedly medieval, as noblemen are said to have dispatched messengers with moves to rivals who lived at considerable distance—all without benefit of convenient and standardized notation. Today, correspondence chess includes communications by postal means, by telephone, radio, telex and telegraph, and, of course, by computer. There has even been a simultaneous exhibition match by satellite TV.

The rules for these contests vary and are not even fully standardized within each form of correspondence. In general, they attempt to approximate tournament chess as closely as possible, while still taking advantage of the opportunity provided by the communication system, and the more leisurely pace of such games.

In team telephone and telex matches, variations from the rules and normal time controls are minimal. Players are held strictly to the normal rules by an on-site director, and moves are communicated to the opponent by messengers and runners. One of the few differences between these competitions and games in a tournament hall is that neither player is charged with the time used in this communication. Each player, therefore, gains some extra reflection time, which is usually somewhat balanced by a faster-than-normal time control.

In correspondence chess, however, and in other forms designed to take more than an afternoon or evening to complete, the rules have to be substantially different. There is no way, for example, to enforce rules against researching openings and endings or against manipulating pieces before deciding on a move. These practices are, therefore, virtually encouraged in the interest of more accurate, perfect chess, unhindered by the relentless ticking of the chess clock or the other pressures of the tournament hall.

Nevertheless, each player is expected to rely on his or her own resources, memory, talent, and library. Consulting another person is strictly unethical and a proven violation is usually cause for forfeiture. Similarly, using a chess computer or program for analysis is unethical, and this practice may carry severe penalties.

Time limits, of course, have to be different from over-the-board (OTB) chess. Typically, neither player is charged for the time moves spent in the control of the postal service. Some organizations require that a player respond to a move within two to four days of receiving it. Even more commonly, players are given a time budget to use at their discretion, e.g., 30 days in which to make 10 moves. Most contests allow limited time-outs for vacations, illness, or other emergencies.

A special difficulty in correspondence chess is in illegal, illegible, or ambiguous moves. It is a nuisance to receive such a move, as clarification can take a week or more of transit time, during which the game is stalled. Such moves are sometimes caused by an inaccurate position on a player's board, for example, after someone has played through some variations without resetting the game position accurately.

In such situations, whatever their cause, USCF correspondence chess rules do not call for an application of a touch-move analogy. If a piece has been moved to an impossible square, for instance, the player makes any legal move. The tournament director, however, may impose a time penalty and/or warning for the delay caused by a faulty transmission.

Each organization that sponsors correspondence chess tournaments, including USCF, publishes detailed rules.

12

BLITZ CHESS

Blitz Chess is also known as five-minute chess, the time limit being G/5. As each game takes no longer than ten minutes, it has long been popular for fun games when time is limited, such as during lunch breaks or between rounds of slower tournaments. Some chess clubs hold weekly round robin Blitz tournaments, some of which include almost twenty games in one night.

The USCF does not presently rate Blitz games. They are, however, rated by the World Blitz Chess Association, headed by Grandmaster Walter Browne. The WBCA also issues a Blitz magazine and has successfully encouraged the organization of Blitz events during many major tournaments in the U.S. The recently adopted FIDE Blitz Rules (see Chapter 22) are substantially patterned after WBCA Blitz Rules. For current information on Blitz events or rules, contact WBCA at 8 Parnassus Rd., Berkeley, CA 94708, or the USCF office.

USCF BLITZ RULES

The following USCF Blitz rules are intended to be as similar as possible to regular USCF rules in order to minimize confusion.

1. Scorekeeping. As in Quick Chess, scorekeeping is not required and all rules pertaining to it are irrelevant.

2. Claim of insufficient losing chances. The regular USCF rule (see Chapter 1, 14H1) is modified as follows: A player must have less than *one minute* of remaining time to make a claim. This means that if the claim is denied (see 14H4b), one minute is subtracted from claimant's time, causing an automatic loss. It is still possible to temporarily deny a claim that has some merit (see 14H4c and 14H4d), impose no penalty, and watch the progress of the game for a possible subsequent ruling of a draw.

3. All other rules. All other regular USCF rules for sudden death play apply also to Blitz. Some of the most pertinent are as follows:

Illegal move penalty (11D). A player who makes an illegal move in Blitz and punches the clock does not forfeit. Instead, two minutes are added to the opponent's remaining time.

Correcting illegal move (11D1 or 16D3). If an illegal move in Blitz is not corrected before the opponent of the player who made the illegal move completes two moves, then the illegal move stands, and there is no time adjustment.

Triple occurrence of position (14C8). A player may be awarded a draw in Blitz by triple repetition of position based on the observation of a director, deputy, or impartial witness(es). A player may stop both clocks to see a director in order to demonstrate the ability to force a triple occurrence of position.

Both flags down (14G or 16T). A Blitz game is drawn if both flags are down. If a player claims a win on time with his or her flag still up but does not stop the clock in time to prevent the flag from falling, the game is drawn.

Removing player's hand from clock (16C). Each player in a Blitz game must remove his or her hand from the clock button after depressing the button and must keep the hand off the clock until it is time to press it again.

Operating clock (16D1). Each player in a Blitz game must handle the clock with the same hand that moves the pieces.

Picking up clock (16D2). Each player in a Blitz game is forbidden to pick up the clock.

13

ROUND ROBIN PAIRING TABLES

The following pairing tables are used for round robin tournaments. The player with the first number in each pairing has the white pieces. Pairing numbers are assigned by lot at the beginning of the event, unlike Swiss tournaments in which pairing numbers are determined by ratings.

The advantage of these Crenshaw-Berger tables over other tables is that they allow the reduction of the distortion of color assignments in cases when a player withdraws in the first half of a tournament with an even number of players. In such an event, players are already assigned unequal blacks and whites, and the withdrawal of one player could mean, for example, that some competitors would actually play two more blacks than whites.

The Crenshaw-Berger system for color equalization minimizes these inequities. The general principles are as follows:

1. If no one withdraws before playing at least half the scheduled games, there are no color changes. ("Half" is always rounded up, so, for example, 6 is half of 11.)

2. If one player withdraws before playing half the schedule, some colors are reversed in the last rounds.

3. The maximum number of color changes is two for any player.

4. The tournament director may reschedule any games provided that the games in the starred (*) rounds—those involving color reversals—are played after all players have completed half their games.

Each of the following charts applies to an odd and even number of players. If the number of competitors is an odd one, the final position in the tournament is a bye, but the player scheduled for the bye does not get a scoring point for that round. If there is such a bye in a tournament, no color reversals should be made.

Table A
3 or 4 players

Round	Pairings
1	1–4 2–3
2	3–1 4–2
3	1–2 3–4

Colors in the third round are determined by toss, unless one player has withdrawn after the first game. In that case, the director assigns colors in the third game so that each remaining player has at least one black and one white in the tournament.

Table A (*cont.*)

Withdrawn player	Reversals
1	none
2	4–3
3	2–1
4	none

Table B
5 or 6 players

Round	Pairings		
1	3–6	5–4	1–2
2	2–6	4–1	3–5
3	6–5	1–3	4–2
4	6–4	5–1	2–3
5°	1–6	2–5	3–4

°Color reversals should be made in the fifth round if someone withdraws before playing three games:

Withdrawn player	Reversals	
1	5–2	4–3
2	4–3	
3	none	
4	6–1	5–2
5	6–1	
6	none	

Table C
7 or 8 players

Round	Pairings			
1	4–8	5–3	6–2	7–1
2	8–7	1–6	2–5	3–4

Table C (*cont.*)

Round	Pairings			
3	3–8	4–2	5–1	6–7
4	8–6	7–5	1–4	2–3
5*	2–8	3–1	4–7	5–6
6*	8–5	6–4	7–3	1–2
7*	1–8	2–7	3–6	4–5

*Color reversals should be made in the last three rounds if someone withdraws before playing four games:

Withdrawn player	Reversals			
1	7–2	5–4		
2	6–3			
3	5–4	7–2	2–1	
4	6–3	3–7	7–2	
5	8–1	7–4	4–6	6–3
6	8–2	5–4		
7	8–1	6–3		
8	none			

Table D
9 or 10 players

Round	Pairings				
1	5–10	6–4	7–3	8–2	9–1
2	10–9	1–8	2–7	3–6	4–5
3	4–10	5–3	6–2	7–1	8–9
4	10–8	9–7	1–6	2–5	3–4
5	3–10	4–2	5–1	6–9	7–8
6	10–7	8–6	9–5	1–4	2–3
7*	2–10	3–1	4–9	5–8	6–7
8*	10–6	7–5	8–4	9–3	1–2
9*	1–10	2–9	3–8	4–7	5–6

Table D (*cont.*)

° Color reversals should be made in the last three rounds if someone withdraws before playing five games:

Withdrawn player	Reversals
1	9–2 7–4
2	8–3 6–5
3	7–4 9–2 2–1
4	6–5 8–3 3–9 9–2
5	9–2 2–1 7–4 4–8 8–3
6	10–2 8–5 5–7 7–4
7	10–1 6–5 9–4 4–8 8–3
8	10–2 7–4
9	10–1 8–3 6–5
10	none

Table E
11 or 12 players

Round	Pairings					
1	6–12	7–5	8–4	9–3	10–2	11–1
2	12–11	1–10	2–9	3–8	4–7	5–6
3	5–12	6–4	7–3	8–2	9–1	10–11
4	12–10	11–9	1–8	2–7	3–6	4–5
5	4–12	5–3	6–2	7–1	8–11	9–10
6	12–9	10–8	11–7	1–6	2–5	3–4
7	3–12	4–2	5–1	6–11	7–10	8–9
8	12–8	9–7	10–6	11–5	1–4	2–3
9°	2–12	3–1	4–11	5–10	6–9	7–8
10°	12–7	8–6	9–5	10–4	11–3	1–2
11°	1–12	2–11	3–10	4–9	5–8	6–7

°Color reversals should be made in the last three rounds if someone withdraws before playing six games:

Table E (*cont.*)

Withdrawn player	Reversals
1	11–2 9–4 7–6
2	10–3 8–5
3	9–4 7–6 11–2 2–1
4	8–5 10–3 3–11 11–2
5	7–6 11–2 2–1 9–4 4–10 10–3
6	10–3 3–11 11–2 8–5 5–9 9–4
7	12–1 11–4 4–10 10–3 9–6 6–8 8–5
8	12–2 7–6 10–5 5–9 9–4
9	12–1 8–5 11–4 4–10 10–3
10	12–2 9–4 7–6
11	12–1 10–3 8–5
12	none

Table F
13 or 14 players

Round	Pairings						
1	7–14	8–6	9–5	10–4	11–3	12–2	13–1
2	14–13	1–12	2–11	3–10	4–9	5–8	6–7
3	6–14	7–5	8–4	9–3	10–2	11–1	12–13
4	14–12	13–11	1–10	2–9	3–8	4–7	5–6
5	5–14	6–4	7–3	8–2	9–1	10–13	11–12
6	14–11	12–10	13–9	1–8	2–7	3–6	4–5
7	4–14	5–3	6–2	7–1	8–13	9–12	10–11
8	14–10	11–9	12–8	13–7	1–6	2–5	3–4
9	3–14	4–2	5–1	6–13	7–12	8–11	9–10
10	14–9	10–8	11–7	12–6	13–5	1–4	2–3
11°	2–14	3–1	4–13	5–12	6–11	7–10	8–9
12°	14–8	9–7	10–6	11–5	12–4	13–3	1–2
13°	1–14	2–13	3–12	4–11	5–10	6–9	7–8

° Color reversals should be made in the last three rounds if someone withdraws before playing seven games:

Table F (*cont.*)

Withdrawn player	Reversals
1	13–2 11–4 9–6
2	12–3 10–5 8–7
3	13–2 2–1 11–4 9–6
4	12–3 3–13 13–2 10–5 8–7
5	13–2 2–1 11–4 4–12 12–3 9–6
6	12–3 3–13 13–2 10–5 5–11 11–4 8–7
7	13–2 2–1 11–4 4–12 12–3 9–6 6–10 10–5
8	14–2 12–5 5–11 11–4 10–7 7–9 9–6
9	14–1 13–4 4–12 12–3 11–6 6–10 10–5 8–7
10	14–2 12–5 5–11 11–4 9–6
11	14–1 13–4 4–12 12–3 10–5 8–7
12	14–2 11–4 9–6
13	14–1 12–3 10–5 8–7
14	none

Table G
15 or 16 players

Round	Pairings							
1	8–16	9–7	10–6	11–5	12–4	13–3	14–2	15–1
2	16–15	1–14	2–13	3–12	4–11	5–10	6–9	7–8
3	7–16	8–6	9–5	10–4	11–3	12–2	13–1	14–15
4	16–14	15–13	1–12	2–11	3–10	4–9	5–8	6–7
5	6–16	7–5	8–4	9–3	10–2	11–1	12–15	13–14
6	16–13	14–12	15–11	1–10	2–9	3–8	4–7	5–6
7	5–16	6–4	7–3	8–2	9–1	10–15	11–14	12–13
8	16–12	13–11	14–10	15–9	1–8	2–7	3–6	4–5
9	4–16	5–3	6–2	7–1	8–15	9–14	10–13	11–12
10	16–11	12–10	13–9	14–8	15–7	1–6	2–5	3–4
11	3–16	4–2	5–1	6–15	7–14	8–13	9–12	10–11
12	16–10	11–9	12–8	13–7	14–6	15–5	1–4	2–3
13°	2–16	3–1	4–15	5–14	6–13	7–12	8–11	9–10

Table G (*cont.*)

Round	Pairings							
14°	16–9	10–8	11–7	12–6	13–5	14–4	15–3	1–2
15°	1–16	2–15	3–14	4–13	5–12	6–11	7–10	8–9

° Color reversals should be made in the last three rounds if someone withdraws before playing eight games:

Withdrawn player	Reversals
1	15–2 13–4 11–6 9–8
2	14–3 12–5 10–7
3	13–4 11–6 9–8 15–2 2–1
4	12–5 10–7 14–3 3–15 15–2
5	11–6 9–8 15–2 2–1 13–4 4–14 14–3
6	10–7 14–3 3–15 15–2 12–5 5–13 13–4
7	9–8 15–2 2–1 13–4 4–14 14–3 11–6 6–12 12–5
8	14–3 3–15 15–2 12–5 5–13 13–4 10–7 7–11 11–6
9	16–1 15–4 4–14 14–3 13–6 6–12 12–5 11–8 8–10 10–7
10	16–2 9–8 14–5 5–13 13–4 12–7 7–11 11–6
11	16–1 10–7 15–4 4–14 14–3 13–6 6–12 12–5
12	16–2 11–6 9–8 14–5 5–13 13–4
13	16–1 12–5 10–7 15–4 4–14 14–3
14	16–2 13–4 11–6 9–8
15	16–1 14–3 12–5 10–7
16	none

Table H
17 or 18 players

Round	Pairings								
1	9–18	10–8	11–7	12–6	13–5	14–4	15–3	16–2	17–1
2	18–17	1–16	2–15	3–14	4–13	5–12	6–11	7–10	8–9

Table H (*cont.*)

Round				Pairings				
3	8–18	9–7	10–6	11–5	12–4	13–3	14–2	15–1	16–17
4	18–16	17–15	1–14	2–13	3–12	4–11	5–10	6–9	7–8
5	7–18	8–6	9–5	10–4	11–3	12–2	13–1	14–17	15–16
6	18–15	16–14	17–13	1–12	2–11	3–10	4–9	5–8	6–7
7	6–18	7–5	8–4	9–3	10–2	11–1	12–17	13–16	14–15
8	18–14	15–13	16–12	17–11	1–10	2–9	3–8	4–7	5–6
9	5–18	6–4	7–3	8–2	9–1	10–17	11–16	12–15	13–14
10	18–13	14–12	15–11	16–10	17–9	1–8	2–7	3–6	4–5
11	4–18	5–3	6–2	7–1	8–17	9–16	10–15	11–14	12–13
12	18–12	13–11	14–10	15–9	16–8	17–7	1–6	2–5	3–4
13	3–18	4–2	5–1	6–17	7–16	8–15	9–14	10–13	11–12
14	18–11	12–10	13–9	14–8	15–7	16–6	17–5	1–4	2–3
15°	2–18	3–1	4–17	5–16	6–15	7–14	8–13	9–12	10–11
16°	18–10	11–9	12–8	13–7	14–6	15–5	16–4	17–3	1–2
17°	1–18	2–17	3–16	4–15	5–14	6–13	7–12	8–11	9–10

° Color reversals should be made in the last three rounds if someone withdraws before playing nine games:

Withdrawn player	Reversals
1	17–2 15–4 13–6 11–8
2	16–3 14–5 12–7 10–9
3	15–4 13–6 11–8 17–2 2–1
4	14–5 12–7 10–9 16–3 3–17 17–2
5	13–6 11–8 17–2 2–1 15–4 4–16 16–3
6	12–7 10–9 16–3 3–17 17–2 14–5 5–15 15–4
7	11–8 17–2 2–1 15–4 4–16 16–3 13–6 6–14 14–5
8	10–9 16–3 3–17 17–2 14–5 5–15 15–4 12–7 7–13 13–6

Table H (*cont.*)

Withdrawn player	Reversals
9	17–2 2–1 15–4 4–16 16–3 13–6 6–14 14–5 11–8 8–12 12–7
10	18–2 16–5 5–15 15–4 14–7 7–13 13–6 12–9 9–11 11–8
11	18–1 10–9 17–4 4–16 16–3 15–6 6–14 14–5 13–8 8–12 12–7
12	18–2 11–8 16–5 5–15 15–4 14–7 7–13 13–6
13	8–1 12–7 10–9 17–4 4–16 16–3 15–6 6–14 14–5
14	18–2 13–16 11–8 16–5 5–15 15–4
15	18–1 14–5 12–7 10–9 17–4 4–16 16–3
16	18–2 15–4 13–6 11–8
17	18–1 16–3 14–5 12–7 10–9
18	none

Table I
19 or 20 players

Round	Pairings
1	10–20 11–9 12–8 13–7 14–6 15–5 16–4 17–3 18–2 19–1
2	20–19 1–18 2–17 3–16 4–15 5–14 6–13 7–12 8–11 9–10
3	9–20 10–8 11–7 12–6 13–5 14–4 15–3 16–2 17–1 18–19
4	20–18 19–17 1–16 2–15 3–14 4–13 5–12 6–11 7–10 8–9
5	8–20 9–7 10–6 11–5 12–4 13–3 14–2 15–1 16–19 17–18
6	20–17 18–16 19–15 1–14 2–13 3–12 4–11 5–10 6–9 7–8
7	7–20 8–6 9–5 10–4 11–3 12–2 13–1 14–19 15–18 16–17
8	20–16 17–15 18–14 19–13 1–12 2–11 3–10 4–9 5–8 6–7
9	6–20 7–5 8–4 9–3 10–2 11–1 12–19 13–18 14–17 15–16
10	20–15 16–14 17–13 18–12 19–11 1–10 2–9 3–8 4–7 5–6
11	5–20 6–4 7–3 8–2 9–1 10–19 11–18 12–17 13–16 14–15
12	20–14 15–13 16–12 17–11 18–10 19–9 1–8 2–7 3–6 4–5
13	4–20 5–3 6–2 7–1 8–19 9–18 10–17 11–16 12–15 13–14

Table I (*cont.*)

Round	Pairings									
14	20–13	14–12	15–11	16–10	17–9	18–8	19–7	1–6	2–5	3–4
15	3–20	4–2	5–1	6–19	7–18	8–17	9–16	10–15	11–14	12–13
16	20–12	13–11	14–10	15–9	16–8	17–7	18–6	19–5	1–4	2–3
17°	2–20	3–1	4–19	5–18	6–17	7–16	8–15	9–14	10–13	11–12
18°	20–11	12–10	13–9	14–8	15–7	16–6	17–5	18–4	19–3	1–2
19°	1–20	2–19	3–18	4–17	5–16	6–15	7–14	8–13	9–12	10–11

° Color reversals should be made in the last three rounds if someone withdraws before playing ten games:

Withdrawn player	Reversals
1	19–2 17–4 15–6 13–8 11–10
2	18–3 16–5 14–7 12–9
3	17–4 15–6 13–8 11–10 19–2 2–1
4	16–5 14–7 12–9 18–3 3–19 19–2
5	15–6 13–8 11–10 19–2 2–1 17–4 4–18 18–3
6	14–7 12–9 18–3 3–19 19–2 16–5 5–17 17–4
7	13–8 11–10 19–2 2–1 17–4 4–18 18–3 15–6 6–16 16–5
8	12–9 18–3 3–19 19–2 16–5 5–17 17–4 14–7 7–15 15–6
9	11–10 19–2 2–1 17–4 4–18 18–3 15–6 6–16 16–5 13–8 8–14 14–7
10	18–3 3–19 19–2 16–5 5–17 17–4 14–7 7–15 15–16 12–9 9–13 13–8
11	20–1 19–4 4–18 18–3 17–6 6–16 16–5 15–8 8–14 14–7 13–10 10–12 12–9
12	20–2 11–10 18–5 5–17 17–4 16–7 7–15 15–6 14–9 9–13 13–8
13	20–1 12–9 19–4 4–18 18–3 17–6 6–16 16–5 15–8 8–14 14–7

Table I (*cont.*)

Withdrawn player	Reversals
14	20–2 13–8 11–10 18–5 5–17 17–4 16–7 7–15 15–6
15	20–1 14–7 12–9 19–4 4–18 18–3 17–6 6–16 16–5
16	20–2 15–6 13–8 11–10 18–5 5–17 17–4
17	20–1 16–5 14–7 12–9 19–4 4–18 18–3
18	20–2 17–4 15–6 13–8 11–10
19	20–1 18–3 16–5 14–7 12–9
20	none

Table J
21 or 22 players

Round	Pairings
1	11–22 12–10 13–9 14–8 15–7 16–6 17–5 18–4 19–3 20–2 21–1
2	22–21 1–20 2–19 3–18 4–17 5–16 6–15 7–14 8–13 9–12 10–11
3	10–22 11–9 12–8 13–7 14–6 15–5 16–4 17–3 18–2 19–1 20–21
4	22–20 21–19 1–18 2–17 3–16 4–15 5–14 6–13 7–12 8–11 9–10
5	9–22 10–8 11–7 12–6 13–5 14–4 15–3 16–2 17–1 18–21 19–20
6	22–19 20–18 21–17 1–16 2–15 3–14 4–13 5–12 6–11 7–10 8–9
7	8–22 9–7 10–6 11–5 12–4 13–3 14–2 15–1 16–21 17–20 18–19
8	22–18 19–17 20–16 21–15 1–14 2–13 3–12 4–11 5–10 6–9 7–8
9	7–22 8–6 9–5 10–4 11–3 12–2 13–1 14–21 15–20 16–19 17–18
10	22–17 18–16 19–15 20–14 21–13 1–12 2–11 3–10 4–9 5–8 6–7
11	6–22 7–5 8–4 9–3 10–2 11–1 12–21 13–20 14–19 15–18 16–17
12	22–16 17–15 18–14 19–13 20–12 21–11 1–10 2–9 3–8 4–7 5–6
13	5–22 6–4 7–3 8–2 9–1 10–21 11–20 12–19 13–18 14–17 15–16
14	22–15 16–14 17–13 18–12 19–11 20–10 21–9 1–8 2–7 3–6 4–5
15	4–22 5–3 6–2 7–1 8–21 9–20 10–19 11–18 12–17 13–16 14–15
16	22–14 15–13 16–12 17–11 18–10 19–9 20–8 21–7 1–6 2–5 3–4
17	3–22 4–2 5–1 6–21 7–20 8–19 9–18 10–17 11–16 12–15 13–14

Table J (*cont.*)

Round	Pairings
18	22–13 14–12 15–11 16–10 17–9 18–8 19–7 20–6 21–5 1–14 2–3
19°	2–22 3–1 4–21 5–20 6–19 7–18 8–17 9–16 10–15 11–14 12–13
20°	22–12 13–11 14–10 15–9 16–8 17–7 18–6 19–5 20–4 21–3 1–2
21°	1–22 2–21 3–20 4–19 5–18 6–17 7–16 8–15 9–14 10–13 11–12

° Color reversals should be made in the last three rounds if someone withdraws before playing 11 games:

Withdrawn player	Reversals
1	21–2 19–4 17–6 15–8 13–10
2	20–3 18–5 16–7 14–9 12–11
3	19–4 17–6 15–8 13–10 21–2 2–1
4	18–5 16–7 14–9 12–11 20–3 3–21 21–2
5	17–6 15–8 13–10 21–2 2–1 19–4 4–20 20–3
6	16–7 14–9 12–11 20–3 3–21 21–2 18–5 5–19 19–4
7	15–8 13–10 21–2 2–1 19–4 4–20 20–3 17–6 6–18 18–5
8	14–9 12–11 20–3 3–21 21–2 18–5 5–19 19–4 16–7 7–17 17–6
9	13–10 21–2 2–1 19–4 4–20 20–3 17–6 6–18 18–5 15–8 8–16 16–7
10	12–11 20–3 3–21 21–2 18–5 5–19 19–4 16–7 7–17 17–6 14–9 9–15 15–8
11	21–2 2–1 19–4 4–20 20–3 17–6 6–18 18–5 15–8 8–16 16–7 13–10 10–14 14–9
12	22–2 20–5 5–19 19–4 18–7 7–17 17–6 16–9 9–15 15–8 14–11 11–13 13–10
13	22–1 12–11 21–4 4–20 20–3 19–6 6–18 18–5 17–8 8–16 16–7 15–10 10–14 14–9

Table J *(cont.)*

14	22–2 13–10 20–5 5–19 19–4 18–7 7–17 17–6 16–9 9–15 15–8
15	22–1 14–9 12–11 21–4 4–20 20–3 19–6 6–18 18–5 17–8 8–16 16–7
16	22–2 15–8 13–10 20–5 5–19 19–4 18–7 7–17 17–6
17	22–1 16–7 14–9 12–11 21–4 4–20 20–3 19–6 6–18 18–5
18	22–2 17–6 15–8 13–10 20–5 5–19 19–4
19	22–1 18–5 16–7 14–9 12–11 21–4 4–20 20–3
20	22–2 19–4 17–6 15–8 13–10
21	22–1 20–3 18–5 16–7 14–9 12–11
22	none

Table K
23 or 24 players

Round	Pairings											
1	12–24	13–11	14–10	15–9	16–8	17–7	18–6	19–5	20–4	21–3	22–2	23–1
2	24–23	1–22	2–21	3–20	4–19	5–18	6–17	7–16	8–15	9–14	10–13	11–12
3	11–24	12–10	13–9	14–8	15–7	16–6	17–5	18–4	19–3	20–2	21–2	22–23
4	24–22	23–21	1–20	2–19	3–18	4–17	5–16	6–15	7–14	8–13	9–12	10–11
5	10–24	11–9	12–8	13–7	14–6	15–5	16–4	17–3	18–2	19–1	20–23	21–22
6	24–21	22–20	23–19	1–18	2–17	3–16	4–15	5–14	6–13	7–12	8–11	9–10
7	9–24	10–8	11–7	12–6	13–5	14–4	15–3	16–2	17–1	18–23	19–22	20–21
8	24–20	21–19	22–18	23–17	1–16	2–15	3–14	4–13	5–12	6–11	7–10	8–9
9	8–24	9–7	10–6	11–5	12–4	13–3	14–2	15–1	16–23	17–22	18–21	19–20
10	24–19	20–18	21–17	22–16	23–15	1–14	2–13	3–12	4–11	5–10	6–9	7–8
11	7–24	8–6	9–5	10–4	11–3	12–2	13–1	14–23	15–22	16–21	17–20	18–19
12	24–18	19–17	20–16	21–15	22–14	23–13	1–12	2–11	3–10	4–9	5–8	6–7
13	6–24	7–5	8–4	9–3	10–2	11–1	12–23	13–22	14–21	15–20	16–19	17–18
14	24–17	18–16	19–15	20–14	21–13	22–12	23–11	1–10	2–9	3–8	4–7	5–6

Table K

Round	Pairings											
15	5–24	6–4	7–3	8–2	9–1	10–23	11–22	12–21	13–20	14–19	15–18	16–17
16	24–16	17–15	18–14	19–13	20–12	21–11	22–10	23–9	1–8	2–7	3–6	4–5
17	4–24	5–3	6–2	7–1	8–23	9–22	10–21	11–20	12–19	13–18	14–17	15–16
18	24–15	16–14	17–13	18–12	19–11	20–10	21–9	22–8	23–7	1–6	2–5	3–4
19	3–24	4–2	5–1	6–23	7–22	8–21	9–20	10–19	11–18	12–17	13–16	14–15
20	24–14	15–13	16–12	17–11	18–10	19–9	20–8	21–7	22–6	23–5	1–4	2–3
21°	2–24	3–1	4–23	5–22	6–21	7–20	8–19	9–18	10–17	11–16	12–15	13–14
22°	24–13	14–12	15–11	16–10	17–9	18–8	19–7	20–6	21–5	22–4	23–2	1–2
23°	1–24	2–23	3–22	4–21	5–20	6–19	7–18	8–17	9–16	10–15	11–14	12–13

° Color reversals should be made in the last three rounds if someone withdraws before playing 12 games:

Withdrawn player	Reversals
1	23–2 21–4 19–6 17–8 15–10 13–12
2	22–3 20–5 18–7 16–9 14–11
3	21–4 19–6 17–8 15–10 13–12 23–2 2–1
4	20–5 18–7 16–9 14–11 22–3 3–23 23–2
5	19–6 17–8 15–10 13–12 23–2 2–1 21–4 4–22 22–3
6	18–7 16–9 14–11 22–3 3–23 23–2 20–5 5–21 21–4
7	17–8 15–10 13–12 23–2 2–1 21–4 4–22 22–3 19–6 6–20 20–5
8	16–9 14–11 22–3 3–23 23–2 20–5 5–21 21–4 18–7 7–19 19–6
9	15–10 13–12 23–2 2–1 21–4 4–22 22–3 19–6 6–20 20–5 17–8 8–18 18–7
10	14–11 22–3 3–23 23–2 20–5 5–21 21–4 18–7 7–19 19–6 16–9 9–17 17–8

Table K (*cont.*)

11	13–12 23–2 2–1 21–4 4–22 22–3 19–6 6–20 20–5 17–8 8–18 18–7 15–10 10–16 16–9
12	22–3 3–23 23–2 20–5 5–21 21–4 18–7 7–19 19–6 16–9 9–17 17–8 14–11 11–15 15–10
13	24–1 23–4 4–22 22–3 21–6 6–20 20–5 19–8 8–18 18–7 17–10 10–16 16–9 15–12 12–14 14–11
14	24–2 13–12 22–5 5–21 21–4 20–7 7–19 19–6 18–9 9–17 17–8 16–11 11–15 15–10
15	24–1 14–11 23–4 4–22 22–3 21–6 6–20 20–5 19–8 8–18 18–7 17–10 10–16 16–9
16	24–2 15–10 13–12 22–5 5–21 21–4 20–7 7–19 19–6 18–9 9–17 17–8
17	24–1 16–9 14–11 23–4 4–22 22–3 21–6 6–20 20–5 19–8 8–18 18–7
18	24–2 17–8 15–10 13–12 22–5 5–21 21–4 20–7 7–19 19–6
19	24–1 18–7 16–9 14–11 23–4 4–22 22–3 21–6 6–20 20–5
20	24–2 19–6 17–8 15–10 13–12 22–5 5–21 21–4
21	24–1 20–5 18–7 16–9 14–11 23–4 4–22 22–3
22	24–2 21–4 19–6 17–8 15–10 13–12
23	24–1 22–3 20–5 18–7 16–9 14–11
24	none

CHAPTER 14

THE SCHEVENINGEN SYSTEM

The Scheveningen is a system for pairing team matches. The idea is that each member of a team contests a game with each member of the other team.

Pairing tables follow, with the teams called A and B, board numbers indicated by the subscript, and the white player indicated first in each pairing.

TABLES FOR THE SCHEVENINGEN SYSTEM

Match on 4 boards

Round 1	Round 2	Round 3	Round 4
$A_1–B_1$	$B_2–A_1$	$A_1–B_3$	$B_4–A_1$
$A_2–B_2$	$B_1–A_2$	$A_2–B_4$	$B_3–A_2$
$B_3–A_3$	$A_3–B_4$	$B_1–A_3$	$A_3–B_2$
$B_4–A_4$	$A_4–B_3$	$B_2–A_4$	$A_4–B_1$

Match on 6 Boards

Round 1	Round 2	Round 3	Round 4	Round 5	Round 6
B_1–A_1	B_2–A_1	A_1–B_3	A_1–B_4	B_5–A_1	A_1–B_6
B_5–A_2	A_2–B_1	A_2–B_2	B_6–A_2	B_4–A_2	A_2–B_3
A_3–B_4	B_3–A_3	B_1–A_3	A_3–B_5	A_3–B_6	B_2–A_3
A_4–B_2	B_4–A_4	B_6–A_4	A_4–B_1	B_3–A_4	A_4–B_5
A_5–B_3	A_5–B_6	B_5–A_5	B_2–A_5	A_5–B_1	B_4–A_5
B_6–A_6	A_6–B_5	A_6–B_4	B_3–A_6	A_6–B_2	B_1–A_6

Match on 8 boards

Round 1	Round 2	Round 3	Round 4	Round 5	Round 6	Round 7	Round 8
A_1–B_1	B_2–A_1	A_1–B_3	B_4–A_1	A_1–B_5	B_6–A_1	A_1–B_7	B_8–A_1
A_2–B_2	B_3–A_2	A_2–B_4	B_1–A_2	A_2–B_6	B_7–A_2	A_2–B_8	B_5–A_2
A_3–B_3	B_4–A_3	A_3–B_1	B_2–A_3	A_3–B_7	B_8–A_3	A_3–B_5	B_6–A_3
A_4–B_4	B_1–A_4	A_4–B_2	B_3–A_4	A_4–B_8	B_5–A_4	A_4–B_6	B_7–A_4
B_5–A_5	A_5–B_6	B_7–A_5	A_5–B_8	B_1–A_5	A_5–B_2	B_3–A_5	A_5–B_4
B_6–A_6	A_6–B_7	B_8–A_6	A_6–B_5	B_2–A_6	A_6–B_3	B_4–A_6	A_6–B_1
B_7–A_7	A_7–B_8	B_5–A_7	A_7–B_6	B_3–A_7	A_7–B_4	B_1–A_7	A_7–B_2
B_8–A_8	A_8–B_5	B_6–A_8	A_8–B_7	B_4–A_8	A_8–B_1	B_2–A_8	A_8–B_3

15

About the United States Chess Federation

186 Route 9W
New Windsor, NY 12553
(914) 562-8350

The United States Chess Federation is the official, not-for-profit U.S. membership organization for chess players and chess supporters of all ages and strengths, from beginners to Grandmasters. The USCF represents the U.S. in the World Chess Federation (FIDE), linking U.S. members to chess players around the world.

BENEFITS OF JOINING THE USCF

Members of the USCF receive an official membership card and are entitled to the following benefits, among others:

- *Chess Life* magazine—Adult and Youth members get *Chess Life* magazine every month—by itself a $35.40 newsstand value! A real treat for players of every age and skill, this internationally acclaimed chess magazine covers all the famous players and top events. Each issue is packed with articles, photos, and great games—with notes that give you insights into winning strategy. *Chess Life* also brings you the best in chess lessons. World-famous masters show you how to win. Other articles give you helpful information—you'll discover which chessplaying computer is right for you. And every month, the Tournament Life section gives you details on official tournaments you can play in—close to home and around the United States.

- *School Mates* magazine—Scholastic members get *School Mates* magazine every other month. Each issue has 16 to 20 pages of news, puzzles, games, and instruction especially for beginning chess players. Learn to play better openings, middlegames, and endgames. Find out how young champions got started! Upcoming tournaments across America are also listed.

- Play in tournaments—Hundreds of tournaments are held each year where USCF members meet and socialize. They play for a weekend or just an evening. Some of these tournaments are attended by hundreds of players—competing for large prize funds—while other events are smaller, usually held on weeknights at local clubs.

- Chess rating service—You can trace your improvement with the USCF's rating service for tournament play. Your updated rating is on your magazine label. It shows how your skill matches up against other chessplayers coast-to-coast, and the system is recognized internationally.

- Correspondence chess—Play officially rated chess by mail! You'll make many new chess friends across the country. Many chess teachers say that our correspondence chess program is the best way to improve your program. In addition to playing chess by mail, you can play chess using an electronic network. There are USCF events offered on CompuServe. Whether you enjoy competing for money prizes, a trophy, or USCF merchandise credit, you'll find a correspondence chess event to your liking with the USCF. And you'll have a ball!

- Chess product discounts—You'll get several catalogs a year, offering the finest chess products from all over the world—at significant, member's-only discounts!

  Whether you're a beginner who wants to learn the basics or an advanced player, we have everything you need. Get it all—from videos, wood sets, and classic chess books to roll-up vinyl boards, chess clocks, and state-of-the-art chess computers.

  Your savings on chess equipment and books alone are more than worth the membership dues! And you always get the USCF No-Risk Guarantee with every order.

- Free literature—You'll enjoy the game more when you find out how easy it is to play and to improve. Many kinds of information are available to members on request—FREE!

- Play chess locally—Meet people of your playing ability for over-the-board play and enjoyment. With 1,700 affiliated chess clubs all over the country, there's one near you.

- Build your mind—Whatever your age, as you play chess, you'll continue to hone your critical thinking skills.

- Support chess—Get the satisfaction of supporting a growing national sport! The USCF is a not-for-profit membership association that supports school chess programs, national championships, and U.S. participation in international competition.

- Indulge yourself—Have some fun! Chess is the ultimate game—you'll get the mental stimulation, excitement, and enjoyment. Membership in the USCF is your best way to get moving in the world's most popular and challenging strategy game.

AFFILIATION

U.S. Chess Federation affiliates form a team of 1,700 chess clubs nationwide that support chess in the U.S. These affiliates are the cornerstone of growth for chess in our country. Any group of chess players may affiliate with the USCF at a small annual fee. The benefits include the following:

- The right to sponsor officially rated tournaments.

- Commissions on certain types of membership dues collected.

- Special discounts on chess books and equipments.

- A monthly copy of *Chess Life*.

- The U.S. Chess Federation rating list and supplements, which update members' ratings based on their play in recent events.

- The right to announce their tournaments in *Chess Life* and a substantial discount on *Chess Life* display advertising for their tournaments.

- Free promotional pamphlets and materials (on request) for use in local promotions.

Affiliates are not agents of the USCF for any purpose.

WHAT IS THE USCF?

The USCF tries to provide everything a chess player needs, from chess sets to effective representation in world chess governance. In between, there's publishing *Chess Life* and *School Mates,* rating games, conducting both correspondence and in-person tournaments of all sorts, certifying tournament directors, making the best chess books and equipment available to members at discount prices, promoting our game in the media, and hundreds of other tasks large and small.

All of this activity is conducted through an office staff of about 35 and thousands of dedicated volunteers around the country, giving of their time, knowledge, and skill so others can enjoy the world's greatest game.

A SHORT HISTORY OF THE U.S. CHESS FEDERATION

The U.S. Chess Federation began in 1939 with the merger of the Western Chess Association and the National Chess Federation. The new national organization had the general aim of promoting the game of chess in the U.S., and the specific purpose of organizing the tournaments of both precursors: the invitational U.S. Championship and the U.S. Open.

The new group began with perhaps 1,000 members, and an annual yearbook. In 1945, the yearbook became a twice-monthly newspaper, improving communication among players and organizers. In 1952, the USCF took its next big step forward, with the institution of a national rating system. This provided the foundation for membership-required tournaments, and led to the establishment of a central office to administer services.

Throughout the 1950s the USCF grew steadily under a succession of dynamic presidents—Jerry Spann, Fred Cramer, and Ed Edmondson. The USCF publication, *Chess Life,* assumed the magazine format it has kept to this day, and membership grew to 4,000.

By the 1960s, membership growth led to rapid expansion of the business office. Under the leadership of Executive Director Ed Edmondson, the Federation moved to larger quarters first in Newburgh, then to its own building in New Windsor, New York. Membership had reached 12,000 when Fischer burst on the scene.

Bobby Fischer's conquest of the World Championship in 1972 led to a vast expansion of chess in the United States and of the Federation. Membership swelled to almost 60,000, services expanded exponentially, and *Chess Life* merged with *Chess Review,* the other major U.S. chess magazine. But the post-Fischer letdown brought a time of troubles.

When Fischer failed to defend his title in 1975, many of those he had drawn to the game fell away. The USCF met this challenge with improved services, promotion, and outreach to the untapped pool of casual players. A solid groundwork was laid for the new opportunities of the 1980s.

The eighties ushered in a new period of growth, due in large part to the progress and spread of chess-playing computers. The USCF took full advantage of the new situation, with an aggressive program of promotion and expansion, finding new ways to spread the word of chess while continuing to serve the loyal core of tournament players. By the end of the decade, membership again approached the peak of the "Fischer boom." By 1993, membership had shot past all previous levels, as a result of well-developed, popular programs.

Amid these changes, the USCF remains fully committed to its traditional goals and programs, balancing excellence, growth, and service to its members.

16

How to Read and Write Chess

Chessplayers have invented several systems of *notation* so they can record the moves of their games. This chapter explains a system that is simple to learn and to use, known as *algebraic* notation.

In this system, each square on the board is given a name. Each *file*, or up-and-down row of squares, is assigned a letter—starting from "a" on white's left-hand side and running through "h." Each *rank*, or side-to-side row, is numbered "1" through "8," starting from the row of squares nearest white and proceeding up the board toward black.

The diagram on page 262 shows how easy it is to find the name of each square.

What square is the white bishop on? First, find out what file it is on—the "b" file. Then check its rank. It's on rank "2." Put these two together, and you have "b2"—that's where the bishop is! How about white's king? It's on "e1." Similarly, the white rook is on "a1," the white knight on "g4," the white queen on "f1," the white pawn on "g5," the black king on "e8," the black queen on "f7," the black pawn on "f6," and the black rook on "h8."

Black

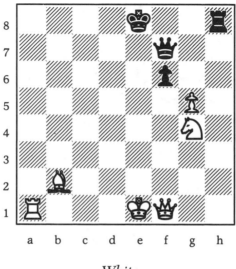

White

To identify the pieces, we use the first letter of each one's name, except that the knight is "N" because "K" is used for the king. No symbol is needed for the pawns.

To record a move, write the letter for the piece that is moving and the name of the square it is moving to. In the diagram, for example, white could move his king one square toward his rook. This is written as "Kd1." Moving the rook forward one square would be written as "Ra2."

Since pawns always stay on the same file (except to capture), we need only record the square a pawn moves to. For example, if the black pawn moves forward one square, that would be "f5." (Remember, black is moving from the top of the board down.)

Captures are recorded using an "x" after the letter for the capturing piece. For instance, if white's bishop captured the black pawn, we would write "Bxf6." When a pawn captures something, we name the file the pawn was on and the square where it makes the capture. If white's pawn captured black's pawn, the move would be "gxf6." If black's pawn captured white's, it would be "fxg5."

The symbol for check is a plus sign. In the example, black could play "Qe6+." How would we record white's knight taking the black pawn with check? The answer is "Nxf6+."

Castling on the *kingside* (as black may do in our example) is written "0-0." White may castle *queenside*, which is written "0-0-0." An easy way to remember is that, in each case, the number of zeros is the same as the number of squares the rook moves in castling.

When a player promotes a pawn, we follow the move with an equal sign and the letter for the piece that the pawn changes into. If black had a pawn on h2 in our example, he could promote it to a queen with "h1=Q."

When it is possible for a player to move more than one of the same type of piece to a square, we must also identify which piece is moving. For example, let's say white has rooks on a1 and d1. If white wants to move one of the rooks to c1, we would have have to write either "Rac1" or "Rdc1," depending on which rook was chosen. Similarly, if black has rooks on h8 and h5 and played one of them to h7, we would write "R5h7" or "R8h7."

Sometimes we comment on the quality of a player's moves by following them with an exclamation mark or a question mark.

!! An excellent move
! A good move
!? An interesting move

?! A dubious move

? A bad move

?? A very bad move

With a little practice, algebraic notation will become second nature to you. Here's a short, silly game you can play over to test yourself. When you are through, you should have reached the position in the diagram:

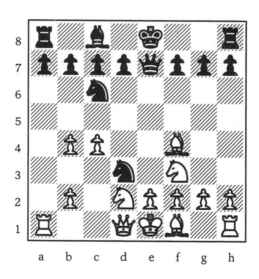

1. d4 Nf6 2. c4 e5 3. dxe5 Ng4 4. Bf4 Bb4+ 5. Nd2 Nc6 6. Nf3 Qe7 7. a3 Ngxe5! 8. axb4?? Nd3 mate.

Some players (and publications) use a system known as "long algebraic." This is identical to algebraic with the addition of identifying the square a piece moved *from* as well as the one it moved *to*. For example, in algebraic the first move for each player might be recorded as "1. d4 Nf6"; in long algebraic, these would be written "1. d2-d4 Ng8-f6."

Other popular systems of chess notation that you ought to know about include "figurine algebraic," which gives a symbol rather than a letter for each piece, and "descriptive," a totally different system. For a free description of these systems, ask for "In Writing" by sending a stamped, self-addressed envelope to U.S. Chess Federation, 186 Route 9W, New Windsor, NY 12553.

Chess is even more fun when you see yourself improving! The following winning tips were written for you by International Grandmaster Arthur Bisguier, former U.S. Champion and six-time U.S. Open Champion. You'll find that the few, expertly written pages of this chapter can help you improve your results dramatically. Read carefully, and you'll have a great surprise for that chess shark at work or for your neighborhood chess champion!

17

TEN TIPS TO WINNING CHESS

by International Grandmaster
Arthur Bisguier

GETTING STARTED

Chess is a game of strategy and tactics. Each player commands an army of 16 *chessmen* — pawns and other pieces (the king, queen, bishops, knights, and rooks).

A well-played chess game has three stages. In the *opening,* the players bring out their forces in preparation for combat. The *middlegame* begins as the players maneuver for position and carry out attacks and counterattacks. The final stage is the *endgame,* when, with fewer pawns and pieces left on the board, it is safer for the kings to come out and join the final battle.

As play proceeds, each player will capture some of the opponent's men; often, the capturing pieces are immediately recaptured. As long as the piece a player gives up is generally equal to the piece he gets in return, we say the players are *exchanging.* If you unintentionally place a piece where it can be captured without getting a piece of equal value in return, we say that you put that piece *en prise.* (This is a French term that literally means "in take.") Sometimes a player may place a piece en prise in order to trick an opponent. If the opponent captures the offered man, it may leave him open to attack.

YOU'RE READY TO GO!

It's time for you to take a look at these ten tips to help you learn some simple ways to win more games:

1. Look at your opponent's move.

2. Make the best possible move.

3. Have a plan.

4. Know what the pieces are worth.

5. Develop quickly and well.

6. Control the center.

7. Keep your king safe.

8. Know when to trade pieces.

9. Think about the endgame.

10. Always be alert.

Don't rush. Take your time and be sure to study the examples carefully. Then go out and practice — and have some fun! If you have trouble reading chess notation, look back at Chapter 16, "How to Read and Write Chess."

1. Look at your opponent's move!

Every time your opponent makes a move, you should stop and think: Why was that move chosen? Is a piece in danger? Are there any other threats I should watch out for? What sort of plan does my opponent have in mind?

Only by defending against your opponent's threats will you be able to successfully carry out your own strategies. Once you figure out what your opponent is attempting to do, you can play to nip those plans in the bud.

Answers to the following examples are after Example L.

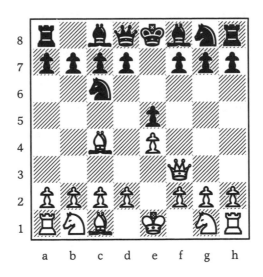

Example A
Black to move

Pretend you're playing black in this position. White has just moved his queen to f3. What's the threat? How should you move to meet his threat?

2. Make the best possible move.

When you are considering a move, ask yourself these questions:

> **a.** Will the piece I'm moving go to a better square than the one it's on now?

> **b.** Can I improve my position even more by increasing the effectiveness of a different piece?

> **c.** Does this move help to defend against my opponent's threats?

> **d.** Will the piece I move be safe on its new square?

> > **i.** If it's a pawn, consider: Can I keep it protected from attack?
> > **ii.** If it's another piece, consider: Can the enemy drive it away, thus making me lose valuable time?

Even if your intended move has good points, it may not be the best move at that moment. Emanuel Lasker, a former world champion, said: "When you see a good move, wait—look for a better one!" Following this advice is bound to improve your chess.

Example B
White to move

You're white in this position. Black has just played cxd4 and is temporarily a pawn ahead. What's the *best* move you can make? Don't be too hasty!

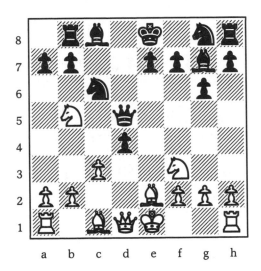

3. Have a plan.

If you threaten something here in one move, something over there in the next move, and so forth, your opponent will have an easy time defending. Your pieces have to work together to be effective. Just imagine each instrument in an orchestra playing a different tune!

When you develop a plan, your men can work in harmony. For example, you might plan to attack your opponent's king; one piece alone probably wouldn't be able to do much, but the combined strength of several pieces makes a powerful attacking force. Another plan could be taking control of all the squares in a particular area of the board.

The chess men are your "team"; to be a good "coach," you have to use all of their strengths together.

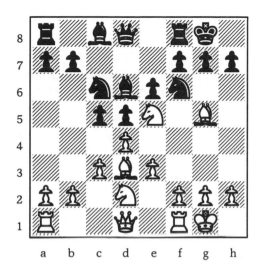

Example C
White to move

Look at this position carefully. What would be a good plan for white? What moves would be involved in carrying out this plan?

4. Know what the pieces are worth.

When you are considering giving up some of your pieces for some of your opponent's, you should think about the *values* of the men, and not just how many each player possesses. The player whose men add up to a greater value will usually have the advantage. So a crucial step in making decisions is to add up the *material*, or value, of each player's men.

The pawn is the least valuable piece, so it is a convenient unit of measure. It moves slowly, and can never go backward.

Knights and bishops are approximately equal, worth about three pawns each. The knight is the only piece that can jump over other men. The bishops are speedier, but each one can reach only half the squares.

A rook moves quickly and can reach every square; its value is five pawns. A combination of two *minor pieces* (knights and bishops) can often subdue a rook.

A queen is worth nine pawns, almost as much as two rooks. It can move to the greatest number of squares in most positions.

The king can be a valuable fighter, too, but we do not evaluate its strength because it cannot be traded.

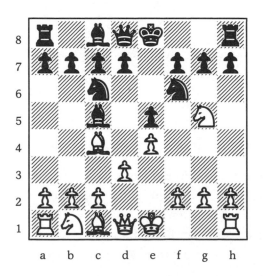

Example D
Black to move

Here's a harder problem that requires you to use several of the tips you've read about so far. Pretend you're playing black in this position. First of all, what is white's threat? Second, what move should you make to meet this threat? Finally, if white went ahead with his "threat" even after you move, what would be the result?

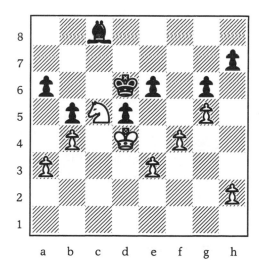

Example E

We know that a knight and a bishop are usually worth about the same. Which would you say is stronger in this position?

Example F
White to move

White is about to make a move here. Is the black knight strong or weak? Would it be better or worse to have a bishop on that square?

5. Develop quickly and well.

Time is a very important element of chess. The player whose men are ready for action sooner will be able to control the course of the game. If you want to be that player, you have to develop your men efficiently to powerful posts.

Many inexperienced players like to move a lot of pawns at the beginning of the game to control space on the chessboard. But you can't win with pawns alone! Since knights, bishops, rooks, and queens can move farther than pawns and threaten more distant targets, it's a good idea to bring them out soon, after you've moved enough pawns to guarantee that your stronger pieces won't be chased back by your opponent's pawns. After all the other pieces are developed, it's easier to see what pawns you should move to fit in with your plans.

It's tempting to bring the queen out very early, because it's the most powerful piece. But your opponent can chase your queen back by threatening it with less valuable pieces. Look at Example A: after 1. ... Nf6, black threatens to drive the white queen away with either 2. ... Nd4 or 2. ... d6 and 3. ... Bg4.

Instead of just moving pieces out, try to determine the best square for each piece and bring it there in as few moves as possible. This may save you from wasting moves later in the game.

6. Control the center.

In many cases, the person who controls the four squares at the center of the board will have the better game. There are simple reasons for this.

First, a piece in the center controls more of the board than one that is somewhere else. As an example, place one knight on a center square and another in one of the corners of the board. The knight in the center can move to eight different squares, while the "cornered" one only has two possible moves!

Second, control of the center provides an avenue for your pieces to travel from one side of the board to the other. To move a piece across the board, you will often have to take it through the center. If your pieces can get to the other side faster than your opponent's pieces, you will often be able to mount a successful attack there before he can bring over enough pieces to defend.

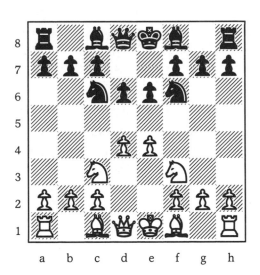

Example G

Each player has moved two knights and two pawns. Which side has better control of the center?

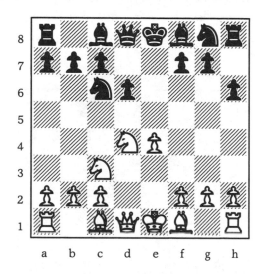

Example H
Once again, think carefully: Which side stands better in the center?
Why?

7. Keep your king safe.

Everyone knows that the object of the game is to checkmate the
opponent's king. But sometimes a player thinks about his own plans
so much that he forgets that his opponent is also king hunting!

It's generally a good idea to place your king in a safe place by castling early in the game. Once you've castled, you should be very careful about advancing the pawns near your king. They are like

bodyguards; the farther away they go, the easier it is for your opponent's pieces to get close to your king. (For this reason, it's often good to try to force your opponent to move the pawns near his king.)

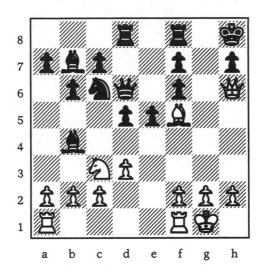

Example I

We've learned many important objectives: advantage in material, better development, control of the center, and now king safety. Which of these is the *most* important?

8. Know when to trade pieces.

The best time to trade men is when you can capture men worth more than the ones you will be giving up, which is called "winning material" (see tip 4, "Know what the men are worth"). But the opportunity to do this may not arise if your opponent is very careful.

Since you will probably have many chances to exchange men on an "even" basis, it's useful to know when you should or shouldn't do this. There are several important considerations.

As a general rule, if you have the initiative (your pieces are better developed, and you're controlling the game), try not to exchange men unless it increases your advantage in some clear way. The fewer men each player has, the weaker the attacking player's threats become, and the easier it is for the defending side to meet these threats.

Another time not to trade pieces is when your opponent has a cramped position with little space for the pieces to maneuver. It's tough to move a lot of pieces around in a cramped position, but easier to move just a few.

One sort of advantage you can often gain by trading pieces is a weakening of your opponent's pawn structure. If, for example, you can capture with a piece that your opponent can only recapture in a way that will give him "doubled pawns" (see glossary), it will often be to your advantage to make that trade.

The player who is ahead in material will usually benefit from trades. It's sort of like basketball or soccer; five players will sometimes have trouble scoring against four opposing players, but take away three from each side and the stronger team will find it easier to score with two players against one.

So, to summarize: It's usually good to trade pieces if your opponent has the initiative, if you have a cramped position, if you can weaken your opponent's pawn structure, or if you are ahead in material. There are exceptions, of course, but following these rules should bring you considerable success.

9. Think about the endgame.

From the time the game begins, you should remember that every move you make may affect your chances in the endgame. For instance, in the earlier parts of the game, a knight and a bishop are about equally powerful. Toward the end of the game, though, when there are fewer men in the way, the bishop can exert its influence in all parts of the board at once, while the knight still takes a long time to get anywhere. So before you trade a bishop for a knight, think not just about the next few moves but also about the endgame.

Pawn structure is crucial in the endgame. When you capture one of your opponent's men with a pawn, you'll often create an open file that will help your rooks and queen to reach your opponent's side of the board, but you may also get doubled pawns. Since doubled pawns cannot defend each other, they are liability in the endgame. If your opponent survives the middlegame, you may have an uphill fight later.

Concentrate on your immediate plans, as well as your opponent's—but always keep the endgame in mind!

Example J
From the very first moves of the game, it's important to have a good pawn formation. How would you assess white's pawn structure in this position?

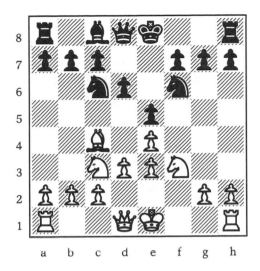

Example K

In the endgame, it's common to see a pawn run to the end of the board and promoted to a queen. So, pawns are a great thing to hang on to. Study this diagram. Who has the "healthier" pawns, white or black?

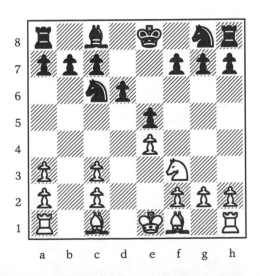

10. Always be alert.

There is a tendency for people to relax once they have reached a good position or to give up hope if their position is very bad. These attitudes are natural, but both lead to bad results.

Many players—even world champions—have achieved winning positions, only to lose because they relaxed too soon. Even the best position won't win by itself; you have to give it some help! In almost any position, the "losing" player will still be able to make threats. The "winning" player has to be alert enough to prevent these positions.

Advice: If you have a better position, watch out! One careless move could throw away your hard-won advantage. Even as you're carrying out your winning plans, you must watch out for your opponent's threats.

Conversely, if you have a worse position, don't give up! Keep making strong moves, and try to complicate the position as much as possible. If your opponent slips, you may get the chance to make a comeback. Remember: Where there's life, there's hope.

So be alert all the time, no matter what the position is like. A little bit of extra care can pay off in a big way.

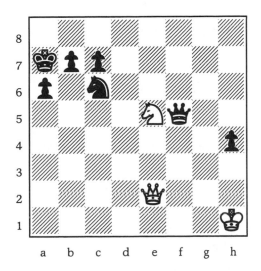

Example L

Black to move

Pretend that you're the general of the black army in the position shown above. You have, as you can see, an easily won game—since you are four pawns ahead. But white has just moved his knight to e5. This looks like a silly move, since you could capture this knight with your own knight or with your queen.

But look again. Don't relax because you're winning too easily! If you captured white's knight with your knight, what would be his best (and surprising) move?

Answers

Example A: White is threatening to play Qxf7 checkmate! Black defends best by moving 1. . . . Nf6. This move meets the threat and develops the knight to a good square.

Example B: White can win his pawn back immediately with a move like 1. Nbxd4. But did you look for a better move? By playing 1. Nc7+, you can win black's queen!

Example C: One good plan for white here would be an attack on black's king. Once he has decided to do this, white should figure out how to bring his pieces to that area of the board. After 1. f4, for example, white can bring his rook to f3 and then to g3 or h3, where it would exert pressure around black's king.

Example D: White's threat here is to play Nxf7, with a double attack on black's queen and rook. Black should simply castle (0-0). Now if white continues with his "threat," black merely captures the knight and the bishop. That continuation would be

1. . . . 0-0 2. Nxf7 Rxf7 3. Bxf7+ Kxf7

You can see that white has traded bishop and knight for black's rook and pawn. That's about an even exchange, except—in the early part of the game especially—these two pieces are often handier than the rook. Note that white has exchanged his only developed pieces, while black has a bishop and two knights ready to attack.

Example E: Here is an example where a knight is better than a bishop. The bishop is trapped behind its own pawns, while the knight is free to hop in and out of black's position. It will be easy to maneuver the knight to f6, and if black defends the pawn at h7 with his king, white's king will enter black's position by way of c5 or e5, with decisive effect.

Example F: The tables turn; black's knight moves so slowly that after 1. h6, the pawn cannot be prevented from reaching the eighth rank and being promoted. If black has a bishop on b6 instead of the knight, he could answer 1. h6 with 1. . . . Bd4+, when the bishop would control the crucial square h8.

Example G: It is easy to see that white has control of the center in this position. His pawns occupy center squares, while black's pawns are not yet involved in the struggle. Note how easy it will be for white to develop his bishops to squares that help control the center, while black's bishops are hemmed in by his own pawns.

Example H: There, too, white has more central control and a freer game. The pawn at e4 attacks two squares on black's half of the board and helps control d5, preventing the pawn on d6 from advancing while providing protection in the event that white plays Nd5. White can put a rook on d1 later to put pressure on the d-file.

Example I: This example shows why king safety is the most important factor. Black is ahead in material by a bishop and a pawn, has control of the center, and has more pieces developed, but this is all worthless because he is unable to prevent white from playing Qxh7, checkmate!

Example J: White has doubled pawns on the e-file, normally a disadvantage. Here, though, the pawn on e3 controls the vital squares d4 and f4. Also, white can mount an attack by putting his rooks and queen on the f-file, which is no longer blocked by one of his pawns.

These doubled pawns could turn out to be weak in the endgame. Therefore, white should avoid unnecessary exchanges and concentrate on winning in the middlegame.

Example K: Black has the "healthier" set of pawns here, since white has doubled pawns on both the a- and c-files. Such pawns cannot protect each other. Also, notice that the trailing or "caboose" pawn must stay forever behind his leader. A set of doubled pawns are worth little more than one pawn.

Example L: Did you get this one? It's a toughy. As black in this superior position, if you capture white's knight on e5 with your knight (1. . . . Nxe5) instead of your queen (1. . . . Qxe5), then white should move 2. Qf2+!

As you can see, this forces black's queen to capture white's queen, placing the white king in stalemate. The game would be a draw!

So stay alert. This type of surprising sacrifice can happen surprisingly often!

Glossary

CENTER. The four squares in the middle of the board.

DEVELOPMENT. The process of moving pieces from their original squares to positions where they can better aid the player's plans.

DOUBLED PAWNS. Two pawns of the same color on the same file. Generally considered a disadvantage because the pawns cannot defend each other.

ENDGAME. Also called "ending," it is the third and final phase of the game, in which each player has relatively few pieces remaining. The *promotion* of pawns is a common goal in the endgame.

FILE. A vertical (up and down) row of squares. The players' kings start the game on the same *file*.

INITIATIVE. Control of the game, usually due to better placement of men and easier access to weaknesses in the opponent's position.

MATERIAL. The chess pieces. The player whose remaining pieces are of greater value is said to have a "material advantage."

MIDDLEGAME. The second phase of the game, in which *develop-*

ment of the pieces has mostly been completed and many pieces are captured or traded as the players pursue their plans.

OPENING. The first phase of the game, in which players concentrate on *development*, gaining room for their pieces to maneuver, and on bringing their kings to safety.

PROMOTION. When a pawn reaches the eighth (last) rank, the player "promotes" it to his choice of a queen, rook, bishop, or knight.

RANK. A horizontal (left to right) row of squares. The pawns start the game on each player's second *rank*.

18

WORLD AND NATIONAL CHAMPIONS

World Chess Champions

Year	Name	Country
1858	Paul Morphy	USA +
1866–1894	Wilhelm Steinitz	Austro-Hungary
1894–1921	Emanuel Lasker	Germany
1921–1927	Jose Raoul Capablanca	Cuba
1927–1935	Alexander Alekhine	Russia-France
1935–1937	Max Euwe	Netherlands
1937–1946°	Alexander Alekhine	Russia-France
1947	Vacant	
1948–1957	Mikhail Botvinnik	Soviet Union
1957–1958	Vassily Smyslov	Soviet Union
1958–1960°	Mikhail Botvinnik	Soviet Union
1960–1961	Mikhail Tal	Soviet Union
1961–1963°	Mikhail Botvinnik	Soviet Union
1963–1969	Tigran Petrosian	Soviet Union
1969–1972	Boris Spassky	Soviet Union

World Chess Champions

Year	Name	Country
1972–1975	Robert James Fischer	United States
1975–1985	Anatoly Karpov	Soviet Union
1985–	Garry Kasparov	Soviet Union

° Indicates a rematch.

+ Indicates unofficial but widely recognized world champion.

World Women's Chess Champions

Year	Name	Country
1927–1944	Vera Menchik	Czechoslovakia
1944–1950	Vacant	
1950–1953	Lyudmila V. Rudenko	Soviet Union
1953–1956	Yelizavyeta Bykova	Soviet Union
1956–1958	Olga Nikolayevna Rubtsova	Soviet Union
1958–1962	Yelizavyeta Bykova	Soviet Union
1962–1978	Nona Gaprindashvili	Soviet Union
1978–1991	Maia Chiburdanidze	Soviet Union
1992–	Xie Jun	China

U.S. Champions

1845–1857—Charles Stanley

1857–1871—Paul Morphy

1871–1890—George H. Mackenzie

1890–1891—Jackson Showalter

1891–1894—Solomon Lipschutz

1894—Jackson Showalter

1894–1895—Albert Hodges
1895–1897—Jackson Showalter
1897–1906—Harry Nelson Pillsbury
1906–1909—Jackson Showalter
1909–1936—Frank J. Marshall
1936—Samuel Reshevsky
1938—Samuel Reshevsky
1940—Samuel Reshevsky
1942—Samuel Reshevsky
1944—Arnold Denker
1946—Samuel Reshevsky
1948—Herman Steiner
1951—Larry Evans
1954—Arthur Bisguier
1957–58—Bobby Fischer
1958–59—Bobby Fischer
1959–60—Bobby Fischer
1960–61—Bobby Fischer
1961–62—Larry Evans
1962–63—Bobby Fischer
1963–64—Bobby Fischer
1965—Bobby Fischer
1966—Bobby Fischer
1968—Larry Evans
1969—Samuel Reshevsky
1972—Robert Byrne (play-off)
1973—John Grefe, Lubomir Kavalek
1974—Walter Browne
1975—Walter Browne

1977—Walter Browne
1978—Lubomir Kavalek
1980—Walter Browne, Larry Evans
1981—Walter Browne, Yasser Seirawan
1983—Walter Browne, Larry Christiansen, Roman
    Dzindzichashvili
1984—Lev Alburt
1985—Lev Alburt
1986—Yasser Seirawan
1987—Nick deFirmian, Joel Benjamin
1988—Michael Wilder
1989—Roman Dzindzichashvili, Yasser Seirawan, Stuart Rachels
1990—Lev Alburt
1991—Gata Kamsky
1992—Patrick Wolff

U.S. Open Champions

1900—Louis Uedemann
1901—N. M. MacLeod
1902—Louis Uedemann
1903—Max Judd
1904—Stasch Mlotkowski
1905—E. F. Schrader
1906—George Wolbrecht
1907—Einar Michelsen
1908—E. P. Elliott
1909—Oscar Chajes
1910—George Wolbrecht

1911—Charles Blake
1912—E. P. Elliott
1913—Bradford Jefferson, Sr.
1914—Bradford Jefferson, Sr.
1915—Jackson Showalter
1916—Edward Lasker
1917—Edward Lasker
1918—Boris Kostic
1919—Edward Lasker
1920—Edward Lasker
1921—Edward Lasker
1922—Samuel Factor
1923—Stasch Mlotkowski, Norman Whitaker
1924—Carlos Torre
1925—Abraham Kupchik
1926—Leon Stolzenberg
1927—Albert Margolis
1928—Leon Stolzenberg
1929—Herman Hahlbohm
1930—Samuel Factor, Norman Whitaker
1931—Samuel Reshevsky
1932—Reuben Fine
1933—Reuben Fine
1934—Reuben Fine, Samuel Reshevsky
1935—Reuben Fine
1936—I. A. Horowitz
1937—D. S. Polland
1938—I. A. Horowitz, Isaac Kashdan
1939—Reuben Fine
1940—Reuben Fine

1941—Reuben Fine
1942—Herman Steiner, Dan Yanofsky
1943—I. A. Horowitz
1944—Samuel Reshevsky
1945—Anthony Santasiere
1946—Herman Steiner
1947—Isaac Kashdan
1948—Weaver W. Adams
1949—Albert Sandrin, Jr.
1950—Arthur Bisguier
1951—Larry Evans
1952—Larry Evans
1953—Donald Byrne
1954—Larry Evans, Arturo Pomar
1955—Nicolas Rossolimo
1956—Arthur Bisguier
1957—Robert Fischer
1958—E. Cobo-Arteaga
1959—Arthur Bisguier
1960—Robert Byrne
1961—Pal Benko
1962—Antonio Medina
1963—William Lombardy
1964—Pal Benko
1965—Pal Benko, William Lombardy
1966—Pal Benko, Robert Byrne
1967—Pal Benko
1968—Bent Larsen
1969—Pal Benko
1970—Bent Larsen

1971—Walter Browne, Larry Evans
1972—Walter Browne
1973—Norman Weinstein
1974—Pal Benko, Vlastimil Hort
1975—Pal Benko, William Lombardy
1976—Anatoly Lein, Leonid Shamkovich
1977—Leonid Shamkovich
1978—Joseph Bradford
1979—Florin Gheorghiu
1980—John Fedorowicz, Florin Gheorghiu
1981—Florin Gheorghiu, Larry Christiansen, Jeremy Silman, Nick deFirmian, John Meyer
1982—Andrew Soltis, William Martz
1983—Larry Christiansen, Viktor Korchnoi
1984—Roman Dzindzichashvili, Sergey Kudrin
1985—Yasser Seirawan, Boris Spassky, Joel Benjamin
1986—Larry Christiansen
1987—Lev Alburt
1988—Dmitry Gurevich
1989—Lev Alburt
1990—Yasser Seirawan
1991—Michael Rohde
1992—Gregory Kaidanov
1993—Alexander Shabalov

U.S. Women's Champions

1937—Adele Rivero
1938—Mona Karff
1940—Adele Rivero
1941—Mona Karff

1942—Mona Karff

1944—Gisela Gresser

1946—Mona Karff

1948—Gisela Gresser, Mona Karff

1951—Mary Bain

1953—Mona Karff

1955—Gisela Gresser, Nancy Roos

1957—Sonja Graf, Gisela Gresser

1959—Lisa Lane

1962—Gisela Gresser

1964—Sonja Graf

1965—Gisela Gresser

1966—Gisela Gresser, Lisa Lane

1967—Gisela Gresser

1969—Gisela Gresser

1972—Eva Aronson, Marilyn Koput

1974—Mona Karff

1975—Diane Savereide

1976—Diane Savereide

1977—Rachel Crotto, Diane Savereide

1978—Rachel Crotto, Diane Savereide

1979—Rachel Crotto

1981—Diane Savereide

1984—Diane Savereide

1986—Inna Izrailov

1987—Anna Achsharumova

1989—Alexey Root

1990—Elena Donaldson

1991—Irina Levitina, Esther Epstein

1992—Irina Levitina

1993—Irina Levitina, Elena Donaldson

19

A Historical Crosstable of the U.S. Chess Federation

Year	U.S. Open Business Meeting	President (1)	Executive Officer (2)	Membership
1940	Dallas, TX	George Sturgis	None	1,000 (appr.)
1941	St. Louis, MO	"	"	"
1942	Dallas, TX	"	"	"
1943	Syracuse, NY	"	"	"
1944	Boston, MA	"	"	"
1945	Peoria, IL	Elbert Wagner	"	"
1946	Pittsburgh, PA	"	"	"
1947	Corpus Christi, TX	"	"	"
1948	Baltimore, MD	"	"	"
1949	Omaha, NE	"	"	"
1950	Detroit, MI	Paul Giers	"	"
1951	Fort Worth, TX	Harold Phillips	"	"
1952	Tampa, FL	"	"	1,127
1953	Milwaukee, WI	"	Kenn. Harkness	1,496
1954	New Orleans, LA	"	"	2,184
1955	Long Beach, CA	Frank Graves	"	2,408

Year	U.S. Open Business Meeting	President (1)	Executive Officer (2)	Membership
1956	Oklahoma City, OK	"	"	2,220
1957	Cleveland, OH	"	"	2,100
1958	Rochester, MN	Jerry Spann	"	2,668
1959	Omaha, NE	"	"	3,820
1960	St. Louis, MO	"	Frank Brady	4,579
1961	San Francisco, CA	Fred Cramer	"	5,543
1962	San Antonio, TX	"	Jos. Reinhardt	6,120
1963	Chicago, IL	"	"	7,454
1964	Boston, MA	Ed Edmondson	"	8,383
1965	San Juan, PR	"	Ed Edmondson	8,625
1966	Seattle, WA	"	"	9,466
1967	Atlanta, GA	Marshall Rohland	"	9,943
1968	Snowmass, CO	"	"	11,202
1969	Lincoln, NE	"	"	13,488
1970	Boston, MA	Leroy Dubeck	"	22,623
1971	Ventura, CA	"	"	26,536
1972	Atlantic City, NJ	"	"	30,844
1973	Chicago, IL	Frank Skoff	"	59,250
1974	New York, NY	"	"	59,779
1975	Lincoln, NE	Frank Skoff	Ed Edmondson	51,842
1976	Fairfax, VA	George Koltanowski	"	49,179
1977	Columbus, OH	"	Martin Morrison	46,175
1978	Phoenix, AZ	"	"	48,837
1979	Chicago, IL	Gary Sperling	Gerry Dullea	48,707
1980	Atlanta, GA	"	"	47,805
1981	Palo Alto, CA	"	"	49,628
1982	St. Paul, MN	Tim Redman	"	51,925
1983	Pasadena, CA	"	"	52,576

Year	U.S. Open Business Meeting	President (1)	Executive Officer (2)	Membership
1984	Fort Worth, TX	"	"	53,516
1985	Hollywood, FL	E. Steven Doyle	"	54,599
1986	Somerset, NJ	"	"	55,291
1987	Portland, OR	"	"	55,944
1988	Boston, MA	Harold Winston	Al Lawrence	52,964
1989	Chicago, IL	"	"	51,595
1990	Jacksonville, FL	"	"	52,898
1991	Los Angeles, CA	Maxim Dlugy	"	57,617
1992	Dearborn, MI	"	"	63,279
1993	Philadelphia, PA	"	"	68,746

1. A change of presidents occurs immediately after a business meeting; for example, Tim Redman succeeded Gary Sperling in August 1981, but Sperling chaired the 1981 meeting.

2. Until Ed Edmondson was named executive director in 1967, this position was called business manager.

20

INTERNATIONAL (FIDE) LAWS OF CHESS

These rules are for international events recognized by the World Chess Federation. The Laws of Chess approved by FIDE General Assembly at Manila in 1992.

THE LAWS OF CHESS

The Laws of Chess cannot cover all possible situations that may arise during a game, nor can they regulate all administrative questions. Where cases are not precisely regulated by an article of the Laws, it should be possible to reach a correct decision by studying analogous situations, which are discussed in the Laws. The Laws assume that arbiters have the necessary competence, sound judgment, and absolute objectivity. Too detailed a rule might deprive the arbiter of his or her freedom of judgment and thus prevent him or her from finding the solution to a problem dictated by fairness, logic, and special factors.

FIDE appeals to all chess players and federations to accept this view.

Any chess federation that already operates or wants to introduce more detailed rules, is free to do so provided:

a. they do not conflict in any way with the official FIDE Laws of Chess;

b. they are limited to the territory of the federation in question; and

c. they are not valid for any FIDE match, championship or qualifying event, or for a FIDE title or rating tournament.

In these Laws, the words "he," "him," and "his" are used indiscriminately to include "she," and "her."

ARTICLE 1. THE CHESSBOARD

The game of chess is played between two opponents by moving pieces on a square board called a "chessboard."

1.1   The chessboard is composed of 64 equal squares alternately light (the "white" squares) and dark (the "black" squares).

1.2   The chessboard is placed between the players in such a way that the near corner square to the right of each player is white.

1.3   The eight vertical columns of squares are called "files."

1.4   The eight horizontal rows of squares are called "ranks."

1.5   The lines of squares of the same color, touching corner to corner, are called "diagonals."

ARTICLE 2. THE PIECES

2.1   At the beginning of the game, one player has 16 light-colored pieces (the "white" pieces) and the other has 16 dark-colored pieces (the "black" pieces).

2.2 These pieces are as follows:

A white king, usually indicated by the symbol:

A white queen, usually indicated by the symbol:

Two white rooks, usually indicated by the symbol:

Two white bishops, usually indicated by the symbol:

Two white knights, usually indicated by the symbol:

Eight white pawns, usually indicated by the symbol:

A black king, usually indicated by the symbol:

A black queen, usually indicated by the symbol:

Two black rooks, usually indicated by the symbol:

Two black bishops, usually indicated by the symbol:

Two black knights, usually indicated by the symbol:

Eight black pawns, usually indicated by the symbol:

2.3   **The initial position of the pieces on the chessboard is as follows:**

ARTICLE 3. THE RIGHT TO MOVE

3.1   The player with the white pieces commences the game. The players alternate in making one move at a time until the game is completed.

3.2   A player is said to "have the move" when his opponent's move has been completed. See Article 6.

ARTICLE 4. THE GENERAL DEFINITION OF THE MOVE

4.1   With the exception of castling (Article 5.1b), a move is the transfer by a player of one of his pieces from one square to another square that is either vacant or occupied by an opponent's piece.

4.2   No piece except the rook when castling (Article 5.1b) and the knight (Article 5.5) may cross a square occupied by another piece.

4.3   A piece played to a square occupied by an opponent's piece captures it as part of the same move. The captured piece must be removed immediately from the chessboard by the player making the capture. See Article 5.6c for capturing en passant.

ARTICLE 5. THE MOVES OF THE PIECES

5.1. The king.

a. Except when castling, the king moves to any adjoining square that is not attacked by an opponent's piece.

b. Castling is a move of the king and either rook, counting as a single move of the king and executed as follows: The king is transferred from its original square two squares toward either rook on the same rank; then that rook is transferred over the king to the square the king has just crossed.

c. If a player touches a rook and then his king, he may not castle with that rook, and the situation will be governed by Articles 7.2 and 7.3.

d. If a player, intending to castle, touches the king first, or king and rook at the same time, and it then appears that castling is illegal, the player may choose either to move his king or to castle on the other side, provided that castling on that side is legal. If the king has no legal moves, the player is free to make any legal move.

e. Castling is illegal:

> **i.** if the king has already been moved, or

> **ii.** with a rook that has already been moved.

f. Castling is prevented for the time being:

> **i.** if the king's original square or the square that the king must cross over or that it is to occupy is attacked by an opponent's piece, or

> **ii.** if there is any piece between the king and the rook with which castling is to be effected.

5.2. The queen.

The queen moves to any square (except as limited by Article 4.2) on the file, rank, or diagonals on which it stands.

5.3. The rook.

The rook moves to any square (except as limited by Article 4.2) on the file or rank on which it stands.

5.4. The bishop.

The bishop moves to any square (except as limited by Article 4.2) on the diagonals on which it stands.

5.5. The knight.

The knight's move is composed of two different steps: first, it makes one step of a single square along its rank or file and then, still moving away from the square of departure, one step of one single square on a diagonal. It does not matter if the square of the first step is occupied.

5.6. The pawn.

a. The pawn may move only forward.

b. Except when making a capture, it advances from its original square either one or two vacant squares along the file on which it is placed, and on subsequent moves it advances one vacant square along the file. When capturing, it advances one square along either of the diagonals on which it stands.

c. A pawn, attacking a square crossed by an opponent's pawn that has been advanced two squares in one move from its original square, may capture this opponent's pawn as though the latter had been moved only one square. This capture may be made only in reply to such an advance and is called an "en passant" capture.

d. On reaching the last rank, a pawn must immediately be exchanged, as part of the same move, for a queen, a rook, a bishop, or a knight of the same color as the pawn, at the player's choice and without taking into account the other pieces still remaining on the chessboard. This exchange of a pawn for another piece is called "promotion" and the effect of the promoted piece is immediate.

e. In a competition, if a new piece required for the promotion is not immediately available, the player may stop his clock and ask for the assistance of the arbiter. The player must complete his move correctly, in the manner specified in Article 5.6d.

ARTICLE 6. THE COMPLETION OF THE MOVE

6.   The move is completed:

6.1   in the case of the transfer of a piece to a vacant square, when the player's hand has released the piece;

6.2   in the case of a capture, when the captured piece has been removed from the chessboard and the player, having placed his own piece on its new square, has released the piece from his hand;

6.3   in the case of castling, when the player's hand has released the rook on the square crossed by the king. When the player has released the king from his hand, the move is not yet completed, but the player no longer has the right to make any move other than castling on that side, if this is legal;

6.4   in the case of the promotion of a pawn, when the pawn has been removed from the chessboard and the player's hand has released the new piece after placing it on the promotion square. If the player has released from his hand the pawn that has reached the promotion square, the move is not yet completed, but the player no longer has the right to play the pawn to another square.

6.5 When determining the prescribed number of moves has been made in the allotted time, the last move is not considered completed until after the player has stopped his clock. This applies to all situations except those governed by Articles 10.1, 10.2, 10.3, 10.4, and 10.6.

ARTICLE 7. THE TOUCHED PIECE

7.1 Provided that he first expresses his intention (e.g., saying *"j'adoube"*), the player having the move may adjust one or more pieces on their squares.

7.2 Except for the above cases, if the player having the move deliberately touches on the board:

> **a.** one or more pieces of the same color, he must move or capture the first piece touched that can be moved or captured; or

> **b.** one of his own pieces and one of his opponent's pieces, he must capture his opponent's piece with his own piece; or if this is illegal, move or capture the first piece touched that can be moved or captured. If it is impossible to establish which piece was touched, the player's piece shall be considered the touched piece.

7.3 If none of the pieces touched has a legal move (or none of the opponent's pieces touched can be legally captured), the player is free to make any legal move.

7.4 If a player wishes to claim that his opponent has violated Article 7.2, he must do so before he himself touches a piece.

ARTICLE 8. ILLEGAL POSITIONS

8.1 If, during a game, it is found that an illegal move was made, the position shall be reinstated to what it was immediately before the illegal move was made. The game shall then continue by applying the rules of Article 7 to the move replacing the illegal move. If the position cannot be reinstated, the game shall be annulled and a new game played.

This applies to all sessions of play and to a game awaiting a decision by adjudication.

8.2 If, during a game, one or more pieces have been accidentally displaced and incorrectly replaced, the position before the displacement occurred shall be reinstated, and the game shall continue. If the position cannot be reinstated, the game shall be annulled and a new game played.

8.3 If a player moves and in the course of this inadvertently knocks over a piece or several pieces, he must reestablish the position on his own time.

8.4 If, after an adjournment, the position is incorrectly set up, the position as it was on adjournment must be set up again and the game continued.

8.5 If, during a game, it is found that the initial position of the pieces was incorrect, the game shall be annulled and a new game played.

8.6 If a game has begun with colors incorrectly reversed, then it shall continue if one quarter of the total time allocated to both players to the first time control has elapsed. Earlier, the arbiter can arrange a new game to start with the correct colors, if the event's timetable is not excessively disrupted.

8.7 If, during a game, it is found that the board has been placed contrary to Article 1.2, the position reached shall be transferred to a board correctly placed and the game continued.

ARTICLE 9. CHECK

9.1 The king is in check when the square it occupies is attacked by one or more of the opponent's pieces; in this case, the latter is or are said to be "checking" the king. A player may not make a move that leaves his king on a square attacked by any opponent's piece.

9.2 Every check must be parried by the move immediately following. If any check cannot be parried, the king is said to be "checkmated" ("mated"). See Article 10.1.

9.3 Declaring a check is not obligatory.

ARTICLE 10. THE COMPLETED GAME

10.1 The game is won by the player who has mated his opponent's king. This immediately ends the game.

10.2 The game is won by the player whose opponent declares he resigns. This immediately ends the game.

10.3 The game is drawn when the king of a player who has the move is not in check and the player cannot make any legal move. The king is then said to be "stalemated." This immediately ends the game.

10.4 The game is drawn when one of the following endings arises:

> **a.** king against king;

> **b.** king against king with only bishop or knight;

> **c.** king and bishop against king and bishop with both bishops on diagonals of the same color. This immediately ends the game.

10.5 A player having a bare king cannot win the game. A draw shall be declared if the opponent of the player with a bare king oversteps the time limit (Article 10.13 and 10.14) or has sealed an illegal move (Article 10.16).

10.6 The game is drawn upon agreement between the players. This immediately ends the game.

10.7 A proposal of a draw under the provisions of Article 10.6 may be made by a player only at the moment when he has just moved a piece. On then proposing a draw, he starts the clock of his opponent. The latter may accept the proposal, which is always to be taken as unconditional, or he may reject it either orally or by completing a move. A draw offer is valid until the opponent has accepted or rejected it.

10.8 If a player delays proposing a draw until after the opponent's clock is running and he is contemplating his move, the opponent may agree to the draw or reject the offer. A player who offers a draw in this manner may be penalized by the arbiter. See Article 16.5.

10.9 If a player proposes a draw while his own clock is running, or after his move has been sealed, the opponent may postpone his decision until after he has seen the player's move.

10.10 The game is drawn upon a claim by the player having the move, when the same position, for the third time,

> **a.** is about to appear if he first writes his move on his score sheet and declares to the arbiter his intention of making this move or;

> **b.** has just appeared, the same player having the move each time.

The position is considered the same if pieces of the same kind and color occupy the same squares and if the possible moves of all the pieces are the same, including the right to castle or to take a pawn en passant.

10.11 If a player executes a move without having claimed a draw for one of the reasons stated in Article 10.10, he loses the right to claim a draw. This right is restored to him, however, if the same position appears again, the same player having the move.

10.12   The game is drawn when a player having the move claims a draw and demonstrates that the last 50 consecutive moves have been made by each side without the capture of any piece and without the movement of any pawn. This number of 50 moves can be increased for certain positions, provided that this increase in number and these positions have been clearly announced by the organizers before the event starts.

10.13   If a player claims a draw under the provisions of Articles 10.10 and/or 10.12, the arbiter must first stop the clocks while the claim is being investigated. In the absence of the arbiter the player may stop both clocks to seek the arbiter's assistance.

> **a.** If the claim is found to be correct, the game is drawn.

> **b.** If the claim is found to be incorrect, the arbiter shall then add five minutes to the claimant's used time. If this means that the claimant has overstepped the time limit, his game will be declared lost. Otherwise, the game will be continued and the player who has indicated a move according to Article 10.10 is obliged to execute this move on the chessboard.

> **c.** A player who has made a claim under these articles cannot withdraw his claim.

10.14   The game is lost by a player who has not completed the prescribed number of moves in this allotted time, unless his opponent has only the king remaining, in which case the game is drawn. See Articles 6.5 and 10.5.

10.15 The game is lost by the player who arrives at the chessboard more than one hour late for the beginning of the game or for the resumption of an adjourned game. The time of delay is counted from the start of the session. However, in the case of an adjourned game, if the player who made the sealed move is the late player, the game is decided otherwise if:

> **a.** the absent player has won the game by virtue of the fact that the sealed move is checkmate; or

> **b.** the absent player has produced a drawn game by virtue of the fact that the sealed move is stalemate, or if one of the positions in Article 10.4 has arisen as the consequence of the sealed move; or

> **c.** the player present at the chessboard has lost the game according to Article 10.14 by exceeding his time limit.

10.16 At the resumption the game is lost by a player whose recording of his sealed move (a) is ambiguous; or (b) would result in a false move, the true significance of which is impossible to establish; or (c) would result in an illegal move.

10.17 The game is lost by a player who during the game refuses to comply with the Laws. If both players refuse to comply with the Laws or if both players arrive at the chessboard more than one hour late, the game shall be declared lost by both players.

ARTICLE 11. THE RECORDING OF GAMES

11.1   In the course of play, each player is required to record the game (his own moves and those of his opponent), move after move, as clearly and legibly as possible in the algebraic notation, on the score sheet prescribed for the competition. It is irrelevant whether the player first makes his move and then records it or vice versa.

11.2   If a player has less than five minutes on his clock until the time control, he is not obliged to meet the requirements of Article 11.1. As soon as the special device (e.g., flag) on the clock indicates the end of his allotted time, the player must immediately complete his record of the game by filling in the moves omitted from his score sheet.

11.3   If both players cannot keep score, the arbiter or his deputy must endeavor to be present and keep score. The arbiter must not intervene unless one flag falls, and until then he should not indicate in any manner to the players how many moves have been made.

11.4   If Article 11.2 does not apply, and a player refuses to record the game according to Article 11.1, then Article 10.17 should be applied.

11.5   If a player does not refuse to comply with the arbiter's request for a completed score sheet, but declares that he cannot complete his score sheet without consulting his opponent's, the request for this score sheet must be made to the arbiter, who will determine whether the score sheet can be completed before the time control without inconveniencing the other player. The latter cannot refuse his score sheet, because the score sheet belongs to the organizers and the reconstruction will be made on his opponent's time. In all other cases the score sheets can be completed only after the time control.

11.6 If, after the time control, one player alone has to complete his score sheet, he will do so before making another move, and with his clock running if his opponent has moved.

11.7 If, after the time control, both players need to complete their score sheets, both clocks will be stopped until the two score sheets are completed, if necessary with the help of the arbiter's score sheet and/or a chessboard under the control of the arbiter, who should have recorded the actual game position beforehand.

11.8 If, in Article 11.6, the arbiter sees that the score sheets alone cannot help in the reconstruction of the game, he will act as in 11.7.

11.9 If it is impossible to reconstruct the moves as prescribed under Article 11.7, the game shall continue. In this case, the next move played will be considered to be the first one of the following time control.

ARTICLE 12. THE CHESS CLOCK

12.1 Each player must make a certain number of moves in an allotted period of time, these two factors being specified in advance. The time saved by a player during one period is added to his time available for the next period.

12.2   Control of each player's time is effected by means of a clock equipped with a flag (or other special device) for this purpose. The flag is considered to have fallen when the arbiter observes the fact, or when the arbiter determines that the allotted time has been exceeded, even though the flag, because of a defect, has not fallen when the end of the minute hand has passed the end of the flag. In cases where no arbiter is present, the flag is considered to have fallen when a claim has been made to that effect by a player.

12.3   At the time determined for the start of the game, the clock of the player who has the white pieces is started. During the game, each of the players, having completed his move, stops his own clock and starts his opponent's clock.

12.4   Every indication given by a clock is considered to be conclusive in the absence of evident defects. A player who wishes to claim any such defect must do so as soon as he himself has become aware of it but not later than immediately after his flag has fallen at the time control. A clock with an obvious defect should be replaced, and the time used by each player up to the time the game was interrupted should be indicated on the new clock as accurately as possible. The arbiter shall use his best judgment in determining what times shall be shown on the new clock. If the arbiter decides to add time used to the clock of one or both of the players, he shall under no circumstances (except as provided for in Article 10.13b) leave a player with:

> **a.** less than five minutes to the time control; or

> **b.** less than one minute for every move to the time control.

12.5 If the game needs to be interrupted for some reason that requires action by the arbiter, the clocks shall be stopped by the arbiter. This should be done, for instance, in the case of an illegal position being corrected, in the case of a defective clock being changed, or if the piece that a player has declared he wishes to exchange for a promoted pawn is not immediately available, or to claim a draw by repetition of position, or under the 50-move rules. If the arbiter is not present, the player may stop both clocks in order to seek the arbiter's assistant.

12.6 In the case of Articles 8.1 and 8.2, when it is not possible to determine the time used by each player up to the moment when the irregularity occurred, each player shall be allotted up to that moment a time proportional to that indicated by the clock when the irregularity was ascertained. For example, after black's 30th move, it is found that an irregularity took place at the 20th move. For these 30 moves the clock shows 90 minutes for white and 60 minutes for black, so it is assumed that the times used by the players for the first 20 moves were as follows:

White $\dfrac{90 \times 20}{30}$ = 60 minutes   Black $\dfrac{60 \times 20}{30}$ = 40 minutes

This rule must not be used to leave a player with less than five minutes to the time control, or less than one minute for every move to the time control. (The most common occasion when this problem arises is immediately after an adjournment when the clock times can be most easily adjusted using the times on the sealed move envelope.)

12.7 A resignation or an agreement to draw (Articles 10.2 and 10.6) remains valid even when it is found later that the flag had fallen.

12.8 If both flags have fallen virtually at the same time and the arbiter is unable to establish clearly which flag fell first, the game shall continue. In this case, if the score sheets cannot be brought up-to-date showing that the time control has been passed, the next move played will be considered to be the first one of the following time control.

12.9 The arbiter shall refrain from calling a player's attention to the fact that his opponent has made a move, or that the player has forgotten to stop his clock after he has made a move, or informing him how many moves he had made, etc.

ARTICLE 13. THE ADJOURNMENT OF THE GAME

13.1 **a.** If a game is not finished at the end of the time prescribed for play, the player having the move must write his move in unambiguous notation on his score sheet, put his score sheet and that of his opponent in an envelope, seal the envelope, and only then stop his clock without starting his opponent's clock. Until he has stopped the clocks, the player retains the right to change his sealed move. If, after being told by the arbiter to seal his move, the player makes a move on the chessboard, he must write the same move on his score sheet as his sealed move.

b. A player having the move who adjourns the game before the end of the playing session will have added to the used time on his clock the whole of the remaining time to end the session.

13.2 Upon the envelope shall be indicated:

    a. The names of the players.

    b. The position immediately before the sealed move.

    c. The time used by each player.

    d. The name of the player who has sealed the move.

    e. The number of the sealed move.

13.3 The arbiter is responsible for the safekeeping of the envelope and should check the accuracy of the information on it.

ARTICLE 14. THE RESUMPTION OF THE ADJOURNED GAME

14.1 When the game is resumed, the position immediately before the sealed move shall be set up on the chessboard, and the time used by each player when the game was adjourned shall be indicated on the clocks.

14.2 The envelope shall be opened only when the player who must reply to the sealed move is present. The player's clock shall be started after the sealed move has been played on the chessboard.

> **a.** If the two players have agreed to a draw and announce their decision to the arbiter, or

> **b.** If one of the players in an adjourned game notifies the arbiter that he resigns,

and it is then found after the envelope has been opened that the sealed move is invalid according to Article 10.16, then in (a) the draw stands, and in (b) the resignation is still valid.

14.3 If the player having to respond to the sealed move is absent, his clock shall be started, but the envelope containing the sealed move shall be opened only when he arrives. The player's clock shall then be stopped and restarted after the sealed move has been played on the chessboard.

14.4 If the player who has sealed the move is absent, the player having the move is not obliged to reply to the sealed move on the chessboard. He has the right to record his move in reply on his score sheet, to seal the score sheet in an envelope, to stop his clock, and to start his opponent's clock. The envelope should then be put into safekeeping and opened on the opponent's arrival.

14.5 If the envelope containing the move recorded in accordance with Article 13 has disappeared:

> **a.** The game shall be resumed from the position at the time of adjournment and with the clock times recorded at the time of adjournment.
>
> **b.** If it is impossible to reestablish the position, the game is annulled and a new game must be played.
>
> **c.** If the time used at the time of the adjournment cannot be reestablished, this question is decided by the arbiter. The player who sealed the move makes it on the board.

14.6 If, upon resumption of the game, the time used has been incorrectly indicated on either clock, and if either player points this out before making his first move, the error must be corrected. If the error is not so established, the game continues without correction unless the arbiter feels that the consequences will be too severe.

14.7 The duration of each resumption session shall be controlled by the wall clock, with the starting time and finishing time announced in advance.

ARTICLE 15. THE CONDUCT OF THE PLAYERS

15.1. Prohibitions.

> **a.** During play, the players are forbidden to make use of handwritten, printed, or otherwise recorded matter, or to analyze the game on another chessboard. They are also for-

bidden to have recourse to the advice or opinion of a third party, whether solicited or not.

b. The use of notes made during the game as an aid to memory is also forbidden, aside from the actual recording of the moves and the times on the clocks.

c. No analysis is permitted in the playing rooms during play or during resumption sessions.

d. It is forbidden to distract or annoy the opponent in any manner whatsoever. This includes the persistent offering of a draw.

15.2 Infractions of the rules indicated in Article 15.1 may incur penalties, even to the extent of the loss of the game. See Article 16.5.

ARTICLE 16. THE ARBITER

An arbiter should be designated to control the competition. His duties are:

16.1 To see that the Laws are strictly observed;

16.2 To supervise the progress of the competition, to establish that the prescribed time limit has not been exceeded by the players, to arrange the order of resumption of play of adjourned games, to see that the arrangements contained in Article 13 are observed, to see that the information on the envelope is correct, to keep the sealed move envelope until the resumption of the adjourned game, etc.;

16.3 To enforce the decisions he may make in disputes that have arisen during the course of the competition;

16.4 To act in the best interest of the competition to ensure that a good playing environment is maintained and that the players are not disturbed by each other or by the audience;

16.5 To impose penalties on the players for any fault or infraction of the Laws. These penalties may include a warning, a time penalty by adding to the player's used time or to his opponent's unused time, or even the loss of the game.

ARTICLE 17. SCORING

For a won game, the winner gets 1 (one) point and the loser 0 (zero); for a draw, each player gets 0.5 (one-half) point.

ARTICLE 18. THE INTERPRETATION OF THE LAWS

In case of doubt as to the application or interpretation of the Laws, FIDE will examine the evidence and render official decisions. Rulings published are binding on all affiliated federations. All proposals and questions about interpretations should be submitted by member federations with complete data.

ARTICLE 19. VALIDITY

The English text is an authentic version of the Laws of Chess, which were adopted by the 1984 FIDE Congress, with amendments approved by the 1992 FIDE Congress. These Laws came into force on January 1, 1993.

21

FIDE–Rated Tournaments

All Tournaments

1. In order to rate an event, at least four of the players must already be FIDE rated. (FIDE Ratings are published every January 1 and July 1. A rating is not official until it has been published. When a player has been inactive for three years, his rating is dropped from the list but remains official.)

2. Rates of play. The following types of events can be rated:

a. The rate of play must not exceed 23 moves per hour at any stage of the game unless specified in the regulations such as for the World Youth Chess Festival.

b. Sudden-death: one-hour chess, in which all the moves must be made within one hour per player, and 30-minute (Rapid) Chess, in which all the moves must be made within one-half hour per player.

3. Laws to be followed:

a. For games under 2a: the normal Laws of Chess.

b. For games played under 2b: The rules of One-Hour and Rapid (30-minute) Chess (see chapter 22)

4. Number of rounds per day:

a. For games played under 2a: Not more than 2 rounds per day, excluding adjourned games.

b. For games played under 2b: Not more than 4 rounds per day for One-Hour Chess; not more than 6 rounds per day for 30-minute chess.

5. Duration of the event: A period not greater than 90 days. Leagues may be rated which last for a period greater than 90 days. The rating list used depends on the event's starting date. For example, the January rating list is used for events with a starting date between January 1 and June 30. The July list is used for events with a starting date between July 1 and December 31.

6. Unplayed games are not counted.

7. Composition of the tournament:

a. If an unrated player scores zero in an event, his score and that of his opponents against him are disregarded.

b. The results in events involving preliminaries and finals are pooled.

c. In a round robin tournament, at least one-third of the players must be rated.

    1) If the event has less than ten players, at least four must be rated.

    2) In a double round robin tournament with unrated participants, there must be at least six players, four of whom must be rated.

8. In a Swiss or team event (except Scheveningen matches), only the games against rated opponents are counted.

    a. For rated players, all games against rated opponents are counted.

    b. For unrated players, results are counted only if the player meets at least four rated opponents in the event.

    c. In the case of a round robin tournament where one or more games are unplayed, the results of the tournament are to be reported for rating as for a Swiss system tournament.

9. FIDE-rated tournament must be FIDE-registered through the national federation, preferably two months before the event.

Futurity Round Robins

1. Futurity round robin event events must consist of at least ten players. Smaller tournaments can be rated, but nine games are needed for a publishable rating.

2. At least a third of the players must be FIDE rated. At least one extra rated player is recommended.

3. A reasonable field of non-FIDE-rated players. Ideally, all players should be capable of scoring 40 percent or more against rated players. Admitting players with USCF ratings below 2000 is not recommended.

FIDE-rated Swiss Tournaments

1. Players' results are rated individually. All games between FIDE-rated players will be rated, but an unrated player must play at least four rated players in order to secure a ratable performance. (A rough measure is performance rating: add 400 points to the ratings of those you beat, subtract 400 from those who beat you, take the rating of those with whom you draw, and average it out. If the result is 2000 or better, the player has a ratable performance.)

2. Swiss results are valid for title norms if the requirements listed in the remainder of this chapter are met. One's own rating is averaged in to determine the "field."

Requirements for International Round Robins and Title Tournaments

The following regulations are the requirements for events in which title results—Grandmaster (GM), International Master (IM), Woman Grandmaster (WGM), Woman International Master (WIM)—(see Chapter 22).

1. Regulations described in the FIDE Handbook under "FIDE Rating Regulations."

2. That it is to be governed by the FIDE Laws of Chess and Rules of Play.

3. That no more than two rounds are played on any day. For a GM result to be possible, no more than two rounds a day for two days shall be played and no more than one round per day in the last three rounds.

4. The speed of play must not exceed 46 moves in two hours at any stage of the game except that a sudden death final time control of at least 30 minutes may be used in a tournament with games lasting at least seven hours. This may not be used in World Championship cycles or in continental championships.

5. The event must be played within a period of 90 days.

6. The tournament should, if possible, be conducted by an International Arbiter.

Composition of a Title Tournament

1. The tournament consists of the player and his opponents.

a. Games played against opponents who do not belong to FIDE federations or who belong to federations that have been temporary excluded are not included.

b. Games played against unregistered computers are not included.

c. Games decided by forfeit, adjudication, or any means other than over-the-board play are not included. Games once started, which are forfeited for whatever reason, shall however be included.

2. The tournament must have at least nine rounds.

3. At least 80 percent of the players must be rated.

a. For GM and IM results, women rated below 2205 are considered to be unrated at 2200.

b. For the period between January 1, 1993, and December 31, 1993 (inclusive), the figure used for an unrated player is 2100. Starting January 1, 1994, the figure used for an unrated player will be 2000.

c. A player may ignore his result(s) against unrated opponents whom he has defeated, provided this leaves him with at least nine games. Nonetheless, the full cross table of the event must be submitted.

d. In zonal tournaments, the limit of 20 percent unrated is waived. See 20b for the figure used for an unrated player in the World Championship and Women's World Championship zonals.

4. At least 50 percent of the players must be titleholders—Grandmaster (GM), FIDE Master (FM), International Master (IM), Woman Grandmaster (WGM), Woman International Master (WIM), Woman FIDE Master (WFM), Honorary Grandmaster (HGM), Honorary Woman Grandmaster (HWGM)—or players with a current rating greater than 2300 (2100 for WGM and WIM results in tournaments exclusively for women).

5. At least one-third of the players shall not come from the same federation as the candidate. Thus, in a nine-round event, there are ten players including the candidate. At least four opponents must be from federations other than his own.

6. Except for Scheveningen-type tournaments, and zonal tournaments of single federation zones, at least three federations must be represented.

7. For a player who shall not come from the host federation, the requirement of section 5 is: No more than two-thirds plus one players shall come from one federation. For example, 9 round $((2 \times 10) + 1)/3$ leads to 7 and 13 rounds $((2 \times 14) + 1)/3$ leads to 10. Provided that at least one-third of the opponents must be from federations other than his own.

8. In any one year, one national championship and also one exclusively for women can be considered to be an international tournament, waiving sections 5, 6, and 7, provided the championship is registered in advance.

9. Swiss system tournaments shall be exempt from the requirements of sections 5 and 7 provided that there are at least 20 FIDE-rated foreign players, at least ten of whom hold GM or IM titles, in the tournament section.

Those who wish to organize a FIDE-rated tournament should contact the USCF for further information.

Determining the Rating Average for a Title Result (Norm)

1. In a round robin tournament, the rating average for title purposes is determined before the start of the tournament.

2. In a Swiss, Scheveningen, or team tournament, the rating average for title purposes is determined once all a player's opponents are established. A candidate then considers himself and all his opponents as a round robin tournament for this purpose.

a. Results against unrated players who score zero are not included in computing title norms in round robin tournaments.

3. For the period between January 1, 1993 and December 31, 1993 (inclusive), the figure used for an unrated player is 2100. Starting January 1, 1994, the figure used for an unrated player will be 2000.

4. One GM aged 55 and over, who in the past qualified at least for the Candidates' Semi-finals, is awarded a temporary Honorary Rating. Only one player in a tournament can hold this title. This Honorary Rating shall be equal to the average rating of the other participants. This is then valid for calculation of the Tournament Category and the rating changes of the other players. However, the GM with Honorary Rating shall have his rating change computed on his actual rating.

Regulations Regarding Title Results and the Award of a Title

1. GM results in tournaments with fewer than three GMs are not valid.

2. WGM results in tournaments with fewer than three of the following are not valid: GMs, IMs, WGMs, or women players rated over 2300.

3. IM results in tournaments with fewer than three IMs or two GMs are not valid.

4. WIM results in tournaments with fewer than three WIMs or two of the following are not valid: GMs, IMs, WGMs, or women players rated over 2300.

5. At least one title result shall be based on a round robin or an Olympiad. Otherwise, the title application shall be based on at least 30 games.

6. At least one title result must be obtained in an event having no more than one round per day.

7. The results supporting a title application must be achieved in events with starting dates that fall within a six-year period.

8. If a result is sufficient for more than one title, then it may be used as part of the application for both.

9. A player who has achieved a title result in the Olympiad before the last round can ignore all his games played subsequently. In such a case, the chief arbiter shall certify the player's result as a valid title result.

10. A title result shall be valid if it was obtained in accordance with the International Title Regulations prevailing at the time of the tournament where the norm was attained.

Tournament Classification

1. To determine the classification of a tournament, the average rating of the players is determined. The categories of International Title Tournaments are given by the chart on pages 334 and 335. This shows the minimum percentage score required to achieve the result when playing in that category.

2. The average rating is the total of the players' ratings (including the title candidate) divided by the number of players.

3. Rounding of the average rating is made to the nearest whole number. The fraction 0.5 is rounded upward.

4. "Chart of Points Required for FIDE International Title Results" table summarizes the scores required, depending on the number of rounds.

CHART OF POINTS REQUIRED FOR

Nr. of part.	games	required players not from one and the same feder.	minimum rated players	number of titleholders all inclusive	FIDE TITLE RESULT	I 2251 2275	II 2276 2300	III 2301 2325
10	9	4	8	5: 3 GM	GM			
				2 GM/3 IM	IM	7	7	6½
11	10	4	9	6: 3 GM	GM			
				2 GM/3 IM	IM	8	7½	7
12	11	4	10	6: 3 GM	GM			
				2 GM/3 IM	IM	8½	8	8
13	12	5	11	7: 3 GM	GM			
				2 GM/3 IM	IM	9½	9	8½
14	13	5	12	7: 3 GM	GM			
				2 GM/3 IM	IM	10	9½	9½
15	14	5	12	8: 3 GM	GM			
				2 GM/3 IM	IM	11	10½	10
16	15	6	13	8: 3 GM	GM			
				2 GM/3 IM	IM	11½	11	10½
17	16	6	14	9: 3 GM	GM			
				2 GM/3 IM	IM	12½	12	11½
18	17	6	15	9: 3 GM	GM			
				2 GM/3 IM	IM	13	12½	12
19	18	7	16	10: 3 GM	GM			
				2 GM/3 IM	IM	14	13½	13
20	19	7	16	10: 3 GM	GM			
				2 GM/3 IM	IM	14½	14	13½

FIDE INTERNATIONAL TITLE RESULTS

CATEGORIES AND AVERAGE RATINGS

IV	V	VI	VII	VIII	IX	X	XI	XII	XIII	XIV	XV	XVI
2326	2351	2376	2401	2426	2451	2476	2501	2526	2551	2576	2601	2626
2350	2375	2400	2425	2450	2475	2500	2525	2550	2575	2600	2625	2650
			7	7	6½	6	6	5½	5½	5	4½	4½
6	6	5½	5½	5	4½	4½	4	4	3½	3	3	
			8	7½	7	7	6½	6	6	5½	5	5
7	6½	6	6	5½	5	5	4½	4	4	3½	3	
			8½	8	8	7½	7	7	6½	6	5½	5½
7½	7	7	6½	6	5½	5½	5	4½	4	4	3½	
			9½	9	8½	8	8	7½	7	6½	6	6
8	8	7½	7	6½	6	6	5½	5	4½	4	4	
			10	9½	9½	9	8½	8	7½	7	6½	6½
9	8½	8	7½	7	6½	6½	6	5½	5	4½	4	
			11	10½	10	9½	9	8½	8	7½	7	7
9½	9	8½	8	7½	7	7	6	6	5	5	4½	
			11½	11	10½	10	10	9	8½	8	7½	7
10	10	9	8½	8	7½	7	6½	6	5½	5	4½	
			12½	12	11½	11	10½	10	9	8½	8	7½
11	10½	10	9½	8½	8	7½	7	6½	6	5½	5	
			13	12½	12	11½	11	10½	10	9	8½	8
11½	11	10½	10	9	8½	8	7½	7	6½	6	5½	
			14	13½	13	12½	11½	11	10½	9½	9	8½
12½	11½	11	10½	9½	9	8½	8	7½	6½	6	5½	
			14½	14	13½	13	12½	11½	11	10½	9½	9
13	12½	11½	11	10½	9½	9	8½	8	7	6½	6	

The average rating consists of a rating figure (from FIDE Rating List) for each player, which have been totalled and then divided by the number of players. Roundings of the average ratings are made to the nearest whole number. The fraction 0.5 is rounded off upward.

22

Special FIDE Rules

(including Titles, Computers, and Faster Play)

FIDE Titles

1. International Grandmaster (GM)—obtained by achieving any of the following:

> **a.** Two or more GM results in events covering at least 24 games and a rating of at least 2500 in the FIDE rating list current at the time the FIDE Congress considers the application, or in the two lists following immediately thereafter.
>
> **b.** Qualification for the Candidates Competition for the World Championship.
>
> **c.** One GM result in a FIDE Interzonal tournament.
>
> **d.** Winning the Women's World Championship match is equivalent to one nine-game GM result.
>
> **e.** Clearing first place in the World Junior Championship is equivalent to one nine-game GM result.

2. International Master (IM)—obtained by achieving any of the following:

a. Two or more IM results in event covering at least 24 games and a rating of a least 2400 in the FIDE rating list current at the time of the FIDE Congress considering the application, or in the two lists immediately following thereafter.

b. First place in any one of the following events:

> **1.** Women's World Championship.
>
> **2.** World Junior Championship.
>
> **3.** Zonal Tournament.
>
> **4.** International Braille Chess Association (IBCA) World Championship (champion is given a rating of 2205).
>
> **5.** International Committee of Silent Chess World Championship.

c. First place in one of the following events, provided the tournament was played with a minimum of 13 games and also 14 contestants:

> **1.** Continental Individual Championship.
>
> **2.** Continental Individual Junior Championship.
>
> **3.** Arab Individual and Junior Championships.

The Deputy President of the Continent may vary the 13-game rule in consultation with the Qualification Commission Chairman and approval by the President.

In the event of a tie for first place in any of the above events in 2b and 2c, each of the tied players shall be awarded the title of International Master, subject to a maximum of three players.

d. Qualification for the Interzonal Tournament of the World Championship cycle.

e. One IM result in the cycle of the Individual World Championship, of no less than 13 games. When such a tournament is played with preliminaries and finals, the results will be pooled.

f. A score of 66⅔ percent or better in a Zonal Tournament of at least nine games. When such a tournament is played with preliminaries and finals, the results will be pooled.

3. FIDE Master (FM)—obtained by achieving any of the following:

a. A rating of at least 2300 after the player has played at least 24 rated games. The national federation is responsible for the payment of the fee established in the financial regulations, upon which the title will be awarded.

b. First place in any of the following events: World Championships for players under-ten to under-eighteen, ICBA World Junior Championship, given a rating of 2205.

c. First place in one of the following events, provided the event was played with a minimum of nine games and also ten contestants:

1. Continental Individual Championship.

2. Continental Junior, Under-16 and Under-14 Championships.

3. Centroamerican-Caribbean Junior Championship;

In the event of a tie for first place in any of the above events, each of the tied players shall be awarded the title of FIDE Master, subject to a maximum of three players.

d. A score of 50 percent or better in a Zonal Tournament of at least nine games. When such a tournament is played with preliminaries and finals, the results will be pooled.

e. Runner-up of IBCA World Championship, given a rating of 2205.

4. Woman Grandmaster (WGM)—obtained by achieving any of the following:

a. Two or more WGM results in events covering at least 24 games and a rating of at least 2300 in the FIDE rating list current at the time of the FIDE Congress considering the application, or in the two lists immediately following thereafter.

b. Qualification for the Candidates' Competition for the Women's World Championship.

c. One WGM result in the cycle of the Individual Women's World Championship, of no less than 13 games. When such a tournament is played with preliminaries and finals, the results will be pooled.

d. Clearing first place in the World Girls' Championship is equivalent to one nine-game WGM result.

5. Woman International Master (WIM)—obtained by achieving any one of the following:

a. Two or more WIM results in events covering at least 24 games and a rating of at least 2200 in the FIDE rating list current at the time of the FIDE Congress considering the application, or in the two lists following immediately thereafter.

b. Qualification for the Interzonal Tournament for the Women's World Championship.

c. First place in any of the following events.

1. World Girls' Championship.

2. Continental Women's Championship, provided the event was played with a minimum of 13 games and also 14 contestants.

3. Arab Women's Championship, provided the event was played with a minimum of 13 games and also 14 contestants.

The Deputy President of the Continent may vary the 13-game rule in consultation with the Qualification Commission Chairman and approval by the President.

In the event of a tie for first place in the above events, each of the tied players shall be awarded the title of WIM, subject to a maximum of three players.

d. One WIM result in the cycle of the Individual Women's World Championship, of no less than 13 games. When such a tournament is played with preliminaries and finals, the results will be pooled.

e. A score of 66⅔ percent or better in a Women's World Championship Zonal Tournament of at least nine games. When such a tournament is played with preliminaries and finals, the results will be pooled.

6. Women's FIDE Master (WFM)—obtained by achieving any one of the following:

a. A rating of at least 2100 after the player has played at least 24 games. The national federation is responsible for the payment of the fee established in the financial regulations, upon which the title will be awarded.

b. First place in any of the following events:

1. World Girls' Championships for players under-ten to under-eighteen.

2. Continental Women's Championship.

3. Continental Girls' Championship.

4. Arab Women's Championship.

5. IBCA Women's World Champion, given a rating of 2205.

For the events 6b3 through 6b5 above, the tournament must be played with a minimum of nine games and ten contestants.

In the event of a tie for first place in events 6b1 through 6b5 above, each of the tied players shall be awarded the title of WFM, subject to a maximum of three players.

c. A score of 50 percent or better in a Woman's Zonal Tournament of at least nine games. When such a tournament is played with preliminaries and finals, the results will be pooled. For players conferred the GM, IM, WGM, or WIM titles conditioned on attaining the minimum rating in the next two FIDE rating lists, a player who achieves the minimum rating in the middle of a rating period may disregard his subsequent tournament results for purposes of the title application.

7. Requirements for the title of International Arbiter (IA)—all of the following:

a. Thorough knowledge of the Laws of Chess and the FIDE Regulations for chess competitions;

b. Absolute objectivity, demonstrated at all times during his activity as an arbiter;

c. Sufficient knowledge of at least one official FIDE language;

d. Experience as chief or deputy arbiter in at least four FIDE-rated events governed by the FIDE Laws of Chess and Rules of Play such as the following:

1. The final of the National Individual Adult Championship (not more than two).

2. All official FIDE tournaments and matches.

3. International title tournaments and matches.

4. International chess festivals with at least 100 contestants.

8. Requirements for Chess Composition titles—: as established by the regulations of FIDE PCCC.

9. Requirements for Correspondence Chess titles—: as established by the regulations of ICCF.

Application Procedure

1. Applications forms for GM, IM, FM, WGM, WIM, WFM, HGM, HWGM, IA, and Rapid Chess Expert titles are printed in the FIDE Handbook. Applications for these titles must be prepared on these forms and all the information required supplied together with the application.

2. An application for title may be submitted to the appropriate judging unit by the federation of the applicant. The national federation is responsible for the fee. Applications can only be considered by the FIDE Congress or Executive Council if received by the judging unit at least thirty days before the meetings.

Computers in FIDE-rated Tournaments

1. Computers will not be eligible to participate in official FIDE tournaments (i.e., World Championship cycle, Olympiads, Continental Team Championships, etc).

2. As of July 1, 1992, all computers will be entitled to be registered with FIDE, and to compete in FIDE-registered and title tournaments (excluding international titled tournaments such as the World Championship cycle, Olympiads, etc.).

3. FIDE-registered computers will be rated and listed in a computers section of the FIDE Rating List, starting with the January 1993 list.

4. Only FIDE-registered computers may acquire FIDE ratings.

5. Effective January 1, 1993, tournaments or matches that include computers that are not FIDE registered will not be rated and will not be valid as international title tournaments.

6. Only one unit of any FIDE registered computer may compete in any FIDE-registered or title tournament.

7. FIDE-registered computers shall count as opponents for title purposes as if they were a member of a different federation from the player.

8. No participant in a FIDE-registered or title tournament may decline to be paired against a computer.

Computer Playing Rules in FIDE Tournaments

These rules are for the operator of a computer participating in a FIDE-rated event.

1. General

1.1 The game shall be played according to FIDE Laws on a tournament chess board and using a tournament clock.

1.2 The operator is regarded as "the computer's player" except that Article 7—"The Touched Piece"—does not apply to the operator. (See Chapter 20 "International (FIDE) Laws of Chess.")

1.3 After the player has made a move, the operator will key it into the computer and record it on the tournament score sheet.

1.4 After the computer has indicated a move, the operator will play it on the tournament board, start the player's clock and record the move on the tournament score sheet.

2. Time Limits

2.1 The move rate set on the computer should allow for the time which will be taken by the operator in transferring moves from and to the tournament board.

2.2 If the computer is becoming short of time, the operator may select a faster move rate that must be kept until the time control has been passed. The operator may then return the computer to the move rate required to reach the next time control. Other variations from the preset parameters are not permitted.

2.3 The operator may not force the computer to move.

3. Rights and Duties of the Operator.

3.1 The operator must obey each instruction of the computer.

3.2 The operator may accept or refuse the player's offer of a draw as provided in the FIDE laws. The player may suggest that the computer should resign, and the operator may resign on behalf of the computer. In each case, before deciding the operator may consult, in the presence of the arbiter, a previously nominated person accepted by the arbiter.

3.3 Only if the computer itself so instructs him may the operator offer a draw, or claim a draw by repetition.

3.4 The operator may change cartridges or other memory only on instructions from the computer.

3.5 If the computer is sealing a move, the arbiter may ask the player to withdraw temporarily to a position from which he cannot see the computer's display of the move to be sealed. The arbiter must check that the instructed move has been recorded on the score sheet. The operator is responsible for maintaining the security of the move indicated on the computer display. At the time of the resumption of the game, it is the responsibility of the operator to ensure that the position has been entered correctly on the computer.

One-Hour and Rapid Chess

These FIDE rules were approved by the 1985 General Assembly (One-Hour Chess) and 1987 General Assembly (Rapid Chess) and amended by the 1989 and 1992 General Assemblies. These rules permit FIDE tournament games to be one or two hours long.

Duration of Play

1. Each player shall make all his moves within sixty, or thirty minutes on the clock, as stipulated in advance of the tournament.

2. Both players shall record the game move by move until one has not more than five minutes left on the clock, then they both may stop recording.

The Clock

3. Each clock must have a special device, usually called a "flag," marking the end of the time control period.

4. Before play begins, the players should inspect the position of the pieces and the setting of the clocks. If they have omitted this, no claim shall be accepted after each player has made his first move, except by mutual agreement.

5. Each player shall handle the clock with the same hand with which he handles his pieces. Exception: it is permitted to perform the castling move by using both hands.

6. The arbiter should stipulate, at the beginning of the tournament, the direction the clocks are to face, and the player with the black pieces shall decide on which side of the board he shall sit.

7. No player is permitted to cover more or less permanently the button of his own clock with one of his fingers.

8. During the game, the clock must not be picked up by either player.

The Won Game

9. A game is won by the player:

> **a.** Who has checkmated his opponent's king.

b. Whose opponent declares that he resigns.

c. Whose opponent's flag falls first, at any time before the game is otherwise ended.

10. A player must claim a win himself by immediately stopping both clocks and notifying the arbiter. To claim a win under Rule 9c, the player's flag must be up and his opponent's flag must be down after the clocks have been stopped. If both flags are down, the game is declared a draw (Rule 11a).

The Drawn Game

11. A game is drawn under the normal rules of chess and also:

a. If both flags are down.

b. A player's flag falls when his opponent cannot possibly checkmate.

c. A player very short of time who is clearly winning.

d. A player very short of time whose opponent is continuing in a dead-drawn position may request a draw, and if the arbiter agrees the game is drawn.

12. A game may also be drawn, but only before the claimant's flag falls, and supported where necessary by a completed score sheet:

a. If the player demonstrates a perpetual check or a forced repetition of position (if this claim is found to be false, his opponent is compensated by having two minutes extra time added).

b. If his opponent has no practical winning chances (if this claim is found to be false, his opponent is compensated by having two minutes extra time added). The following shall be considered positions without "practical winning chances" (provided there is no forced way to win):

> **i.** if claimant has queen vs. queen (or rook or bishop or knight or pawn);

> **ii.** if claimant has a rook vs. rook (or bishop or knight);

> **iii.** if claimant has a bishop (or knight) vs. bishop (or knight);

> **iv.** if claimant has bishop vs. pawn, knight vs. pawn, rook vs. pawn—provided, in all cases, there is no forced win for his opponent;

> **v.** king vs. "a" or "h" pawn and bishop on the wrong diagonal, provided that the king is controlling the promoting square;

> **vi.** in all cases, claimant could have additional pieces.

c. If both kings are in check and a player announces that he is correcting the irregularity, then the last move shall be established and the correct position set up. If this is impossible to do with the last played move of one player, then the game shall be proclaimed a draw.

13. The player with the white pieces is responsible for notifying the arbiter of a drawn game.

The Arbiter

14. In case of a dispute, either player may stop the clocks while the arbiter is being summoned.

15. The arbiter shall not handle the clocks except in the case of a dispute or when both players asked him to do so.

16. Spectators and participants in another game are not to speak or otherwise interfere in a game. If a spectator interferes in any way, such as by calling attention to a flag fall or an illegal move, the arbiter may cancel the game and rule that a new game be played in its stead, as well as expel the offending party from the room. The arbiter, too, must refrain from calling attention to a flag fall or an illegal move, as these are entirely the responsibility of the players.

Miscellaneous

17. If a player accidentally displaces one or more pieces, he shall replace them on his own time. If it is necessary, his opponent may start the player's clock without making a move in order to make sure that the player replaces the displaced pieces on his own time.

18. Play shall be governed by the FIDE Laws of Chess in that they are not inconsistent with these rules.

If a player first touches one piece and then moves another, his opponent should restart the player's clock, if it is necessary, and inform him that he must complete the move in accordance with Article 7.

19. Illegal moves unnoticed by both players cannot be corrected afterwards. Exception: 12c.

20. Before a One-Hour or Rapid Chess Tournament, the organizers should hand out a copy of these rules to each participant; or, if this is not possible, see that a sufficient number of copies of these rules are posted in the playing room at least half an hour before the tournament is to begin.

21. If, after a claim by the opponent, the arbiter agrees:

> **a.** that the player has violated articles 7 or 8 or 17 or 18 of these rules or Article 15.1.d of the Laws of Chess; or

> **b.** that the player has made an illegal move; or

> **c.** that the player for the second or subsequent time:

>> **i.** has violated articles 2 or 5 of these rules;

>> **ii.** or the player has made an ambiguous move, the arbiter may penalize a player by giving two extra minutes to his opponent's time.

(When a special chess clock for Rapid Chess is available, which gives one or both players a continuing further ten seconds per move, the time regulations in these rules shall apply.)

22. Tournament games played under these rules may be rated only in a separate list established for Rapid Chess and One-Hour Chess.

23. In tournaments using 60 minutes per game, no more than three rounds per day may be played; in tournaments using 30 minutes per game, no more than six rounds may be played.

24. Because of the special conditions of Rapid Chess, players should conduct themselves in an ethical manner in the spirit of fair play. Disciplinary measures may be taken by arbiters against erring players.

FIDE Regulations for Five-Minute (Blitz) Chess

These rules were approved by FIDE's General Assembly to permit FIDE tournament games to be played in ten minutes (five minutes for each player). However, the results are rated separately from slower games.

1. Play will be governed by FIDE Rules of Chess except where overridden by the following rules.

2. Each player must make all his moves in the five minutes allotted on his clock.

3. Players do not need to record the moves.

4. A player who has made an illegal move must retract it and make a legal move on his own time.

> **a.** Illegal moves unnoticed by both players cannot be corrected afterwards, nor can they become the basis for making a claim, although a piece once touched must be moved. If no legal move exists with that piece, and the clock has not been hit, any move with another piece may be made.

> **b.** An illegal move is completed when the player neutralizes his clock (starts his opponent's clock) whereupon the opponent may claim a win.

5. All the clocks must have a special device, usually called a "flag" marking the end of the time control period.

6. Claims regarding incorrect piece placement, board orientation, and clock setting cannot be made after either player has made three moves. However, if it is subsequently discovered that the king and queen were set up incorrectly, the player may castle "long" on the kingside and "short" on the queenside.

7. Each player must push the clock with the same hand he uses to move the pieces; exception: during castling, both hands may be used. The arbiter gives a warning after the first infraction, a penalty of one minute added to the innocent party's clock after the second, and loss of the game after the third.

8. The arbiter states, at the start of the event, the direction the clocks are to face. The player with the black pieces decides on which side of the board he will sit.

9. Neither player may touch the clock except to straighten it or to push the button.

    a. If either player knocks over the clock, his opponent gets one extra minute playing time.

    b. If his opponent's clock does not tick, a player may push the opponent's side and re-punch his own side; however, if this procedure is unsatisfactory, he is to call the arbiter.

    c. Each player must always be allowed to push the clock after his move has been made. He may not keep his fingers on the button nor hover over it.

10. If a player displaces one or more pieces, he shall replace them on his own time. If it is necessary, his opponent may start the player's clock without making a move himself in order to make sure that the player uses his own time while replacing the pieces.

11. If a player first touches one piece, then moves another, his opponent can restart the player's clock and make him move the piece first touched.

> **a.** First offense will result in a warning (unless he causes his opponent's flag to fall, in which case the opponent gets one extra minute playing time).

> **b.** Second offense, the offended shall receive one extra minute playing time.

> **c.** Third offense, the offender shall forfeit the game.

> **d.** Thereafter, for repeated offenses, the arbiter may use other penalties, including expelling the offender from the event.

12. If a player promotes a pawn and leaves it on the board, either player may stop the clocks while a replacement piece is found.

13. In case of a dispute, either player may stop the clock while the arbiter is being summoned.

14. The game is won by the player:

> **a.** Who has mated his opponent's king.

> **b.** Whose opponent resigns.

c. Whose opponent's flag falls first, at any time before the game is otherwise ended:

> **i.** provided that he points it out and neutralizes the clocks while his own flag is still up, and

> **ii.** he has sufficient mating material. Mating material requires that a position is possible in which mate-in-one is forced (opponent, to move, cannot avoid mate next move).

d. Whose opponent completes an illegal move, which includes leaving his king in check or moving his king into check, and neutralizes his clock (but only if the player claims the win before he himself has completed his move).

15. The game is drawn:

a. If one of the kings is stalemated.

b. By agreement between the players during the game.

c. If the flag of one player falls after the flag of the other player has already fallen and a win has not been claimed as in 14ci.

d. By perpetual check, repetition of position, and "dead" positions. To claim a draw, a four-time repetition is necessary with the player counting the moves out loud. The claimant must stop the clock after the fourth repetition.

e. If a player's flag has fallen but his opponent has insufficient mating material, as defined in 14cii.

Miscellaneous

16. The arbiter must not interfere in any way with the player of the game unless called upon to make a ruling. In particular, he must not call attention to flag falls or illegal moves.

17. The arbiter must not pick up the clock except in the case of a dispute when both players ask him to do so, at his discretion, to change a defective clock.

18. Spectators, and players in other games, are not to speak or otherwise interfere in a game. If a spectator interferes in any way, such as calling attention to a flag fall, the arbiter may cancel the game and rule that a new game be played in its stead. He may also expel the offending party from the playing room.

19. All decisions of the arbiter are final and non-appealable.

Index

absent player, 62
　　completion of games, 28–29, 55, 126, 313
　　resumed games and, 320
　　see also late arrival at chessboard
accelerated early-round pairings, 79, 98–101
adjourned games, xxvi, 51–58, 61, 98, 148
　　completion of games and, 29–30, 313
　　computer chess and, 152
　　FIDE laws and, 308, 313, 318–22, 325, 328
　　illegal positions and, 57, 308
　　incorrect position and, 21, 57
　　resumption and, 29, 53–54, 56–58, 308, 313, 319–22, 346
adjudicated games, 55, 62, 98, 308
adjustment of pieces and pawns, 18–19
affiliation to USCF, 257–58
algebraic notation, xii, 42, 154–59, 161, 163, 168, 261–65, 314
Allegro Clock, xix, xxiv, 10–11, 39–40, 42, 170–71
allocation of colors, *see* color allocation
all play all (round robin), 126
ambiguity, 230, 351
　　chess pieces and, 313
　　notation and, 159–60, 163, 318–19

sealed move and, xv, 30, 57, 313, 318–19
telephone and voice transmission notation and, 163
announcements, 55, 124–25, 146, 148–49, 173, 176, 185, 218, 320–21
　　checklist and, 192–93
　　of computers entered in tournaments, 149
　　of prizes, 132, 135–37, 139, 195
　　of tiebreaks, 139–40
　　of tournament conditions, 75, 77–78, 83, 257
　　see also notification
appeals, 76, 196, 201, 217, 356
　　of director's decision, xxv, 67–72
　　of special referee, 68–72
　　of tournament's appeal committee, xxv, 68–72
arbiters, 208, 299, 306, 319–23, 328, 332
　　defective clocks and, 316–17, 353, 356
　　duties of, 311, 322–23
　　five-minute chess and, 353–54, 356
　　international (IAs), 215–16, 342–43
　　Rapid and one-hour chess, 347–52
　　score keeping and, 314–15
　　sealed moves and, 319, 321–22, 346
　　see also tournament directors

bishop, xii, 14, 34–35, 40–41, 160, 166, 263, 272–75, 280, 301, 305, 310, 349
black (player with black pieces), 42, 46–47, 90, 105–19, 130, 143, 156, 164–66, 175, 236
  clock facing, 47
  equipment choice of, 164–65, 171
blind players, xiii, 146–49
  sighted players vs., 148
Blitz rules, 128
  FIDE five-minute rules, 233, 352–56
  USCF Blitz rules, 11, 233–35
byes, 174–76
  alternatives to, 92–94
  half-point, xv, xxv, 72–74, 88–93, 102, 120, 124, 141, 174
  irrevocable in last half of tournament, 73
  one-point (or full point), xxvi, 72, 74, 90–94, 142, 174, 176
  round-robin pairings and, 127
  Swiss system, 88–94, 99, 101–2, 105, 116, 118, 125, 130, 141

captain of team, xxvii–xxviii, 130–32
capture, 35–36, 169, 266, 279, 305–7, 311–12
  algebraic notation, 156–58, 262–63
  blind players and, 146
  computer notation of, 158
  English descriptive notation of, 160
  by pawns, 15, 32, 158, 303, 305, 311
  of pieces, 12, 16, 303
  touched piece and, 16, 307
castling, xix, 7, 158–59, 277, 347
  algebraic notation of, 158, 263
  completion of the move, 16, 306
  computer notation of, 159
  draw by repetition and, 32, 311
  English description notation of, 160
  five-minute chess and, 353
  international correspondence notation of, 162
  moves of the pieces, 12–14, 16, 20, 303–4

center, control of, 275–77
changes in tournament plans, 75, 77–78
check, 7, 32, 348–49, 355
  algebraic notation of, 158, 263
  definition of, 23, 309
  English descriptive notation of, 160
checkmate, definition of, 8
chessboards, 4–6, 44, 58, 90, 151–52, 155–56, 185–86
  definition of, 4–5
  equipment standards for, xxviii, 48, 164–69
  facing of clock and, 47, 152
  FIDE laws and, 300, 302, 309, 344–45, 347, 353
  illegal moves and, 22
  visually handicapped players and, 146–48
Chess Life (magazine), 75, 78, 83, 149, 189, 254–55, 257–59
claim of touched pieces, 17–18, 20
classes of players (rating groups), 73, 86–89, 93–94, 120, 122–23, 132–33, 135, 137–38, 225–26
clocks, xiii, 56–58, 94, 97–98, 147–48, 231
  Allegro, xix, xxiv, 10–11, 39–40, 42, 170–71
  analog, 10, 171
  beepers of, 170
  claim of draw, 30–34, 36–40, 310–12, 317–18
  completed game, 24–28, 310–11
  computer chess, 151–52, 344–45
  defects of, 46, 48–49, 316–17, 353, 356
  digital, 10–11, 170–71
  equipment standards for, 47–48, 164, 169–71
  facing of, 47, 152, 347, 353
  FIDE laws, 28, 306–7, 309–25, 328, 344–48, 350–51, 353–56
  five-minute chess, 234–35, 352–56
  handling of, xxiv, 11, 45, 200, 235
  illegal moves and positions, 20–22, 46, 49, 234, 317

Official Rules of Chess, 9–12, 15–17, 20–29, 45–52, 66
  in Rapid and one-hour chess, 346–47, 350–51
  resetting of, 45–51, 56, 97, 147, 317–18, 320
  sudden-death rules and, 9–11, 38, 41, 43, 45–46, 49–50, 234–35
  wall clocks in playing room, 53, 321
  white space of, 46
  see also time controls
clocks, stopping of, xx, 147, 306–7, 316–19
  to call director, xv, 37–38, 43–44, 49, 66, 317
  five-minute chess, 354–55
  forfeits and, xiii, 24–28, 38, 43, 46, 49–50, 57, 61, 66, 152, 348
  game interrupted, xv, 11, 49, 66, 317
  illegal positions, 20–21, 317
  pawn promotion delay, 15–16, 306, 317, 354
  player neglecting, 60
  proposal of draw, xxi, 30–34, 36–38, 98, 312, 317, 348
  sealed move, 52, 97–98, 318–19
club members in Swiss system, 86, 90, 94
club tournaments, directors of, 66, 94, 209, 211
co-champions, 140
Code of Ethics, USCF, xv, 4, 58, 63, 197–204
color allocation, xiv–xv, 175, 178
  coin toss for, 90, 105–6, 127
  Crenshaw-Berger pairing tables, xv, 126–27, 236–51
  priority, 106–7, 113
  Swiss system, xxvi–xxvii, 80, 90, 101, 103–18, 124–25
  team tournaments, 130
colors (chromatic shades), 166–69, 309
  of chessboards, 4, 166–68
  of chess pieces, 166–68
  see also black; white

combined individual-team tournaments, xxvi, 61, 94–95, 102–3, 128–29
commercial computers, 92–93, 150, 152
committees:
  appeals, xxv, 68–72
  rules, xi, xiii
  TDCC, 206, 210, 212, 216–18
  for tournaments, 74
completed games, 126
  FIDE laws, 309–13, 347–48
  five-minute chess, 354–55
  Official Rules of Chess, 23–30, 54–55
  see also check; draws
completion of moves, 119
  blind player and, 146–47
  computer chess, 151, 345
  FIDE laws and, 306–7
  Official Rules of Chess, xx, 16–20, 22–30
  release of piece, 16–17
completion of score sheets:
  FIDE rules, 314
  USCF rules, 26
computer notation, 42, 154, 158–59, 161
computers, 72, 81, 119, 122–23, 221, 223, 230–31
  assistance to humans during games, 58, 61, 150, 231
  player signing non-play list, 149
  rules in FIDE-rated tournaments, xiv–xv, xxviii, 153, 328, 343–46
  rules in USCF-rated tournaments, 92–93, 96–97, 149–53
computers, operators of, 150–52, 344–46
  definition of, 150
  draws and resignation, xxviii, 345–46
  execution of moves, 150–51, 345
conduct of players and spectators:
  behavior of spectators, xxv, 63–65, 323, 350, 356
  FIDE laws, xxviii, 321–22, 356
  Official Rules of Chess, 58–66
  players' responsibilities, xii, xxv, 32, 44, 47, 58–65, 150, 195–204, 321–23

conduct of players and spectators (*cont'd.*)
USCF Code of Ethics, xv, 4, 58, 63, 197–204
consultation, 69–71
computers, xxviii, 58, 61, 150, 231
correspondence chess, 231
during games, xxviii, 58–59, 61–64, 200, 322
correspondence chess, 154, 161–63, 230–32, 255–56, 258, 343
Crenshaw-Berger pairing tables, xv, 126–27, 236–51
cross-round pairings, 93–94
cross-section pairings, xxvi, 94
cumulative scores of opposition tiebreaks, xxviii, 142
cumulative tiebreak system, xiii–xiv, xxviii, 104, 142

decisive game, 23–30
descriptive notation, xii, 42, 154, 159–61, 265
determination and completion of a move, xx, 16–18, 119, 146
diagonals, definition of, 5, 300
diagram of position, 27, 44
digital clocks, 10–11, 170–71
directors, *see* arbiters; tournament directors
disabled players, rules for, xv, 42, 145–49
distribution of cash prizes, 132–34
doubled pawns, 279–80
double forfeit, 120
double round-robin tournaments, 127, 326
draw, agreement to, 31–33, 49, 57
completed games and, 24, 310–11
FIDE laws and, xii, 310–11, 318, 320
five-minute chess and, 355
made in advance, 32
draws, xxviii, 9, 60, 78, 89, 97–98, 120–21, 131, 142–44, 322
claims of, xi, xxi–xxiv, 17–18, 30–43, 49, 57, 73, 171, 310–13, 317–18, 320, 346, 349, 355

completed games, 24, 310–13
computer chess, xxviii, 152, 345–46
50-move, xxi–xxii, 17–18, 35–37, 41, 43, 312, 317
insufficient losing chances in sudden-death, xxii–xxiv, 17–18, 37–41, 171, 234
insufficient material to continue, 29, 34–35
insufficient material to win on time, 35
no progress, 39
175-move, 10, 42, 170
in Rapid and one-hour chess, 348–49
rejecting offer of, 31
repetition of position, *see* repetition of position
sealed moves, 41–42, 97, 320
stopping clocks, xxi, 30–34, 36–38, 98, 312, 317, 348
sudden-death rules, xxii, 10–11, 34, 36–41, 49
due colors, definition of, 105–7
duration of tournament and FIDE-rated tournaments, 45, 324–25, 328, 346–47

elapsed time for reset clocks, 47–48
endgame, 280–81
English descriptive notation, 159–61
en passant captures, 15, 32, 158, 303, 305, 311
entry fees, prizes and, xxv, 74, 135–39
envelope for sealed move, 41–42, 52–54, 56–57, 319–22
equalization of colors, 103–7, 112–13
alternation and, 80, 105–7, 113
Crenshaw-Berger tables and, 127, 236–37
round-robin tournaments and, 127
equipment:
standards for, xxviii, 47–48, 164–71
tournament director's checklist and, 188
USCF membership and, xxviii, 256–58
errors, xxvii, 119

blind players' moves and, 147
in rating assignments, xxv, 83, 88–89
in score sheets, 26–27
established ratings, 222
estimated ratings, 220, 222
ethics and code of ethics, 4, 58, 63, 65, 197–204, 231, 352
Ethics Committee, USCF, 199, 201, 203
evidence in appeals, 67
exceptions in tournament praxis, 78, 173–74
exchange of piece for promoted pawn, 15–16, 160, 163, 263, 281, 305–6, 317, 354
exclusion from events (sanction), 203
experimental programs for computers, 149
expert rating, 225–26
expulsion (sanction), 63, 88–90, 203
external clock used in computer game, 151–52, 344–45

facts in disputes, 67
see also appeals
family members in Swiss system, 90
FIDE (Fédération Internationale des Echecs), 3, 146, 154, 254, 299–356
Blitz rules, 233, 352–56
on computers, xiv–xv, xxviii, 153, 328, 343–46
Laws of Chess, xi–xvi, xx–xxii, xxiv, xxviii, 28, 215, 299–325, 328, 342, 344–48, 350–56
Rapid and one-hour chess rules, 324–25, 346–52
-rated tournaments, xiv–xv, xxv, xxviii, 28, 83–85, 87, 102, 153, 208, 215, 225–26, 324–56
ratings, xxv, xxviii, 83–85, 87, 102, 225–26, 326–27, 330–33, 336–42, 344
Scheveningen tournaments, 330–31
time controls, 28, 306–7, 309–25, 328, 344–48, 350–51, 353–56
titles, 102, 327–44
FIDE master (FM) (title), 329, 338–39, 343

50-move rule, xxi–xxii, 17–18, 35–37, 41, 43, 312, 317
figurine algebraic notation, 158, 265
files:
algebraic notation for, 155, 261–63
definition of, 5, 300
English descriptive notation for, 159
international correspondence notation for, 162–63
see also ranks of chessboard; squares of chessboard
five-minute chess, see Blitz rules
fixing games, penalties for, 32, 63
flag (clocks):
checkmate and, xx, 24, 37
equipment standards for, 169–70
FIDE laws and, 314–16, 318, 347–48, 350, 354–56
five-minute chess and, 235, 354–56
handicapped players and, 147
Official Rules of Chess and, xiii, xx–xxii, 11, 17–18, 24–28, 30–32, 37, 46, 49–50, 147
stalemate and, xx, 30–31
sudden-death rules and, xxii, 37, 39
foreign languages, chess notation and, 155, 160
foreign players in USCF tournaments, xxv, 83–87, 200
forfeit, xv, 49–51, 72, 74, 79, 89, 91, 105, 120, 126, 141, 328, 354
conduct of players and spectators, 58–61, 63
team chess and, 129
on time, xiii, 24–30, 38, 43, 46, 49–50, 57, 61, 66, 152, 348
friends in Swiss system pairings, 90
futurity round robins, 326–27

games:
beginning of, 5–6, 51, 53–54, 75, 90–91, 119, 165–66, 302, 313
completion of, see completed games

games (*cont'd*)
    recording of, xiii, xxi, xxiv, 25–27, 42–45,
        52, 58, 130, 314–15, 322, 345–47,
        352
    scores of, *see* scoring of game
grandmaster (GM) (title), chess ratings of,
        327–32, 334, 336, 342–43

half-point byes, xv, xxv, 72–74, 88–93, 102,
        120, 124, 141, 174
handicapped players, rules for, xv, 42,
        145–49
Harkness tiebreak, xiii, 141
history of chess rule books, xiii-xvi
Holland system of tournaments, xvii, xxvii,
        128
houseman, 66, 72, 92–93, 119, 125, 176
humans vs. computers, rules for, xiv–xv,
        xxviii, 92–93, 96–97, 149–53, 328,
        343–46

I adjust (*j'adoube*), 18–19, 307
illegal moves, xii, 46, 49, 57, 234, 308, 310,
        313, 320, 350–52
    castling and, 20
    correspondence chess and, 232
    five-minute chess and, 352, 355–56
    sudden-death rules and, 20–22, 65, 234
    touched piece and, 21–22
illegal positions, 20–22, 57, 308–9, 317
illegible moves, *see* legibility
individual/team tournaments, xxvi, 61, 94–
        95, 102, 128–29
initial position of pieces, 6, 302
insufficient losing chances in sudden-death,
        xxii–xxiv, 17–18, 37–41, 171, 234
insufficient material to continue, 29, 34–
        35
insufficient material to win on time, 35
interchanges, color allocations and, xxvi,
        103–4, 108–12, 114–18
intermediary pairing numbers, 81
internal clock (computers), 152

international arbiter (IA), 215–16, 342–
        43
international correspondence notation, 154,
        161–63
international grandmaster (GM) (title),
        225–26, 336
International (FIDE) Laws of Chess, xi–
        xvi, xx–xxii, xxiv, xxviii, 28, 215, 299–
        325, 328, 342, 344–48, 350–56
international master (IM) (title), 225–26,
        327, 329–32, 334, 336–38, 342–43
international (FIDE) ratings, xxv, xxviii,
        83–85, 87, 102, 225–26, 326–27, 330–
        33, 336–42, 344
international round-robin tournaments,
        327–28
interpretation of the rules, 65, 76, 323
interruption of game, 49, 317
intervention in game by tournament direc-
        tor, 65–66

j'adoube (I adjust), 18–19, 307

Kashdan system:
    for breaking ties, xiii, 142–43
    for unfinished games, xxvi, 97–98
king, xix–xx, xxii, xxiv, 165–68, 267, 270,
        272, 301, 353–55
    check of, *see* check
    chess notation for, 155, 159, 162, 262
    claim of draw and, 30, 34–35, 41, 310,
        313, 349
    completion of game and, 24, 309–10,
        313, 354–55
    form of, 166
    keeping it safe, 277–78
    movement of, 12–13, 16, 20, 303–4, 306,
        309
    size of, 165
king-side, 158, 160, 263, 353
knights, xii, xxiv, 14, 34–35, 41, 155, 157,
        160, 262, 272–76, 280, 283, 301–3,
        305, 310, 349

ladder down pairings, 118–19
late arrival at chessboard, xxiv, 28–29, 47–
    48, 66, 124, 130, 165, 173, 176–77, 313
    see also absent player
laws of chess, *see* rules of chess
legibility, 232, 313–14
    of score sheet, 42, 314
    of sealed move, 313
lifetime titles, USCF, 225–29
lightning tournaments, *see* Blitz rules
long algebraic notation, 158, 264–65
long diagonals, definition of, 5

major rule changes since last edition of rule
    book, xviii–xxix
masters, xxv, 225–26, 229
matches, 215, 229
    computers vs. computers, 150
    match points and, 144–45
    Scheveningen system and, 252–53, 326,
        330–31
material necessary for mate, xxi–xxii, 35,
    354
materials for pieces and boards, 165–66
Median/Harkness tiebreak, xiii, 140–42
membership:
    reinstatement of, 203
    USCF and, xv, xxviii, 63, 65, 74–75, 130,
        149, 190, 198–99, 203, 205, 254–60
memory-unit exchange, computer chess
    and, 152, 346
microcomputers, *see* computers
misrepresentation, USCF Code of Ethics,
    200
modified median (Skoff) tiebreak system,
    xxviii, 140–42
move (unit of game), 56–58, 302–18, 322,
    345–47, 349–53
    blind players, 146–48
    completion of, *see* completion of moves
    completion of game, 27, 310–13
    completion of score sheets, 42, 44,
        314–15

computer chess, 150–51, 345
    definition of, 12, 303
    determination of, xx, 16–18, 119, 146
    50-move rule, xxi–xxii, 17–18, 35–37, 41,
        43, 312, 317
    handicapped player's communication,
        146–48
    illegal, *see* illegal moves
    move-pair, definition of, 26
    175-move rule, 10, 42, 170
    player having move, 56
    proposal of draw, xxi, xxiv, 31–36, 310–
        12, 349
    quality of, 263–64
    resumption of adjourned game, 29, 56–
        57, 320
    right to move, 302
    sealed, *see* sealed move
    touched piece, *see* touched piece
movement of pieces, 97, 159, 318
    algebraic notation and, 42, 156–57
    correspondence chess and, 162
    English descriptive notation, 159
    five-minute chess and, 352–56
    pieces and, 12–22, 32, 45–47, 146–47,
        230–31, 263, 302–9, 312, 350

NC (no computer) announcements, 149
noncommercial use agreement, chess com-
    puters and, 149
norm point requirements:
    FIDE titles, 327, 330–31, 334–35
    USCF lifetime titles, 227–29
notation, xii–xiii, 10, 42, 52, 154–63, 168,
    230, 261–65, 267, 314, 318–19
notes used during games, 58, 321–22
notification:
    of delay in resumption of adjournment,
        29
    to director of result of game, 58, 320
    of player ratings, 87
    of sanctions, 204
    see also announcements

objectivity, tournament directors and, 66
odd man:
    round-robin pairings and, 237
    Swiss system and, 102–5, 118
Official Rules of Chess, xiii, xx–xxv, 3–76,
    147
one-hour and Rapid chess rules, 324–25,
    346–52
175-move rule, 10, 42, 170
one-point byes, xxvi, 72, 74, 90–94, 142,
    174, 176

packing list for tournament directors,
    187–90
pairing and pairings, xiv-xv, xxvi–xxviii, 48,
    51, 65, 72, 125–32, 172, 174–80, 195,
    207–8
    class pairings, 122–23
    combined individual and team, 94–95,
        102–3
    computers in tournaments, xiv, xxviii,
        92–93, 119, 122–23, 149–50, 153
    Crenshaw-Berger round-robin table, xv,
        126–27, 236–51
    Look Ahead method, xxvii, 112–18
    plus-two method, 95
    Swiss system, xviii, xxvi–xxvii, 79–125,
        127–28, 130, 236
    team vs. team, 128–32, 252–53
    Top Down method, xxvii, 113–14
    unfinished games, xxvi, 54–55, 97–98,
        118
    unreported results, xxvii, 119–22
pairing card, 176–80, 208
    Swiss system, xiii, 80–82, 97, 99–100, 119
    team tournaments, 130
pairing score, definition of, 26
parameter settings, computer chess and,
    150, 345
pawn, 35–36, 41, 168, 272, 274–81, 283,
    301–3, 311–12, 349
    algebraic notation and, 155–59, 262–63
    in endgame, 280–81

English descriptive notation for, 159–60
    moves of, 14–16, 19–20, 32, 305–6, 312
    promotion of, see promotion of pawns
penalties, 31–32, 44–45, 126, 135, 232, 351
    blind players and, 147
    for consulting with computer, 58, 150
    duties of arbiter and, 311
    failure to notify of delay and, 29
    for false claim of draw, xxi, xxiii, 31, 35–
        36, 39, 41, 311
    five-minute chess and, 353–54
    for groundless appeal, 68, 70
    for illegal moves, 22, 234
    for prohibited conduct, xii, 32, 44, 47,
        58–63, 65, 150, 322–23
    tournament director's responsibility for,
        xii, xxiii, 4, 47, 58, 67–68, 70–71, 120,
        151
perfect scores, Swiss system and, 78–79,
    98–99, 101, 104
perpetual check, 32, 348, 355
personal computers, see computers
pieces, xii, 5–8, 154–60, 300–13
    chessboard, 6, 302
    claim of draw, 40, 310–12, 349
    definition of, 6–7
    equipment standards, xxviii, 164–68
    FIDE laws and, xx, 300–312, 317, 345,
        347, 350, 353–54
    50-move rule, 35–36, 41
    movement of, see movement of pieces
    promotion of pawn, 15–16, 19–20, 317
    touched, see touched piece
    trading of, 278–80
    values of, 271–72, 279
place prizes, 84, 133, 137–39
planning of tournaments, 180–86, 190–92
players:
    alertness of, 281–83
    conduct of, xii, 32, 44, 47, 58–65, 150,
        195–204, 321–23
    rights and responsibilities of, xv, 67–71,
        76, 195–97

tips for, 266–88
tournament directors as, 66, 205, 207, 217–18
playoffs, 139, 144
Policy Board, USCF, xiv, 199, 201–4, 217
position diagram, 27, 44
position of chessboard in play, 4, 146
positions (game positions), 6, 42–44, 60, 62, 64, 66, 302, 315, 346–47, 353, 355
blind player's board, 146–48
claim of draw and, 35–36, 38, 40, 42–43, 311–12, 346, 349
completion of the game, 311–13
correspondence chess, 232
illegal, 20–22, 57, 308–9, 317
reconciliation of, 151
repetition of, *see* repetition of position
resumption of adjourned game, 56–57, 319–21, 340
postal chess, correspondence chess and, 154, 161–63, 230–32, 255–56, 343
prearranged game results, 32
preference not to play a computer, 149
pre-tournament literature, 78, 132
priority of color, 106–7, 113
prizes, 4, 54, 63, 84–86, 195, 218–19
based on number of entries, xxv, 74, 135–39
based on number of points, xxviii, 138–39
class, 73, 86, 88, 93, 122–23, 132–33, 135, 137–38
computer chess, 150
effect of pairings on, 119, 121
guidelines for, 74, 84, 132–39
indivisible, 136–37, 139–40
payment of, 74, 132–35
pooled, 132
scholastic, 94, 136
tournaments and, xxvi, 68, 73–74, 84, 86, 88–89, 92–94, 101, 119, 121–23, 125–26, 128–29, 131–40, 142, 213–14, 219, 255
withdrawal from tournament and, 135

probation (sanction), 202–3
procedures, USCF Code of Ethics and, 200–202
program modules, computer chess and, 152
prohibited conduct of players or spectators, xii, 32, 44, 47, 58–65, 150, 321–23
promotion of chess, 258, 260
promotion of pawns, 15–16, 19–20, 158, 160, 163, 263, 281, 305–7, 317, 354
proportions of chessboards, 167–68
protest, continuing play and, 68
provisional rating, 220, 222

quads, definition of, 126
queen, xx, 40–41, 159, 166–68, 272, 275, 280–81, 283, 301, 349, 353
form of, 166
moves of, 13, 304
pawn promotion and, 15–16, 281, 305
queen-side, 158, 263, 353
Quick Chess, xix, 10, 84, 219–21, 224, 229, 234
time pressure and, 219
see also sudden-death rules

radio notation, 163
rank in Swiss system tournaments, 80–81, 99, 102–3
ranks of chessboard, 156–62
algebraic notation, 156–58, 261
computer notation, 158, 161
definition of, 5, 300
English descriptive notation, 159–60
international correspondence notation, 162
see also files; squares of chessboard
Rapid and one-hour chess rules, 324–25, 346–52
rating system, 38, 63, 68, 126–31, 173–75, 177–78, 200, 219–33
chess ratings and, 219–29
class prizes and, 73, 123, 133, 137–38
computers vs. humans and, xxviii, 150

rating system (*cont'd*)
  due colors and, 107, 113–14
  FIDE-rated tournaments and international ratings, xiv–xv, xxv, xxviii, 28, 83–85, 87, 102, 153, 208, 215, 225–26, 324–56
  foreign or FIDE ratings, 83–87
  handicap effect in, 223–24
  multiple USCF ratings, 83
  players without USCF ratings, 83–87, 90–91, 129
  rating floor, 224–25
  round robins and, 126–27, 326–27
  Swiss system and, xviii, xxvi–xxvii, 80–94, 97–105, 107–13, 118–20, 123, 236, 327
  team tournaments and, 129–31
  tiebreaks and, 13, 143
  USCF system and, xii, xix, xxv–xxvii, 61, 70, 80–94, 97–105, 139, 150, 205, 209, 219–32, 255, 257–59, 327
  value of colors and value of ratings and, xxvi–xxvii, 108–12
  see also classes of players
reconciliation of positions, computer chess and, 151
recording of games, xiii, xxi, xxiv, 25–27, 42–45, 52, 58, 130, 314–15, 322, 345–47, 352
reentries, xxvi, 101–2
refusal to play a computer, 149
registration, 90–91, 131, 173, 191
regulations, *see* rules of chess
reinstated games, illegal positions, 20
release of piece, completion of move and, 16–17
re-pairing round, xxvii, 118–19, 121
repetition of position, xii, xxi, 32–34, 43, 234–35, 311, 346, 348
  five-minute chess, 355
  regular time control, 317
  sudden-death time control, 17–18, 34, 234–35
reprimand (sanction), 202

requirements of FIDE international titles, 327–28
resetting computer, 151–52
resignation of game, 8–9, 54
  completed game, 24, 309, 348
  computer chess, xxviii, 152, 345–46
  conduct of player, 62
  fallen flag, 49, 318
  five-minute chess, 354
  sealed move, 57, 320
results, *see* scoring of game
resumption of adjourned games, 29, 53–54, 56–58, 308, 313, 319–22, 346
reversals of colors, round-robin pairings and, 237–51
rights of players, xv, 67–71, 76, 195–97
rooks, xix, xxiv, 7, 40–41, 157, 272, 275, 280, 301, 303–6, 349
  moves of, 12–14, 16, 20, 263, 303–4, 306
  pawn promotion, 305
round-robin pairing tables, xv, 124–25, 236–51
round-robin tournaments, xvii, xxvii, 77–78, 124–28, 144–45, 209, 326–28, 330–32
rounds, xxvi, 172–77, 228, 252–53, 325, 328–30, 332, 351
  byes in, *see* byes
  last, *see* tournaments, last round of
  round-robin tournaments, 127, 328
  starting times for, 51, 94, 97, 122, 173–77, 179, 196–97
  Swiss system and, xvi–xvii, 78–81, 89–94, 97–101, 103, 105–25, 138, 141–42, 237
  tournament director's checklist, 191–92
rules of chess, 197
  evolution of, ix–xxix
  FIDE, xi–xvi, xx–xxii, xxiv, xxviii, 28, 215, 299–325, 328, 342, 344–48, 350–56
  interpretation of, 65, 76, 323
  official, xiii, xx–xv, 3–76, 147
  and regulations for tournaments, xi–xix, xxi–xxiv, 26, 45, 51, 61, 65, 68–70, 72–74, 77–153, 172–86, 200

of Swiss system, xi–xii, xxvi–xxvii, 79–80
tournament director's responsibility for,
xiii, xx–xxv, 3–4, 28–31, 42, 47, 51, 58,
66–68, 70, 74, 76, 145–47, 172, 195,
207–8, 217–18

sanctions, USCF Code of Ethics and, 63,
198–204
Scheveningen system, 252–53, 326, 330–31
scholastic chess, 80, 93–95, 128–29, 136–37
School Mates (magazine), 189, 255, 258
score group, definition of, 102–3
score sheets, 33–34, 169, 208, 311, 348
blind players, 147–48
opponent's, 26–27, 43–44, 314–15
prohibited conduct, 58
recording of games, xiii, xxi, xxiv, 26–27,
42–45, 314–15, 345–46
resumption of adjourned games, 56, 320
sealed move, 52, 56, 318–20
sudden-death rules, xv–xvi, xxiv, 36, 43
time forfeit, 25–27, 43
scoring of game, xii, 130–31, 147–49, 168–
69, 178–79, 196, 234–35
adjournment, 52
computers, 96–97, 151
due colors, 106
FIDE laws, 323, 325
FIDE-rated tournaments, 325, 327, 345
five-minute chess, 234
notice to arbiter, 58, 320
Official Rules of Chess, 9–10, 65
pairings, xxvii, 26, 80, 89, 98–99, 102–4,
106–7, 119–23, 125, 237
round robins, 126, 144–45
Swiss system, xxviii, 79–80, 89, 94–99,
102–4, 106–7, 119–23, 125, 130, 138,
141–44
tiebreaks, 104, 141–45
tournament results, 73, 89, 97, 208, 219
sealed move, xii, xv, 97–98, 318–22, 346
absence of envelope in, 41–42, 321
adjournment of game, 29, 52–54, 318–19

completion of games, 29–30, 310, 313
definition of, 52
resignation of game, 57, 320
resumption of adjourned game, 29, 53,
56–57, 313, 319–22
sealing move early, 52
senior directors, xxv, 211–13
senior masters, xxv, 225–26
sighted players, blind players vs., 148
skittles room, 182, 184
Skoff (modified median) tiebreak system,
xxviii, 140–42
solicited and unsolicited advice, *see* conduct
of players and spectators
Solkoff system, xiii, xxviii, 142
Sonneborn-Berger system tiebreak, xiii,
143–44
special referee, xxv, 68–72
see also appeals
spectators, 125, 164, 186
conduct of, xxv, 63–65, 323, 350, 356
fall of flag and, 25, 28, 350
five-minute chess and, 356
houseman and, 92
illegal moves and, 22, 350
sportsmanship, 58, 65, 196, 200
squares of chessboard, 155–59, 162–63,
275, 303
algebraic notation for, 155–58, 261
definition of, 4, 300
English descriptive notation for, 159
equipment standards and, 167–68
Official Rules of Chess and, 4–5, 14
see also files; ranks of chessboard
staff-meeting checklist, 193–94
stalemate, xx, 17, 30–31, 313
definition of, 30, 310
five-minute chess and, 355
standards, 198–200
for equipment, xxviii, 47–48, 164–71
for tournaments, 4, 58, 61, 63–64, 198–
99, 202–3
USCF Code of Ethics and, 199–200

start of game, 119, 313
  requirements, 90–91, 316
  starting times, 51, 53–54, 75, 90, 94
stationery supplies, tournament director's
  checklist and, 187–89
Staunton pattern chess pieces, 165–66
sudden-death rules, 9–11, 17–18, 20–22,
  34–43, 45–46, 49–50, 55, 65, 171
  FIDE laws, 324
  USCF rules, xv–xvi, xix–xxiv, 234–35
supplies, tournament director's checklist,
  188
suspension, *see* sanction
Swiss system, ix–xviii, xxvi–xxviii, 174, 211
  FIDE ratings, 83–84, 87, 102, 326–27,
    330–31
  team tournaments, 94–95, 102–3
  tiebreaks, xiv, 104, 140–44
  tournaments, xi, xxvi–xxvii, 77–128, 130,
    138, 140–44, 209, 236–37, 326–27,
    330–31
symbols for pieces, xii, 5–6, 154–55, 160,
  301–2

tape recorders, 147
teams:
  captains of, xxvii–xxviii, 130–32
  team chess and, 61, 128–32, 252–53
  telephone chess and, 230–31
  tiebreaks and, 131, 144–45
  tournaments and, xxvi, 61, 94–95, 102–3,
    127–32, 209, 326, 330–31
telecommunications, correspondence chess
  and, 230–31
telephone chess, 163, 230–31
telephone notation, 163
temporary adjudications, 98
temporary rating adjustments, 100
threefold occurrence, *see* repetition of position
throwing games, penalties for, 63
tiebreak system, xiii–xiv, xxviii, 13, 104,
  139–45

co-champion, 140
indivisible prizes, 136–37, 139–40
  team, 131, 144–45
time allotment for tournament, 45, 324–25,
  328, 346–47
time controls, xx–xxi, 49–53, 60–61, 63–66,
  219, 274
  adjourned games, 29, 52–53, 55, 318–19
  appeal of tournament director's ruling
    on, 68
  blind players, 147–48
  claims of draw, xxi, 30–40, 317
  claims of time forfeits, xiii, 24–30, 38, 43,
    46, 49–50, 57, 61, 66, 152, 348
  completed game, 23–29, 310, 312–13
  completion of move, 16–18, 307
  computer chess, 151–52, 345
  correspondence chess, 231–32
  illegal moves and positions, 20–22, 46,
    309, 317
  playoffs, 139
  recording games, 25–27, 42–44, 58, 314–
    15, 322
  resumption of adjourned games, 29, 56–
    57, 313, 319–21
  sudden-death rules, xv–xvi, xix–xxiv,
    9–11, 21, 38–40, 45–46, 49–50, 55, 65,
    171
  team telephone chess, 231
  tournament director's responsibility, 28–
    29, 53, 65–66, 68, 97, 316–17, 322–
    23
  see also clocks
tips to winning chess, 266–88
touched piece:
  blind players and, 146
  computer chess and, 151, 345
  correspondence chess and, 232
  FIDE laws and, xx, 307–8, 345, 350, 354
  five-minute chess and, 354
  Official Rules of Chess and, xx, 16–22, 31
tournament directors (TDs), 131, 139–41,
  231

adjournment of games, 29, 52–58, 98, 319–21

announcements, 149, 218

assistants, 65, 207–8, 211

associate national (ANTDs), 213–15

authority of, 70–71, 74

calculating players' ratings, xii, xxv–xxvi, 80–89

certification of, 72, 74, 205–18

checklist, 187–94

chief, 65, 68, 70, 76, 207, 211, 214

clocks, xv, 10–11, 31, 46–51, 56, 66, 97, 170–71, 316–18, 321–23

completion of games, 24–30, 54, 309, 311–12

computer chess, 149–51

conduct, 58–66, 198–200, 216

counting moves in sudden-death, xxii, 35 37

declaring draws, xii, xxi–xxiv, 33–42, 66, 73, 97–98, 120, 171, 235, 317, 320

declaring game over, 55

delegation of authority, 65

disciplining of, 217–18

discretion of, 4, 19, 42, 47, 58, 62, 67, 70–71, 74

equipment standards, 164–65, 170–71

fall of flag, 17, 24–26, 31, 37, 46, 316, 318

50-move, 35–36, 41

illegal moves, 21–22, 57, 65

local, 210–11

national (NTDs), 213–15

Official Rules of Chess, xiii, xx–xxv, 3–4, 28–31, 47, 51, 58, 65–76

players' rights, 67–71, 76, 195–96

round-robin tournaments, 127, 237

rules for handicapped or disabled players, 42, 145–47

score sheets, xxi, 25–26, 42–45, 52, 208

senior, xxv, 211–13

sudden-death rules, xxii–xxiii, 10–11, 21, 34–43, 65

Swiss system, xxvii, 78–90, 92–99, 102–5, 107–10, 112–15, 118–23, 141

time trouble, 28, 53, 66

in well-run tournaments, 172–82, 184–85

see also arbiters

tournaments, xxi–xxviii, 35, 50–55, 213–15, 236–37

cancellation of, xxv, 75

categories, 208–9

clocks, 48, 50

computer chess rules, xiv–xv, xxviii, 92–93, 96–97, 149–53, 328, 343–46

correspondence chess, 258

equipment standards for, 164

FIDE-rated, xiv–xv, xxv, xx–viii, 28, 83–85, 87, 102, 153, 208, 215, 225–26, 324–56

planning of, 180–86, 190–92

players' rights and responsibilities, 195–97

regulations and guidelines for, xi–xix, xxi–xxiv, 51, 65, 68–70, 72–74, 77–153, 172–86, 200

score sheets, xxi, 45

set-up for, xxix, 74, 180–86

sponsors, 74, 198–200

standard of conduct at, 4, 58, 61, 63–64, 198–99, 202–3

time controls, 28, 51

time limits at, 45, 51, 324–25, 328, 346–47

USCF Code of Ethics, 199–200

USCF membership, xv, 74, 149, 255, 257–60

USCF-rated, xii, xix, xxv–xxvii, 61, 70, 80–94, 97–105, 139, 150, 205, 209, 219–32, 255, 257–59, 327

well-run, 172–86

tournaments, last round of, 54–55, 62–63, 73

color allocation in, 106, 237

pairings in, 55, 89, 95, 106–7, 118, 122, 125, 237

tournaments, last round of (*cont'd*)
   tiebreaks in, 142
   tournament director's checklist and, 192
tournaments, withdrawal from, xxvii, 29, 97,
      118–19, 124, 126–27, 135, 141, 179,
      185, 196
   and round-robin pairing tables, xv,
      236–51
transpositions in pairings, Swiss system and,
      xxvi, 103–5, 108–12, 114–18, 121
trophies, 136–37

unbalanced Holland, definition of, xxvii,
      128
unfinished games, xxvi, 54–55
   color allocations and, 118
   Swiss system and, 97–98, 118
United States chess champions, 289–95
United States Chess Federation (USCF),
      3–4, 10–11, 39–40, 72–154, 166–67,
      170, 195, 265, 330
   Blitz rules of, 11, 233–35
   Code of Ethics, xv, 4, 58, 63, 197–204
   Computer Rating Agency, 150
   correspondence chess, 232, 255–56
   history of, 258–60, 296–98
   lifetime titles, 225–29
   membership in, xv, xxviii, 63, 65, 74–75,
      130, 149, 190, 198–99, 203, 205,
      254–60
   Policy Board of, xiv, 199, 201–4, 217
   ratings, xii, xix, xxv–xxvii, 61, 70, 80–94,
      97–105, 139, 150, 205, 209, 219–32,
      255, 257–59, 327
   sanctions, 63, 198–204
   tournament regulations and guidelines,
      xi–xxiv, 26, 45, 61, 65, 68–70, 72–74,
      77–153, 200
   about USCF, 254–60
unplayed games, xxvi, xxviii, 72–74, 97, 105,
      124, 141, 143, 325

unrated players, 129, 220, 222
   FIDE-rated tournaments and, 325–26,
      329, 331
   prizes and, 84–86, 139
   Swiss system and, xxvii, 80–87, 90–91,
      104, 112, 123, 143
unreported results, xxvii, 119–22

validity:
   of FIDE laws, 323
   of wall-chart ratings, 88
variations:
   and exceptions in tournament praxis, 78,
      173–74
   in Swiss system pairings, 95, 99–102,
      105–7, 111–12, 120, 130
violations of USCF Code of Ethics, 201
visibility of clocks, 47
visually handicapped players, xiii, 146–49

wall chart, 65, 72, 81, 86, 88, 91, 94, 96–97,
      130–32, 175, 177–80, 184–85, 197,
      208
wall clocks, 53, 321
well-run tournament, 172–86
white (player with white pieces), 90, 105–
      18, 130, 175, 236
   beginning game, 46–47, 302
   equipment, 5, 165–66
   right to move, 302
witnesses in appeals, 69
woman grandmaster (WGM) (title), 327,
      329, 331–32, 339–40, 342–43
woman international master (WIM) (title),
      327, 329, 332, 340–43
women's FIDE master (WFM) (title), 329,
      341–43
World Blitz Chess Association (WBCA),
      233
world chess champions, 288–89
World Chess Federation, *see* FIDE